The Ultimate Collection of Fun Things to Do in Retirement

Your Roadmap to Explore the World, Spark Creativity, Expand Your Mind, Uncover Hidden Talents, Make New Friends, and Savor Your Golden Years

The Great Retirement Escape

Retirement Reinvented

Copyright © 2024 by Lara West

The content contained within this book may not be reproduced, duplicated, stored in a retrieval system, or transmitted in any form or by any means, electronic, mechanical, photocopying, recording, or otherwise, without direct written permission from the author or the publisher.

Legal Notice:

This book is copyright-protected. It is only for personal use. You cannot amend, distribute, sell, use, quote, or paraphrase any part, or the content within this book, without the consent of the author or publisher.

Disclaimer Notice:

Please note the information contained within this book is for educational and entertainment purposes only. All readers/viewers of this content are advised to consult their doctors or qualified health professionals regarding specific health questions before beginning any fitness or lifestyle program.

The content within this book has been derived from various sources. All effort has been executed to present accurate, up-to-date, reliable, and complete information. No warranties of any kind are declared or implied. Readers acknowledge that the author is not engaged in the rendering of legal, medical, or professional advice. Neither Lara West nor the publisher takes any responsibility for possible health consequences of any person reading or following the information in this educational content.

By reading this document, the reader agrees that under no circumstances is the author responsible for any losses, direct or indirect, that are incurred as a result of the use of the information contained within this document, including, but not limited to, errors, omissions, or inaccuracies.

Contents

The Great Retirement Escape
Your Guide to Journeys Across the Globe, Adventures Close to Home, Inspiring Outdoor Activities, and Fun Active Lifestyle for Your Best Years Yet

1. Introduction — 2
2. Designing Your Dream Retirement: A Blueprint for Adventure and Fulfillment — 5
   - 2.1 Charting Your Path to an Epic Retirement Adventure
   - 2.2 Maximizing Your Adventures with Minimal Spending
   - 2.3 Essential Digital Tools for Modern Retirees
   - 2.4 Balancing Safety with Adventure
3. Pathways to Wellness: Inspiring Journeys for a Healthy and Active Retirement — 25
   - 3.1 Finding Peace: Mindfulness and Meditation Retreats
   - 3.2 Golf as a Social Game: Connection, Fitness, and Fun
   - 3.3 Refreshing Waters: Water Aerobics, Swimming, and Cold Plunges

3.4 Floating into Wellness: The Sensory Deprivation Experience

3.5 Fitness at Home: Online Classes and Resources

3.6 Gardening for Fitness, Mindfulness, and Growth

3.7 Tai Chi and Qigong: Gentle Movements for Strength and Balance

3.8 Paddling to Health: Kayaking, Canoeing, and Paddleboarding

3.9 Nordic Walking: A Whole-Body Approach to Staying Active

3.10 Leisurely Rides: Scenic Biking Routes for Casual Cyclists

3.11 Cross-Country Skiing: A Workout for Winter Wellness

3.12 Cooking for Health: Fun Workshops and Classes

3.13 Relax, Renew, Rebalance: Spa and Hot Springs Escapes

4. The World at Your Fingertips: Senior-Friendly Destinations, Budgets, and Beyond   53

   4.1 The Best Senior-Friendly Travel Destinations Worldwide

   4.2 The Best Travel Times for an Unforgettable Experience

   4.3 Group Travel: Finding Retirement Travel Clubs

   4.4 Solo Travel: Exploring the World on Your Own Terms

   4.5 A Comprehensive Guide to Traveling with Physical Limitations

   4.6 Seeing the World Without Breaking the Bank

5. Epic Journeys of a Lifetime: Unforgettable Travel Experiences … 70

    5.1 Eco-Tourism: Environmentally Conscious Travel

    5.2 Voluntourism: Combining Travel with Volunteer Work

    5.3 Senior Safari Adventures: Planning the Trip of a Lifetime

    5.4 Sea Voyages and River Cruises: Unlocking Unforgettable Adventures

    5.5 Top Historical Landmarks for Your Global Bucket List

    5.6 Cultural European Tours for the Curious Retiree

    5.7 Learning While Traveling: Cultural Exchange Programs

    5.8 Savoring the World Through Food and Wine Adventures

6. Sky High & Deep Dive: Adventure-Fueled Experiences … 101

    6.1 Skydiving and Paragliding: Thrills in the Sky

    6.2 Scuba Diving: Exploring Underwater Worlds

    6.3 Motorcycle Road Trips: On the Open Road with Confidence

    6.4 Hot Air Balloon Rides: Seeing the World from Above

    6.5 White Water Rafting: Riding the Waves of Adventure

    6.6 Mountain Biking for the Energetic Retiree

    6.7 Soaring Through the Skies with Zip-Lining

7. The Great Outdoors: Exploring Nature's Wonders … 119

7.1 Bird-Watching: Connecting with Nature's Winged Wonders

7.2 Fishing and Boating: Relaxing by the Water

7.3 Exploring the Wonders of National Parks

7.4 Hidden Treasures: The Exciting World of Treasure Hunting

7.5 Camping and Glamping: Relaxing Outdoor Retreats

7.6 Charting the Course: Planning Your Dream RV Adventure

7.7 Horseback Riding: Essentials for a Safe and Enjoyable Experience

7.8. Exploring the Night Sky: Stargazing and Astronomy Clubs

8. Conclusion — 137

Resources — 139

   Chapter 2.

   Chapter 3.

   Chapter 4.

   Chapter 5.

   Chapter 6.

   Chapter 7.

References — 158

Retirement Reinvented

Your Inspiring Guide to Creative Expression, Intellectual Growth, Entrepreneurial Ventures, and Leaving a Legacy for a Fulfilling and Meaningful Life After Work

1. Introduction — 164

2. From Worker to Creator: Crafting Your New Re-   170
   tirement Identity and Rhythm
   - 2.1 Overcoming the Fear of the Unknown
   - 2.2 Rebranding Your Identity in Retirement
   - 2.3 Embracing a New Rhythm: Crafting Your Retirement Week
   - 2.4 Time Management Tips for an Unstructured Day
   - 2.5 Setting Up Your Morning Routine for an Energized Start

3. Intellectual Pursuits: Mindful Exploration and Life-   182
   long Learning
   - 3.1 Fluency on Your Terms: Exploring New Languages
   - 3.2 Expand Your Horizons with Online Learning
   - 3.3 Tech Savvy Seniors: Mastering New Gadgets
   - 3.4 Brain Games and Puzzles for Daily Mental Exercise
   - 3.5 Video Games for Intellectual Engagement
   - 3.6 The Joy of Playing Chess in Local Clubs
   - 3.7 Organizing a Local Bridge Club
   - 3.8 Attending Workshops and Lectures

4. Creative Expression: Finding Joy Through Imagina-   204
   tion
   - 4.1 Exploring Art Forms: From Painting to Digital Creativity
   - 4.2 Creating Melodies and Memories
   - 4.3 Photography Classes: Capturing Life's Moments
   - 4.4 Crafting Stories: Creative Writing Workshops

5. Socializing and Building New Connections   219
   - 5.1 Hosting Parties and Theme Nights

    5.2 Sharing Stories and Opinions in Book and Film Clubs

    5.3 Dance Lessons: In Rhythm with Your Community

    5.4 Connecting Online in Virtual Meetups

    5.5 Rediscovering Romance in Retirement

6. Community Engagement and Leadership   233

    6.1 Volunteering: A Powerful Way to Give Back and Connect with Your Community

    6.2 Participating in Seasonal Local Events and Festivals

    6.3 Starting a Small Non-profit Organization

    6.4 Creating a Garden for a Thriving Community

    6.5 Running for a Local Office: Leading with Purpose

    6.6 Mentoring the Younger Generation: Shaping the Future Through Guidance

7. Home-Based Hobbies: Inspirations in the Heart of Your Home   253

    7.1 Home Gardening: Creating Your Peaceful Oasis

    7.2 Creating Personal Touches: Adventures in DIY Home Decor

    7.3 World Cuisines: Virtual Cooking Classes

    7.4 Home Brewing and Wine Making: Crafting Your Beverages

    7.5 Beginner's Guide to Baking Artisan Breads

8. Entrepreneurial Endeavors and Part-Time Work   273

    8.1 Starting a Small Business in Retirement: Turning Your Passion into Profit

    8.2 Starting a Blog, Vlog, or Podcast: Share Your Journey and Earn Along the Way

    8.3 Transforming Your Hobbies into Income Streams

      8.4 Part-Time Jobs That Don't Feel Like Work: Enjoying Your Second Act

      8.5 Freelancing: Flexibility and Freedom

9. Building Your Legacy for Future Generations   294

      9.1 Legacy Projects: Making a Lasting Impact

      9.2 Teaching Workshops and Classes

      9.3 Crafting Your Ethical Will

      9.4 Building a Family Tree

      9.5 Engaging in Philanthropy: Small Acts, Big Impacts

10. Conclusion   304

References   306

About the Author   311

Also by Lara West   313

The Great Retirement Escape

Your Guide to Journeys Across the Globe, Adventures Close to Home, Inspiring Outdoor Activities, and Fun Active Lifestyle for Your Best Years Yet

Lara West

Chapter One

Introduction

So, you've finally done it. You've handed over the keys to the office, given the farewell speech, either tearfully endless or joyfully brief, and walked out into the brave new world of retirement. This is the moment you've been waiting for, but now what? Are you supposed to sit on a porch swing and count the days like you're waiting for the end credits to roll? Hardly! Retirement is not the end of the road; it's the start of an exhilarating adventure. As you embark on this exciting journey, allow me to be your guide to help you navigate the twists and turns, uncover new passions, and fully embrace the limitless possibilities that lie ahead. Together, we'll explore how to make this chapter the most fulfilling and vibrant time of your life.

But first, let me introduce myself. I'm a woman in my early 60s, a business owner, a wife, and a mother. I adore my life, family, and business. I'm very active and always hungry for new experiences. And I plan to keep it that way throughout my 60s, 70s, and beyond. My husband, in his mid-60s, shares my enthusiasm for art, music, sports, travel, and intellectual pursuits. Together, we're committed to living a vibrant and adventurous life, and we will not let something as trivial as retirement slow us down. In fact, during one of those epiphany moments—when friends around us started retiring—I realized I wanted more freedom in our retirement years, soaking up every bit of joy, adventure, and creativity that retirement years offer. As I delved into what "retire" truly meant, I realized it was never something nature intended for us. The word itself, rooted in stepping back or withdrawing, didn't sit right with me. I didn't want to withdraw from life as I aged; I wanted to embrace it more fully. That's when I started devouring books, articles, and every piece of research I could find on making the most of this new chapter. What I found was electrifying. I discovered that retirement offered the opportunity for more joy, adventure, and creativity than at any other time in my life. And I knew I had to share this with others. Nature didn't design us to fade away; it designed us to grow, to flourish, and to live with purpose. Retirement, as I see it, is the beginning of a time to truly thrive.

This book is a result of my journey into planning for a fulfilling retirement. Its purpose is simple: to provide you with a joyful, creative, and adventurous roadmap for your retirement. We'll explore a wide variety of activities that cater to different interests, physical abilities, and budgets. From adrenaline-pumping adventures to serene, soul-soothing hobbies, there's something here for everyone. And don't worry, there's not a single mundane or trivial suggestion in sight.

As I began gathering information for this book, I realized something exciting. I had collected so much valuable content—enough to fill two books! Rather than overwhelm you with everything at once, I split the material into two separate books. This way, each can focus more deeply on specific areas of life in retirement.

The book you're holding now is dedicated to travel, outdoor adventures, health, and staying active—all the physical and adventurous pursuits that keep life exciting and fulfilling. Whether you're dreaming of exploring new destinations, hiking beautiful landscapes, or keeping your body and mind sharp through fitness, this book is your ultimate guide to making the most of your time outdoors and on the move.

I understand that not everyone may be solely interested in physical adventure or travel. That's why the second book, *Retirement Reinvented: Your Inspiring Guide to Creative Expression, Intellectual Growth, Entrepreneurial Ventures, and Leaving a Legacy for a Fulfilling and Meaningful Life After Work,* focuses on intellectual pursuits, creative expression, community building, and entrepreneurship—perfect for those looking to continue growing, learning, and connecting in meaningful ways. Each book offers a unique approach to thriving in retirement, allowing you to choose the path that speaks to you most.

But why limit yourself to one? For the most well-rounded and enriching retirement experience, I encourage you to explore both books. Together, they will create a complete guide to living a life filled with adventure, growth, and lasting connections. Whether you're drawn to outdoor exploration, the quiet satisfaction of creative and intellectual engagement, or both, these books will inspire you to make the most of this exciting chapter.

So, here's my call to action: approach your retirement with an adventurous spirit. Be open-minded and be willing to try new things. Use this book as your guide to explore the multitude of options available. To make these golden years the best years yet, let's redefine the idea of retirement. Let's think of retirement not as an end, but as a fantastic beginning. Let's embrace these years with enthusiasm and make them truly unforgettable. Buckle up; it's going to be a fantastic ride! Let's go!

Chapter Two

Designing Your Dream Retirement: A Blueprint for Adventure and Fulfillment

You know that feeling when you walk into a room and forget why you're there? Well, that's how some folks approach retirement—except the room is the rest of your life, and you're not entirely sure what to do next. But let's flip that script. Picture yourself waking up every day, filled with anticipation of the possibility of starting a new hobby, meeting interesting people, or finally visiting your dream location. Sounds thrilling, right? That's what planning your adventure-filled retirement is all about.

2.1 Charting Your Path to an Epic Retirement Adventure

Define Bold and Clear Goals

Defining clear objectives for your retirement is like plotting a course for a fabulous journey. Start by identifying your passions and interests. Are you a thrill-seeker who's always wanted to sky dive, or do you find joy in more serene pursuits like painting or gardening? Creating a retirement bucket list can be a fun way to get started. Jot down everything you've ever wanted to do—no matter how outlandish it seems. Then, try visualizing a typical day in your retirement. Are you strolling through a local farmer's market or taking a cooking class in Tuscany? These exercises help bring your goals into sharper focus.

Once you have a list of potential goals, it's time to prioritize them. Not all dreams are created equal—some may be more workable than others, based on your resources and physical abilities. Rank your goals by considering what excites you the most, what's achievable given your current situation, and what aligns best with your long-term plans. This ranking helps maintain focus and motivation, ensuring that your most cherished dreams don't get lost in the shuffle.

Setting SMART Goals

Setting SMART goals is crucial in making your retirement dreams a reality. SMART stands for **Specific, Measurable, Achievable, Rel-**

evant, and **Time-bound**. By breaking your goals down into these components, you create a clear path toward success. Let's explore each element in more detail with examples to help you create well-structured, attainable goals.

- **Specific**: The first step is to make your goal clear and specific. A vague goal like "I want to stay active" doesn't provide direction or motivation. Instead, try to specify exactly what you want to achieve. For example, "I want to walk 10,000 steps every day" or "I want to swim for one hour three times a week" makes it crystal clear what you're aiming for. Another example: instead of "I want to volunteer," try "I want to volunteer at the local animal shelter for five hours a week."

- **Measurable**: To know if you're making progress, your goals need to be measurable. This means putting numbers or milestones on your goals so you can track your advancement. Instead of saying "I want to read more books," make it measurable: "I want to read 24 books this year." This allows you to track your progress (two books per month) and celebrate small wins along the way. If you want to improve your fitness, set a measurable goal like "I want to lower my cholesterol to below 200 in six months."

- **Achievable**: While it's great to aim high, your goals should also be realistic and achievable given your circumstances. For example, if you've never hiked before, a goal of climbing Mount Kilimanjaro next year will be unrealistic. A more achievable goal would be "I want to hike five beginner trails this year." This way, you're pushing yourself instead of setting up for disappointment. Keep in mind your current health, time, and resources, and make sure your goals fit within those constraints.

- **Relevant**: Your goals should align with your overall vision for retirement and your personal interests. Ask yourself if the goal is meaningful and whether it brings you closer to your broader objectives. For example, if your broader vision is to stay socially engaged, a goal like "I want to take a photography class" may not align as well as "I want to join a photography club where I can meet new people." Ensuring your goals are relevant to your values will make them more motivating and worthwhile.

- **Time-bound**: Finally, always attach a timeline to your goals. Without deadlines, it's easy to procrastinate or lose motivation. Instead of saying "I want to learn a new language," try "I want to complete an introductory Italian course within the next six months." This gives you a sense of urgency and a clear deadline to work towards. A time-bound goal like "I want to complete a 5K run in the next three months" gives you a reason to stay committed.

Creating SMART goals will not only give your retirement plans structure but also boost your motivation and chances of success. Whether it's traveling, volunteering, learning a new skill, or improving your health, SMART goals provide a framework to turn your dreams into reality. By being specific, measuring your progress, setting achievable targets, ensuring relevance, and giving yourself deadlines, you'll be well on your way to a fulfilling and adventurous retirement!

Visualization Techniques

Visualization techniques can be incredibly powerful in turning your retirement dreams into reality. A vision board is a great tool for this. Grab some magazines, scissors, and glue, and start cutting out images and words that represent your goals. Arrange them on a board where you can see them every day. If you prefer a digital approach, there are plenty of free apps that make it easy to create a virtual vision board. Apps like **Canva, Pinterest,** and **Adobe Spark** allow you to gather images, words, and inspirational quotes that resonate with your goals. Simply drag and drop your selections onto a digital canvas, and arrange them in a way that feels meaningful to you. Whether you choose a traditional board or a digital one, the key is to place it somewhere you'll see it every day. This constant visual reminder helps keep your aspirations at the forefront of your mind.

Journaling is another effective technique that can help turn your retirement dreams into actionable steps. Start by writing down your retirement goals, but don't stop there. Dive deeper by creating detailed descriptions of what achieving each goal would look and feel like. Imagine the sights, sounds, fragrances, and emotions associated with your ideal retirement life. For instance, if your goal is to travel more, describe the destinations you want to visit, the experiences you hope to have, and the sense of adventure and fulfillment that comes with exploring unknown places. This kind of vivid writing brings your aspirations to life, making them more tangible and real.

Setting clear, prioritized, and achievable goals is the first step toward a retirement filled with adventure and fulfillment. These practices can provide a motivational boost when you need it most. Whether you're dreaming of skydiving, painting, or traveling, having a well-defined and emotionally charged plan can make those dreams a reality. Pour a cup of coffee, or a glass of wine, grab that pen or laptop, and get ready to create a dream plan to embark on the most exciting chapter of your life!

2.2 Maximizing Your Adventures with Minimal Spending

Assess Financial Resources

Let's face it, the idea of a retirement filled with endless adventures sounds delightful until you start thinking about the price tag. But don't worry, you can have your cake and eat it too. The first step is to assess your financial resources. Start by taking a thorough inventory of your savings, investments, and retirement accounts. If you have a pension, Social Security benefits, or income from rental properties, be sure to include these as well. It's also important to consider any potential sources of income you might tap into during retirement, such as part-time work, consulting, or freelancing. Take a realistic look at what you're spending now and how it might change when you retire. Will you downsize your home? Travel more? By understanding all of your financial resources, you can form a picture of what's feasible and prioritize your spending on the activities that matter most to you. To simplify this process, consider working with a financial advisor or using online retirement calculators like those available through **Fidelity** or **Vanguard** to give you a clearer idea of your retirement income potential.

Create a Retirement Budget

Creating a retirement budget is the next logical step after assessing your financial resources. While this may sound tedious, think of it as your roadmap to financial freedom during retirement—it's how you'll ensure you're living comfortably while still having enough to fund those dream vacations or new hobbies. Start by listing your **fixed expenses**, such as rent or mortgage payments, property taxes, utilities, groceries, and healthcare costs. Keep in mind that healthcare can become a larger expense as you age, so you may want to allocate a generous portion of your budget to medical care and insurance premiums.

Next, consider your **variable expenses**, which include things like dining out, entertainment, hobbies, travel, and any new recreational activities you plan to pick up during retirement. It's important to strike a balance between your everyday needs and the things that bring you joy. This is where budgeting gets fun—you can earmark a portion of your income for adventures and hobbies that enhance your life. Want to take an annual vacation or buy a new camera for your photography hobby? Include those in your budget!

When drafting your budget, don't forget to include an **emergency fund** for unexpected costs like home repairs or medical emergencies. This safety net can help prevent financial stress when life throws an unexpected curveball. Consider using financial planning tools to track your expenses, visualize your budget, and help you stay on course. With a well-planned budget, you can enjoy your retirement without worrying about overspending—allowing you to live large while keeping your finances in check.

Financial Planning Tools

Financial planning tools can be incredibly useful for planning and keeping your finances in check. Apps like **Rocket Money, You Need a Budget (YNAB), Empower (formerly Personal Capital), Simplifi, PocketSmith, and Tiller** can help you manage your funds more effectively. These tools allow you to track your spending, set financial goals, and even get alerts when you're veering off course. It's like having a financial advisor in your pocket, minus the hefty fees. By leveraging these resources, you can ensure your funds are allocated wisely, allowing you to indulge in adventures without financial stress.

Cost-Saving Tips for Retirees

Now, who doesn't love a good bargain? Cost-saving tips for activities can help you stretch your dollars further, sacrificing none of the fun. The first and easiest step is to take full advantage of **senior discounts**. These perks are available in more places than you might think. From discounts at local theaters, movie cinemas, and restaurants to reduced rates for public transportation and museums, every little savings can add up over time. For instance, **AARP (**American Association of Retired Persons) and other senior organizations often offer special discounts at hotels, car rental companies, and even retail stores, making membership a great investment. Please refer to the **Resources Chapter** for a list of organizations offering worldwide resources, advocacy, services, and discounts for seniors.

Another savvy strategy is to plan your trip during **off-peak or shoulder seasons**. Traveling just before or after peak tourist times allows you to save money on flights, accommodations, and attractions while avoiding the crowds. For instance, visiting popular European cities in early spring or late autumn often results in lower costs and a more relaxed experience. Tools like **Google Flights**, **Skyscanner**, and

Kayak can help you find the best deals on flights, especially if you're flexible with your travel dates. Booking mid-week can sometimes save you a significant amount on airfare as well.

When it comes to accommodations, consider alternatives like **Airbnb** for longer stays, as they often offer better rates than hotels. However, don't overlook the benefits of contacting hotels directly, as many now offer lower rates when booked through their websites. Some hotels might even throw in extras like free breakfast or room upgrades. **Hostels** can also be a great option—they aren't just for backpackers anymore! Many now offer private rooms at affordable rates.

Using price comparison websites is a powerful tool for saving money on everything from flights to accommodations. Websites like **Google Flights, Skyscanner, and Kayak** allow you to compare prices across different airlines and booking platforms, helping you find the best deals on airfare. By setting up alerts for price drops, you can track fluctuations and book your tickets when rates are at their lowest. Similarly, for accommodations, platforms like **Booking.com, Airbnb, and Hotels.com** offer comprehensive searches that let you filter by price, amenities, and reviews. When booking car rentals, **Rentalcars.com** and **Expedia** can help you compare prices across multiple rental agencies, ensuring you get the best deal. With a few clicks, you can quickly evaluate options and make informed choices that save you time, effort, and money—leaving more in your budget for those unforgettable experiences.

For activities, **local attractions** can offer fantastic budget-friendly entertainment. Check out free or low-cost events like community festivals or outdoor concerts. Many museums and galleries offer free admission days or senior discounts. Nature lovers can take full advantage of **hiking trails, parks, and nature reserves**, often free or requiring only a small entrance fee. For example, in the U.S., you can purchase a **National Parks Senior Pass**, granting lifetime access to over 2,000 national parks and recreation sites for a one-time fee. This is perfect for nature lovers who want to explore hiking trails, parks, and reserves without constantly worrying about entrance fees.

For meals, **eating like a local** is key to saving money and experiencing the true flavor of a place. Avoid touristy restaurants and opt for local markets, street food, or eateries where the locals dine. Not only are they more affordable, but they also offer a more authentic culinary experience. Shop for breakfast items or snacks at local grocery stores to cut down on dining costs.

Technology is your best friend when traveling on a budget. Apps like **Hopper** can predict the best time to book flights, while **Hotel-Tonight** offers last-minute accommodation deals. Digital maps, such as **Google Maps**, can help you navigate new cities with no need for pricey guided tours—simply create your own route with points of interest, hidden gems, and local eateries.

Another option to save on recreational activities is to join **local clubs or community centers**. Many offer low-cost or free classes and workshops in activities such as painting, dancing, or gardening. These are not only budget-friendly but also a great way to socialize and make new friends who share your interests.

Take advantage of online resources and apps like **Meetup.com** or **Eventbrite** to find free events and gatherings in your area. Whether it's a group hiking trip, a photography workshop, or a book club meeting, these platforms are treasure troves of budget-friendly activities that can enrich your retirement experience. With a bit of planning and creativity, you can enjoy an active and fulfilling retirement without breaking the bank.

To illustrate, let's take a real-life example. When my husband and I decided to take a month-long trip to Europe, we didn't want to drain our savings. We started by creating a detailed budget, allocating funds for flights, accommodations, and daily expenses. Then we booked flights during the off-peak season and took advantage of senior discounts on car rentals. We found great deals on **Booking.com**, allowing us to stay in lovely, affordable accommodations. We also stayed a few times in charming and budget-friendly Airbnb rentals. By using **Rocket Money** to track our spending daily, we managed to stick to our budget without sacrificing experiences. The result? A fantastic, memorable trip that didn't break the bank.

So, as you can see, maximizing your adventures with minimal spending is entirely possible. With careful planning, smart budgeting, and a little creativity, you can make your retirement dreams a reality without financial stress.

2.3 Essential Digital Tools for Modern Retirees

Basic Technology Skills

So, you've packed away the office supplies, handed over your work badge, and are ready to embrace retirement. No more after-hours calls and deadline emails! But don't toss that smartphone and tablet aside just yet! These gadgets are about to become your best retirement friends. First, let's talk about mastering the basics. You might think you know your way around a smartphone, but do you? Can you download apps and use them fast and efficiently? How comfortable are you navigating the app store to find new tools to enhance your day-to-day life? Can you manage different social media platforms like

Facebook or Instagram (they keep changing all the time) to stay connected with friends and family? Do you know how to troubleshoot when something goes awry? Understanding how to reset your device, update software, or fix common glitches will save you from unnecessary frustration.

Beyond these, there are a few more tech-related questions to ask yourself. Are you familiar with cloud storage? With photos, documents, and apps accumulating on your devices, learning to use cloud services like **Google Drive or iCloud** can ensure your files are safe and accessible from anywhere. Do you know how to maximize your device's security settings? Keeping your data safe with strong passwords and two-factor authentication is essential.

To answer these questions and build your skills, start by doing some research. Search for online tutorials and videos on platforms like **YouTube**, which have step-by-step guides on everything from basic smartphone use to more advanced troubleshooting. Websites like **TechBoomers** and **Seniors Guide to Computers** offer free courses specifically designed for older adults wanting to boost their tech literacy. You can also explore free courses on **Udemy** or **Coursera** that cover smartphone and tablet basics. By taking advantage of these resources, you'll be mastering your devices and apps in no time, making your retirement both connected and exciting.

Technology for Travel and Leisure

Learning to use navigation apps like **Google Maps, Apple Maps, MapQuest, Waze, CoPilot GPS, RoadTrippers, Alltrails, and Citymapper** (for public transportation) can turn a simple walk in the park into an exciting treasure hunt for new places to explore. Just type in your destination, and you're off on a smooth, worry-free journey.

There's nothing like the thrill of dreaming up and booking your next adventure. But without the right prep, that excitement can fade fast. Thankfully, we've got travel apps to save the day. They cover everything, from trip planning **(GoogleTravel, TripCase, Wanderlog)** to booking attractions **(Viator, Steller, Culture Trip)**, flights, hotels, or rental cars **(Hopper, HotelTonight, TripAdvisor, Airbnb, Booking.com, Expedia, Hotels.com, Kayak, VRBO)**, to currency conversions **(Xe)**, to dining **(WorldofMouth, OpenTable, EatWith)**, making trips smoother and more budget-friendly and helping you find unique accommodations and hidden gems in any city.

And for the bookworms out there, an e-reader apps like the **Kindle, Google Play Books, Apple Books, Nook, Kobo, and Libby** can store thousands of books, offering endless entertainment without the bulk. Imagine sitting by a serene lake, or on a transatlantic flight, flipping through the latest bestseller on your e-reader. Pure bliss.

Staying Connected

Staying connected has never been easier, thanks to technology. Platforms like **Skype and Zoom** have become indispensable, especially for those of us with family and friends scattered across the globe. A quick video call can bridge the miles, making it feel like your loved ones are right there with you. Social media platforms like **Facebook, WhatsApp, and X (formerly Twitter)** offer a fantastic way to stay updated with what's happening in your friends' and family's lives. Sharing photos **(KwikPic, Instagram, Google Photos)**, commenting on posts, and even creating your own retirement blog **(Squarespace, Wix, Pixpa, Blogger, Hostinger, BTW)** can keep you engaged and socially active.

Health Management Apps

Health management is another area where technology shines. With the plethora of health and wellness apps available, managing your health has never been more convenient. Apps like **MyFitnessPal, Noom, FIIT** can help you track your diet and exercise routines, while others like **Medisafe** remind you to take your medications on time. **HealthTap** provides a personalized answer from doctors in less than 24 hours. **Headspace, Calm, and Insight Timer** have hundreds of guided meditations. And **Apple Fitness Plus, BetterMe, Glo, and SWEAT** track your progress and help you learn new workouts.

Fitness trackers, such as **Fitbit, Apple Watch, and Oura Ring**, monitor your steps, heart rate, and even your sleep patterns. These gadgets can be particularly useful for staying on top of your health goals. Imagine going for your morning walk, glancing at your wrist, and seeing that you've already hit your step goal for the day. It's a small but satisfying victory that keeps you motivated.

As you can see, digital tools can truly enhance your retirement, helping you stay close to loved ones, manage your health, and make the most of your travels. But remember, while these gadgets and apps are great, it's just as important to take time away from the screen. Balance is key—use technology to enrich your life, but don't forget to unplug and savor the moments that make your life special. Power up when you need to, and also make sure to set the devices aside and enjoy the sights and sounds of the world around you.

2.4 Balancing Safety with Adventure

Routine Medical Check-ups

Let's talk about the tightrope walk of balancing safety with adventure. First and foremost, routine medical check-ups are non-negotiable. Think of them as the pit stops on your grand adventure. Regular visits to your healthcare provider ensure you catch any potential issues early, keeping you on the road to a healthy retirement. Discuss your physical activities and future plans with your doctor to ensure they are safe for your specific health conditions. This proactive approach not only maintains your health but also gives you peace of mind, knowing you're fit to tackle whatever adventure comes your way.

Risk Assessment for Activities

Not all of us are in peak physical condition, and that's perfectly okay. The key is adapting activities to match your physical abilities. If hiking up a mountain sounds daunting, opt for a nature walk on a flat trail. Love the idea of cycling but worried about balance? Consider an electric bike. Swimming can be gentle laps in a pool instead of battling ocean waves. If getting on the floor is challenging, you can do chair yoga. There are always modifications and alternatives available, ensuring you can still take part in activities that bring you joy. The goal is to stay active in a way that is safe and feels good to you.

Now picture this: you're all set to hike up a scenic trail, your backpack is stocked, your boots are laced, and then it dawns on you—what if something goes wrong? Don't let that thought send you diving under the covers. Instead, let's tackle risk assessment head-on. Start by considering the activity at hand. Hiking, for example, might seem straightforward but involves risks like uneven terrain, weather changes, and wildlife encounters. Assess the difficulty level of the trail and your fitness level. Ask yourself, do you have the stamina for a five-mile hike, or should you start with something shorter?

If you're planning to travel abroad, research your destination. Know the local customs, understand the political climate, and be aware of any health advisories and the necessary vaccines. For example, in some countries, it's crucial to avoid certain areas after dark, or perhaps it's customary to dress modestly. These minor adjustments can make a big difference. Consider other potential risks like natural disasters, unfamiliar legal systems, and the possibility of scams or petty crime. Knowledge isn't just power—it's your ticket to a safe and enjoyable adventure.

Safety Measures and Emergency Preparedness

Safety measures and precautions are your best friends when it comes to enjoying activities without the looming shadow of danger. For instance, if you're into cycling, wearing a helmet isn't just a good idea; it's a must. Invest in good-quality gear—from helmets and gloves to reflective clothing. And don't forget to check your bike's brakes and tires before hitting the road. If you're planning on cycling long distances, consider carrying a small repair kit that includes tire patches, a multi-tool, and a portable pump. For night rides, make sure to have proper lights—both front and rear—to ensure visibility to others on the road.

When trying out new sports, following your instructor's advice is critical. Whether it's scuba diving, rock climbing, or skiing, these experts know their stuff, and following their guidance can prevent mishaps. Ask questions if you're unsure about a technique or piece of equipment. Get familiar with the terrain and weather conditions before heading out, especially for activities or areas where the environment can change unexpectedly.

Safety is key to enjoying a road trip without unexpected hassles. Before you hit the road, make sure your car is in top shape. Check the oil, tires, and brakes, and don't forget to ensure your spare tire is ready for action. Pack an emergency kit with essentials like a first aid kit, flashlight, jumper cables, and extra water. For longer trips, include a portable battery charger for your devices, a blanket, and extra snacks.

It's also essential to keep a friend or family member informed about your travel plans. Before heading out, share your route, accommodations, and general itinerary with someone back home. Check in regularly, especially if you're moving between different locations. For longer trips or more adventurous travel, consider using a location-sharing app like **Google Maps** or **Find My Friends** so loved ones can track your whereabouts in real time. This way, if you experience any unexpected changes or delays, someone will know your general location and can raise an alert if necessary. It's an extra layer of security that gives both you and your family peace of mind during your travels.

For all activities, don't underestimate the importance of staying hydrated and applying sunscreen, even on cloudy days or when engaging in water sports. Having a reliable first-aid kit and basic first aid knowledge can also come in handy, whether you're hiking, camping, or simply spending a day at the beach.

Emergency preparedness is the foundation of safe adventuring. Picture yourself hiking on a beautiful trail when you twist your ankle—what's your plan? Being prepared for these situations can make all the difference. Always carry a well-stocked first aid kit, whether you're hiking, biking, or traveling. Your kit should include essentials like adhesive bandages, antiseptic wipes, gauze, medical tape, pain relievers, and blister pads. It's equally important to know the basics of first aid: how to clean and dress a wound, properly bandage a sprain, and recognize signs of dehydration or heatstroke. Having these skills ensures you can handle minor injuries on the spot and prevent them from becoming bigger issues.

Besides your first aid kit, make sure to have a list of local emergency contacts handy. If you're traveling abroad, familiarize yourself with the local emergency services number—the equivalent of 911—so you can act quickly in a crisis. It's also a good idea to store important numbers, like your doctor's, your travel insurance company's, and the nearest embassy or consulate, in both your phone and on paper, in case your phone dies or gets lost.

To prevent being left in a vulnerable situation with a dead phone, carry a small power bank to ensure your device stays charged. A portable charger can be a lifesaver when you're out in nature or traveling in remote areas with no access to electricity. Having backup power ensures that you can make emergency calls, use offline maps, or access important information at any time.

Another smart move is to download offline maps and health-related apps, which can guide you to the nearest medical facility or help you find your way, even if you don't have cell service. But sometimes, technology can only take you so far, and an old-fashioned paper map can be a real lifesaver. I remember one time when my husband was mountain biking in a new area while I was hiking. We had no cellular service, and he ended up taking a wrong turn and getting lost. Fortunately, he had a trail map with him and used it to navigate his way back to the parking lot, where I had been waiting anxiously for what felt like ages. His paper map saved the day when digital tools couldn't. A funny fact: that area was around a lake on Vancouver Island called the Lost Lake, which we now call the "Lost and Found" Lake.

With these precautions in place—whether digital or traditional—a little foresight can turn a potential disaster into a manageable inconvenience, allowing you to continue your adventure safely and confidently.

When engaging in outdoor adventures, it's also essential to be prepared for potential encounters with wildlife. Whether you're hiking in a national park, camping, or exploring a remote trail, understanding the local fauna and how to react to encounters can ensure both your safety and the safety of the animals. Always research the wildlife in the area you're visiting, including any potential dangers like bears, mountain lions, or snakes. Carry bear spray in areas known for bear activity and store food properly in bear-proof containers or hang it from a tree to avoid attracting wildlife to your campsite. When hiking, make noise periodically to avoid surprising animals, especially in dense forests or near water sources. If you encounter wildlife, remain calm, keep your distance, and never approach or feed the animals. Many parks provide specific guidelines for handling wildlife encounters, so be sure to review these before heading out. Your awareness and preparedness can prevent dangerous situations while allowing you to peacefully enjoy the natural beauty of your surroundings.

Insurance and Legal Considerations

Now, let's talk about the not-so-glamorous but utterly crucial topic of insurance and legal considerations. Imagine you're on a dream vacation in Bali, and you suddenly need medical attention. Travel insurance can be a lifesaver, covering everything from medical emergencies to trip cancellations. Make sure your travel insurance includes medical evacuation—you don't want to be stuck with a hefty bill if you need to be flown back home. It should also cover any unexpected incidents like trip cancellations or lost luggage. Being prepared helps you focus on the excitement of your adventure rather than worrying about the "what-ifs."

For those engaging in activities like skiing or scuba diving, check if your insurance covers these high-risk activities. Medical insurance is equally important. Ensure you have a plan that covers regular check-ups and emergencies. And don't overlook legal considerations. If you're planning to drive in a foreign country, ensure you have the appropriate licenses and understand local driving laws. Ignorance isn't bliss when it comes to legal matters—it's a recipe for trouble.

Please refer to the **Resources Chapter** for insurance companies' recommendations.

As you plan your retirement adventures, remember that a bit of forethought and preparation can turn potential risks into manageable challenges. Embrace the thrill, but keep safety at the forefront. Your golden years are meant to be enjoyed, and a well-balanced approach ensures that every adventure is both exhilarating and safe.

Chapter Three

Pathways to Wellness: Inspiring Journeys for a Healthy and Active Retirement

R etirement is the perfect time to focus on health and wellness, and there are countless ways to do so. Many people think that health and wellness are all about hitting the gym or sticking to a healthy diet, and while those are important, let's take a broader, more mindful approach. After all, no adventure, contribution, or new passion can truly flourish if your health is not in good shape. That's why I'm starting with this essential chapter on health and wellness—a strong foundation is key to enjoying all the experiences retirement has to offer. Without it, even the grandest travel plans or the most exciting new hobbies can become challenging. Taking time to invest in both your physical and mental well-being is crucial. In this chapter, we'll dive into mindfulness, movement, nutrition, and other wellness practices that can support you in improving and maintaining your health, bring peace to your mind, and joy to your heart so you can fully embrace this next chapter of life with vitality. Let's start with an often-overlooked, yet incredibly powerful, tool: mindfulness.

3.1 Finding Peace: Mindfulness and Meditation Retreats

Exploring the benefits of mindfulness and meditation is like opening a treasure chest of mental and physical health rewards. Imagine reducing stress so effectively that you forget what it even felt like in the first place. Mindfulness and meditation help you achieve just that. These practices improve focus, allowing you to savor each moment more fully. They also help with emotional regulation—suddenly, those little annoyances that once ruffled your feathers become as insignificant as a speck of dust. The benefits are scientifically backed, with many studies showing how mindfulness can lower blood pressure, reduce anxiety, and improve sleep quality.

Finding the right retreat is crucial. You don't want to end up in a place where the "meditation leader" is more interested in your wallet than in your well-being. Ensure the leaders are qualified; a good retreat will have experienced instructors with credentials in mindfulness and meditation practices, like Certified Mindfulness Teacher or Certified Mindfulness Informed Professional.

Look for retreats that offer a serene environment, whether it's a mountainside sanctuary or a peaceful beach resort. Activities should include guided meditations, yoga sessions, and some time for silent reflection. You might enjoy healthy cooking classes that focus on nourishing both body and mind or journaling workshops that help you explore your thoughts and emotions in a supportive environment. Nature walks, creative arts sessions, and mindful movement practices such as Tai Chi could also be part of the experience, offering a holistic approach to rejuvenation and inner peace.

There are many types of retreats, from weekend getaways to week-long immersions. Please refer to the **Resources Chapter** for some popular retreats known for their serene environments and experienced instructors.

Preparing for a retreat involves more than just packing your yoga pants and a comfy sweater. Mentally, approach the experience with an open mind and a heart ready to embrace tranquility. Physically, pack light but smart. Comfortable clothing is a must, along with any personal items that help you relax, like a scented candle, a favorite book, or a journal. Bring a reusable water bottle and some healthy snacks. Expect to disconnect from the digital world—most retreats encourage limited use of phones and other devices to help you immerse yourself fully in the experience.

Integrating practices into daily life ensures that the peace and focus you gain from the retreat don't fade away once you return home. Start with a daily routine; even five minutes of mindfulness each morning can set a positive tone for the day. Many apps, like **Headspace, Insight Timer, and Calm,** offer guided meditations perfect for beginners. Local community centers or yoga studios often provide mindfulness classes, allowing you to practice in a supportive environment. Over time, these practices can become as natural to you as brushing your teeth, providing lasting benefits for your mental and physical health.

3.2 Golf as a Social Game: Connection, Fitness, and Fun

So you pictured yourself on a lush green course, a gentle breeze on your face, and the satisfying sound of a well-struck ball, and you've decided to take up golf. Excellent choice! Golf is the perfect blend of exercise, relaxation, and social interaction. The game's beauty lies in its simplicity and complexity, making it engaging for newbies and seasoned players alike.

Let's start with the basics. First, understand the equipment. You'll need a set of golf clubs, which typically includes drivers, irons, wedges, and a putter. You don't need to buy the most expensive set. Beginners can start with a basic set and upgrade later as their skills improve. You'll also need balls, tees, and gloves—nothing too fancy at first, just the essentials to get started.

Understanding the basic rules and etiquette is equally important. Know when to be quiet, where to stand, and how to keep score. These small details contribute to the overall experience and enjoyment of the game, and they help maintain the respect and rhythm that golfers value.

A great way to kick-start your golfing journey is by taking beginner classes. Many golf courses and clubs offer lessons specifically designed for new players, where you'll learn proper technique, how to swing, and course strategies. Plus, an instructor can help you correct mistakes early on, making the learning process smoother and more enjoyable.

The physical benefits of golf are many. Walking the course improves muscle tone and balance without the jarring impact of more intense sports. Swinging the club engages various muscle groups and enhances flexibility. But it's not just about the body. Golf is a mental game, requiring concentration and strategic thinking. The serene outdoor environment also offers a pleasant break, allowing you to soak in nature while you play.

Golfers can adapt the game to suit their fitness levels. Not everyone can walk 18 holes, and that's okay. Golf carts are a great way to get around the course without overexerting yourself. If a full course seems too daunting, start with a shorter, 9-hole course. Senior-friendly equipment, like lighter clubs with larger grips, can make the game more accessible and enjoyable. These small adjustments ensure you can enjoy the game without straining your body, making it a lifelong sport.

One of the best aspects of golf is its social nature. Joining a local golf club can open up a world of new friendships and social opportunities. Many clubs offer group clinics, perfect for learning the game and meeting people. Weekly tournaments and social gatherings provide additional chances to mingle. Whether you're playing a round with old friends or joining a foursome with new acquaintances, golf offers countless opportunities for social interaction. And the clubhouse is always a great spot for post-game drinks and banter.

3.3 Refreshing Waters: Water Aerobics, Swimming, and Cold Plunges

There's something truly magical about being in the water, where every movement feels fluid and weightless. The gentle embrace of the water creates a sense of calm and freedom, offering a unique combination of relaxation and invigoration. When you're gliding effortlessly through the water, feeling the light resistance as you move, your joints thank you with every stroke. These activities provide a low-impact workout that's perfect for aging bodies. The buoyancy of the water reduces the stress on your joints and musculoskeletal system, making it an ideal exercise if you suffer from arthritis or other joint issues. The resistance water offers helps build strength and improve flexibility without the risk of injury that comes with high-impact exercises.

Pool-Based Water Aerobics and Swimming

Starting a water aerobics or swimming routine doesn't require much. Grab a comfortable swimsuit, water shoes for better traction, and a pair of goggles if you plan to swim laps. You might also want to invest in some pool noodles or water dumbbells to add variety to your workouts, however they are available in most pools. When you're in the water, safety is paramount. Make sure the pool has a lifeguard on duty and always inform someone of your swim schedule. Start slowly and gradually increase the intensity of your workouts as your body adapts. Whether you're doing structured water aerobics classes or swimming laps at your own pace, consistency is key to reaping the benefits.

Warm water exercises add another layer of benefit. Exercising in a heated pool can help relax muscles and ease joint pain, making your workout even more effective. The warmth also increases blood flow, aiding in quicker recovery post-exercise. Finding a pool that offers warm water sessions can be very beneficial if you deal with chronic pain or stiffness. Some community centers and health clubs have specific times when they heat their pools to cater to those needing that extra comfort.

Cold Water Swimming and Outdoor Plunges

For those seeking a more exhilarating experience, cold-water swimming and outdoor plunges offer a thrilling way to engage with nature while boosting overall health. Swimming in lakes, rivers, or the ocean adds an extra dimension of freedom compared to a pool environment. But it's the cold water that truly provides unique benefits—enhancing circulation, reducing inflammation, and even boosting mental clarity and resilience. Cold-water exposure has been linked to improved immune function and mood, making it a fantastic option for retirees looking to keep their bodies and minds sharp.

If you're ready to try cold-water swimming, safety is crucial. Start by ensuring you're familiar with the location—research local conditions and currents, and never swim alone. Gradually acclimate to cold water by starting with shorter dips and slowly increasing the duration as your body adjusts. Experts recommend beginning with water temperatures around 10-15°C (50-59°F), which can provide the benefits of cold exposure without overwhelming your system. Begin with brief dips lasting 10 to 30 seconds, and over time, you can work up to 1-2 minutes as your tolerance increases. It's important to always listen to your body and exit the water if you begin to feel too uncomfortable. Have warm, dry clothing ready when you exit the water to prevent excessive chilling, and consider using a wetsuit for longer swims.

The Finnish Sauna Tradition of Cold Plunges

For centuries, Finland and Russia have upheld the invigorating tradition of alternating between hot saunas and icy cold plunges. After spending time in the heat of a sauna, locals take a brief, shocking dip into a nearby frozen lake or a cold-water pool, embracing the sharp contrast in temperatures. This practice stimulates circulation, promotes deep relaxation, and even relieves chronic aches and pains, making it a perfect wellness ritual for retirees.

This tradition has expanded beyond the Nordic regions, and many modern wellness centers worldwide now offer these experiences. Facilities often provide sauna rooms paired with ice-cold plunge pools, allowing you to enjoy the therapeutic benefits without venturing into the wild. These sauna-and-plunge sessions are ideal for improving circulation, boosting the immune system, and enhancing mental clarity while providing a unique and rejuvenating experience.

If you're new to cold plunges, start by immersing yourself for no longer than 30 seconds to 1 minute in water temperatures ranging from 10-15°C (50-59°F). Gradually, you can increase the time as your body becomes accustomed to the cold.

Before incorporating cold-water plunges or outdoor swimming into your routine, consult with a healthcare provider, especially if you have any underlying health conditions like heart issues or respiratory problems. Cold exposure can be a shock to the system, so ensuring your body is ready for this practice will keep you safe while maximizing the health benefits.

3.4 Floating into Wellness: The Sensory Deprivation Experience

For those looking to explore a more meditative, introspective pathway to wellness in water, sensory deprivation floats offer a deeply relaxing and rejuvenating experience. When you're drifting effortlessly in a saltwater float pod, completely free of external distractions, your senses have a chance to rest and reset. The water, infused with high concentrations of Epsom salts, creates a buoyancy that makes you feel weightless, while the isolation chamber eliminates outside noise, light, and even the sense of touch. Floating in these specialized pods can have profound effects on both mental and physical health, making it a perfect practice for retirees seeking inner peace, pain relief, and overall well-being.

I discovered the magic of sensory deprivation a few years ago, and it quickly became a vital part of my self-care routine. There's a sensory deprivation center where I live, and after just one session, I was hooked. I remember stepping out of the pod feeling like a new person—completely refreshed, with a clear mind and relaxed body. I felt as though I'd hit a reset button. Needless to say, I immediately purchased a membership and now make it a priority to float twice a month. Each session feels like a retreat—a space where I can unwind and let go of the stresses of everyday life. It's become a sanctuary for me, a place where both my body and mind can truly rest.

The benefits of sensory deprivation floats are well-documented. Physically, the absence of gravity allows your muscles and joints to fully relax, which can be especially beneficial for those dealing with arthritis, chronic pain, or tension. The magnesium in the Epsom salts also helps soothe sore muscles and reduce inflammation. Mentally, sensory deprivation offers a unique opportunity to quiet the mind, which can reduce stress and anxiety, and promote a deeper sense of relaxation. Studies have shown that regular float sessions can help lower cortisol levels, improve sleep quality, and even spark creativity by providing a space for uninterrupted thought.

Getting started with sensory deprivation floating is as easy as finding a wellness center or spa that offers float therapy. These facilities often provide private float pods or rooms where you can enjoy a session in complete solitude. The typical float lasts between 60 and 90 minutes, although shorter or longer sessions are available depending on personal preference. Before entering the float pod, take a quick shower and put on earplugs to block out any lingering noise. Once inside the pod, the temperature of the water and air is set to match your body's temperature, creating a seamless transition between the two and enhancing the sensation of weightlessness.

As with any new wellness practice, it's important to consult with your doctor before trying sensory deprivation floats, especially if you have any health concerns like claustrophobia, low blood pressure, or skin sensitivities to salt. The ideal water temperature for floatation therapy is typically set between 93.5°F and 96°F (34°C to 35.5°C), which matches skin temperature, allowing for the perfect float experience. Start with shorter sessions of around 30 to 45 minutes, gradually increasing to the standard 60-90 minute float as your body becomes accustomed to the practice.

Floating in sensory deprivation pods can be a refreshing addition to your wellness journey, offering a unique blend of physical relief and mental clarity. If you're interested in floating but don't have a local center, keep in mind that this practice has become increasingly popular worldwide, and you can plan to visit a floating center during your travels. See the **Resources Chapter** for a list of some floating centers worldwide.

3.5 Fitness at Home: Online Classes and Resources

If you prefer to stay active without leaving the comfort of your home, online workout classes are perfect for you. Selecting appropriate workouts is crucial. **Yoga** is an excellent choice for flexibility and relaxation, while **chair yoga** offers a gentler alternative for those with mobility issues. If you're looking for something more dynamic,

Pilates strengthens core muscles and improves posture. **Tabata** is a high-intensity interval training that can be adapted to your fitness level, and **low-impact aerobics** keeps the heart pumping without too much strain. **Strength training** with light dumbbells can help maintain muscle mass and bone density, which is super important as we age.

The beauty of modern technology is that you have countless online platforms at your fingertips. Websites like **YouTube** offer free classes on anything from yoga to dance workouts. Platforms such as **Peloton** and **Daily Burn** provide live classes and on-demand videos, allowing you to follow along in real-time or at your convenience. These platforms often include progress tracking features, so you can see how much you've improved over time. Apps like **Apple Fitness Plus, MyFitnessPal, BetterMe, and FitOn** also offer curated workout plans tailored to your goals and fitness levels, making it easier than ever to stay on track.

Creating a home gym doesn't require a lot of space or a large investment. Start with minimal equipment like resistance bands, which are versatile and easy to store. A yoga mat and a sturdy chair (for chair yoga) are also great additions. You can use dumbbells of various weights for a wide range of exercises. The key is to have your equipment easily accessible so that you're more likely to use it regularly.

Safety is just as important when working out at home as in the gym. Always begin with a proper warm-up to prepare your muscles and joints. Understand your body's limits and avoid pushing yourself too hard. Start slow and gradually increase the intensity of your workouts. If you're unsure about a specific exercise or routine, seek professional advice. Personal trainers can offer virtual consultations to ensure you're performing exercises correctly, minimizing the risk of injury.

3.6 Gardening for Fitness, Mindfulness, and Growth

Stepping into my garden with the morning dew on the leaves and the fresh scent of the earth all around is my perfect moment of pure connection with nature. But gardening is not just a pleasant pastime; it's a full-body workout wrapped in nature's embrace. There are a few options to start a senior-friendly garden. **Raised beds** are very popular and for a good reason—they bring the soil to you, so no more bending and stooping. **Container gardening** is another fantastic option, allowing you to grow plants on patios or balconies with minimal effort. These methods make gardening accessible and enjoyable, no matter your physical condition.

The physical activities involved in gardening are deceptively beneficial. Digging, planting, weeding, and harvesting might seem like simple tasks, but they engage multiple muscle groups and improve flexibility and strength. Each movement, from pushing a wheelbarrow to pulling out weeds, contributes to overall fitness. It's like hitting the gym but with the added bonus of fresh air and sunshine. Plus, the satisfaction of seeing your hard work bloom into beautiful flowers or tasty vegetables is a reward in itself.

That said, safety is key when gardening, especially for us, seniors. Always take precautions to prevent overexertion or injury. First, protect yourself from the sun by wearing a wide-brimmed hat, sunglasses, and sunscreen with at least SPF 30, especially during midday hours when the sun's rays are strongest. Stay hydrated, as gardening is physically demanding, especially on hot days. Take regular breaks in the shade to avoid heat exhaustion.

When using tools, opt for ergonomically designed tools with padded grips to minimize strain on your hands and wrists. Wearing gloves can protect your skin from thorns, blisters, or insect bites. Bend from your knees, not your back, when lifting heavy items like bags of soil or plants, and use a kneeling pad or gardening stool to reduce pressure on your knees during tasks that require crouching. Consider installing a drip irrigation system to reduce the need for heavy watering cans or hoses.

Incorporating mindfulness into your gardening practice can elevate this activity from a hobby to a form of therapy. Focus on the sensory experiences—the texture of the soil, the vibrant colors of the flowers, and the songs of the birds. These moments of mindfulness help you stay present and grounded, reducing stress and enhancing emotional well-being. Gardening becomes more than just a task; it's an opportunity to connect deeply with nature and find peace in the process.

Community gardening offers another layer of benefits. Participating in a community garden can increase social interaction, allowing you to share gardening responsibilities and learn from others. It's a collaborative effort that fosters a sense of belonging and mutual support. You don't need a space at home to enjoy the fruits of your labor. Community gardens provide plots for you to cultivate your plants, and the shared environment creates opportunities for friendships and community building.

3.7 Tai Chi and Qigong: Gentle Movements for Strength and Balance

Tai Chi and Qigong are ancient Chinese practices where you move like water, flowing smoothly from one pose to another. Originating centuries ago, Tai Chi is a martial art focused on slow, deliberate movements, while Qigong combines breathing techniques with gentle motions. Both are rooted in the principles of balance, flexibility, and inner peace, making them beneficial for seniors. The deliberate pace of

Tai Chi and Qigong helps improve balance and strength without the strain of high-impact exercises. Plus, the focus on mindful movement can enhance mental clarity and reduce stress.

Embarking on the journey of Tai Chi and Qigong offers a unique blend of physical and mental enrichment. As you delve into the basics, focusing on your alignment and breath, you'll gradually see your flexibility and strength enhance. What's important about these practices is their versatility; they can be adapted for standing or seated positions. Their slow, graceful motions serve as a meditative exercise, nurturing both your body and mind.

Finding classes and resources tailored to seniors can enhance your learning experience. Look for local community centers or senior centers that offer Tai Chi and Qigong classes. Many instructors specialize in teaching older adults, ensuring the movements are safe and effective. Online resources, such as instructional videos, video courses on **Udemy**, and virtual classes, can also be valuable. **YouTube** or dedicated Tai Chi platforms like **Taichiapp.com** provide step-by-step guides you can follow at your own pace. Choose instructors with experience in senior fitness to ensure you're getting the most appropriate and beneficial instruction.

Integrating Tai Chi and Qigong into your daily routine can bring lasting benefits. Start your morning with a short session to set a calm and focused tone for the day. Incorporate the practices into your evening routine to unwind and prepare for a restful night. Regular practice can help maintain your physical health and enhance mental tranquility. Consider joining a local group for regular sessions, which can provide a sense of community and additional motivation. The gentle, rhythmic movements can become a cherished part of your daily life, supporting you on your retirement journey.

3.8 Paddling to Health: Kayaking, Canoeing, and Paddleboarding

Kayaking, canoeing, and paddleboarding are fantastic ways to stay fit, connect with nature, and find peace of mind, all while engaging in a low-impact, full-body workout. These activities are perfect for retirees looking to explore new adventures while promoting physical and mental well-being. They provide excellent cardiovascular exercise without putting undue strain on your joints. They engage your core, arms, and back muscles, improving balance and flexibility while also building upper body strength. For those dealing with arthritis or joint pain, paddling can offer a gentle yet effective way to stay active while reducing the impact on knees and hips compared to land-based exercises. Beyond the physical benefits, spending time on the water can enhance mental well-being. The fluid, repetitive motions involved in paddling make these activities a calming form of exercise, reducing stress as you glide across calm lakes, rivers, or coastal waters. Studies have shown that being near or on water can lower stress levels, improve mood, and promote a sense of calm. Whether you're navigating a quiet river in a kayak, paddling across a glassy lake on a stand-up paddleboard (SUP), or exploring winding waterways in a canoe, these activities offer a unique opportunity to escape the hustle and bustle of everyday life and reconnect with nature.

Getting started with paddling is both accessible and affordable, making it a perfect hobby for retirees looking to enjoy the outdoors. You don't need a lot of experience or expensive gear to begin; starting with a leisurely kayak or canoe trip on a calm lake or river is a great way to ease into the sport. For beginners, however, it's highly recommended to take a safety course offered by kayak and canoe clubs. These courses teach essential skills such as paddling techniques, safety measures, and handling various water conditions, ensuring your time on the water is enjoyable and worry-free. Many outdoor centers and national parks also offer rentals and guided tours, allowing you to explore new areas with confidence while learning from experienced instructors.

For those seeking a bit more adventure, paddleboarding (SUP) is a fantastic way to challenge your balance and engage your core. While it may look difficult at first, paddleboarding is surprisingly easy to pick up with a bit of practice. Beginners can start by kneeling on the board before standing up, giving you time to get comfortable with the movements.

Kayaking, canoeing, and paddleboarding can also be tailored to your fitness level. If you're looking for a more challenging workout, choose a faster-paced paddle along a coastal route or a river with gentle currents. If relaxation is your goal, a slow-paced paddle across a peaceful lake at sunset offers the perfect blend of exercise and tranquility.

Safety is paramount when paddling. Always check the weather forecast before heading out and avoid paddling in rough conditions if you're not experienced. Stick to calm waters when you're starting and paddle with a buddy or join a group. Most importantly, take your time and enjoy the journey—paddling is as much about the peaceful moments as it is about the physical activity. If you don't have local waterways, consider making paddling part of your next vacation. Many popular travel destinations now offer kayak or paddleboard rentals, making it easy to explore new areas by water, even while traveling.

I still remember my first time in a kayak—gently gliding across a quiet lake, the sounds of nature all around me, and a deep sense of peace settling in as I moved with the water. What began as a weekend adventure quickly turned into a regular hobby. Living on Vancouver Island, my husband and I make it a point to explore the island's many lakes and rivers. Kayaking has become our way of staying fit while embracing the natural beauty of the island, and every paddle through these picturesque waters brings us closer to the outdoor paradise we're lucky to call home.

3.9 Nordic Walking: A Whole-Body Approach to Staying Active

Nordic walking offers a powerful blend of physical and mental health benefits that can transform your retirement years. By using specially designed poles, this activity engages not only your legs but your upper body and core, providing a full-body workout. It improves cardiovascular health, strengthens muscles, and enhances mood, all while enjoying time spent outdoors. Nordic walking groups and clubs offer both physical exercise and the camaraderie of like-minded individuals. Whether it's a leisurely walk through a local park or a more challenging trail, Nordic walking caters to various fitness levels, ensuring everyone can participate and experience the rewards.

The term "Nordic walking" originates from Finland, where it was developed as a form of off-season training for cross-country skiers in the early 20th century. Skiers needed a way to maintain their fitness levels during the snow-free months, and they discovered that walking with poles, mimicking the movement of cross-country skiing, provided an excellent cardiovascular and full-body workout. Over time, this training method became popular outside the skiing community, evolving into what we now know as Nordic walking.

Finding the right group to walk with can make the experience even more enjoyable. Local community centers, senior groups, or online platforms like **Meetup.com** are great resources for finding Nordic walking clubs that match your fitness level and interests. Some clubs focus on easygoing walks, perfect for those who prefer a relaxed pace and enjoy chatting along the way. Others might cater to more adventurous walkers, offering routes with gentle inclines or longer distances that push your limits. Joining a club not only provides motivation but also introduces you to new trails and destinations you might not have discovered on your own. Plus, the social aspect adds a layer of fun and accountability, making it easier to stay committed to a regular walking routine.

Having the right equipment is key to getting the most out of your Nordic walking experience. First, you'll need a quality pair of Nordic walking poles, which are designed to provide support and engage your upper body. Make sure they are adjustable for your height and have comfortable grips. Appropriate footwear is also essential—sturdy, comfortable shoes with good grip and support will make your walks more enjoyable and help prevent injury. Dressing in layers is important and hydration is just as crucial in Nordic walking as it is in hiking. A small backpack can carry your essentials, including snacks, water, a first-aid kit, and your phone.

Whether you're walking in a local park or on a forest trail, safety and etiquette ensure everyone enjoys the experience. Stick to marked trails to protect the environment and avoid getting lost, and always let someone know your route and estimated return time, especially if walking alone. The "Leave No Trace" principle is vital—pack out all trash, respect wildlife, and leave natural areas as you found them. Proper etiquette on shared trails includes yielding to other hikers and bikers, staying to the right, and maintaining control of your poles to avoid obstructing others. Carry a whistle or signaling device for emergencies, and always be mindful of your surroundings, especially in more remote areas.

Nordic walking is an accessible and effective way to stay active while exploring the great outdoors. It provides a low-impact workout that's gentle on the joints yet highly effective for building strength and improving cardiovascular health. For retirees, it offers the perfect balance between fitness, fun, and social interaction, helping you stay engaged with your community and the natural world. With the right gear, a little preparation, and a supportive walking group, Nordic walking can become a rewarding part of your routine, giving you both physical and emotional benefits.

3.10 Leisurely Rides: Scenic Biking Routes for Casual Cyclists

The gentle breeze against your skin as you cycle down a charming path, sunlight filtering through the leaves, creating patterns of light and shadow. That's the beauty of casual cycling. Choosing the right bicycle can make this vision a reality. For older adults, comfort and safety are paramount. A step-through frame, which allows you to easily mount and dismount, can be very helpful. Ergonomic handlebars reduce strain on your wrists, and a cushioned saddle ensures you won't be wincing in pain after a long ride. Consider bikes with wider tires for stability and shock absorption, and don't forget to look for models with gears that can handle various terrains without requiring Herculean effort. E-bikes are also worth considering—they provide an extra boost on tough inclines or longer rides, making cycling more accessible and enjoyable. My husband, who's an avid cyclist, switched to an e-bike a few years ago and finds it a great workout that allows him to explore so much more without overexertion.

Now that you've got the perfect bike, where should you ride? Scenic routes can turn a simple bike ride into a breathtaking adventure. You don't even need to travel far—many cities and towns have beautiful bike paths waiting to be explored. Local routes can be just as stunning and provide a great way to discover the hidden gems in your own backyard. For example, in Victoria, British Columbia, where we live, the **Galloping Goose Trail** is a perfect spot for cyclists of all levels. Stretching over 34 miles, it winds through urban landscapes, forests, and waterfront areas, offering a peaceful escape while staying close to home. Whether you want a quick ride or a long day on the trail, it's a fantastic way to experience the beauty of Vancouver Island without having to venture too far.

The **Confederation Trail** on Prince Edward Island is a must, with over 270 miles of flat, easy riding through charming villages and lush landscapes. The **Icefields Parkway** in Alberta offers a more challenging ride with breathtaking views of the Rockies, glaciers, and turquoise lakes.

For those in the USA, in the East, the **Virginia Creeper Trail** offers a gentle, 34-mile ride through forests and farmlands. In the Midwest, the **Katy Trail** in Missouri provides 240 miles of scenic beauty, winding through small towns and along the Missouri River. On the West Coast, the **Monterey Bay Coastal Recreation Trail** offers stunning views of the ocean and plenty of spots to stop and enjoy the scenery.

Over in Europe, the **Danube Cycle Path** is one of the continent's most popular routes, stretching from Germany to Hungary along the beautiful Danube River. In France, the **Loire Valley** offers a picturesque ride through vineyards, historic castles, and quaint villages. These scenic paths offer a stunning journey that connects with nature and nourishes the soul. Whether you're exploring local trails or traveling to renowned routes across the globe, there's always a scenic ride waiting for you.

Joining local cycling clubs can enhance your biking experience. These clubs often organize regular rides, providing a fantastic opportunity to meet new people and stay motivated. Whether you're a newbie or a seasoned cyclist, there's likely a group that matches your pace and interests. Participating in group rides adds a social element to your fitness routine, turning solitary exercise into a shared adventure. The camaraderie and friendly competition can make each ride more enjoyable and rewarding.

Preparation and safety should never be an afterthought. Always wear a well-fitted helmet; it's the simplest way to protect yourself. Visibility gear, like reflective vests and lights, ensures that you're seen by motorists, especially in low-light conditions. Before each ride, give your bike a quick once-over—check the brakes, tires, and chain to ensure everything is in working order. Carry a small toolkit for minor repairs and a first-aid kit for any unexpected scrapes. Hydration is key, so bring along an extra water bottle. With these precautions, you can pedal away with peace of mind, ready to soak in the beauty and freedom that scenic biking offers.

3.11 Cross-Country Skiing: A Workout for Winter Wellness

Cross-country skiing is an excellent way to stay active and embrace the beauty of winter landscapes. Unlike downhill skiing, cross-country skiing is a low-impact, full-body workout that is gentle on the joints while effectively engaging muscles across your entire body. This activity improves cardiovascular health, boosts endurance, and strengthens major muscle groups like your core, arms, and legs. Skiing at your own pace also allows you to adjust the intensity, making it accessible to a wide range of fitness levels.

If you're new to cross-country skiing, start by selecting the right equipment. You'll need a set of lightweight skis, poles, and boots specifically designed for this type of skiing. Skis should be matched to your height, weight, and skill level to ensure smooth movement across the snow. It's a good idea to rent equipment from a local ski shop before committing to a purchase, especially as you're learning the basics.

Once you have the gear, look for beginner-friendly trails with groomed tracks that make it easier to glide and maintain balance. Local parks, nature reserves, and ski resorts often have trails designated for cross-country skiing. Most locations will offer trails rated by difficulty, so start with flat or gently rolling terrain until you feel comfortable with your movements. Taking a lesson from a local instructor or joining a cross-country skiing club can also help you quickly learn proper techniques like how to glide efficiently, use your poles for momentum, and climb small hills.

It's essential to take a few precautions to ensure a safe and enjoyable experience. Because this activity can be physically demanding, always warm up with light stretching before hitting the trails. Pay attention to your body's signals, and pace yourself—especially if you're just starting or returning to skiing after a long break. Hydration is key even in colder weather, so bring water or a sports drink with you. It's also important to protect yourself from the elements. Dress in layers so you can adjust your warmth as you build up a sweat on the trails. A moisture-wicking base layer, an insulating mid-layer, and a waterproof outer layer will help keep you dry and comfortable throughout your adventure. Sunscreen is a must, as UV rays can reflect off the snow, and sunglasses will shield your eyes from glare. Make sure you have a map of the trails or use a GPS app, particularly if you're skiing in a remote area.

One of the best parts of cross-country skiing is exploring beautiful winter trails at your own pace. Many ski resorts and parks across the **USA, Canada, and Europe** offer designated cross-country skiing routes, ranging from easy loops to more challenging paths through forests and open fields. In the USA, popular spots include the groomed trails at **Methow Valley in Washington** and **Devil's Thumb Ranch in Colorado**, where skiers can glide along picturesque snow-covered landscapes. Canada also offers spectacular cross-country skiing opportunities, with **Banff National Park** and **Gatineau Park near Ottawa** providing stunning views of snow-capped mountains and frozen lakes.

For those looking to venture further, Europe boasts incredible cross-country skiing destinations as well. In **Norway**, the trails around **Lillehammer and Sjusjøen** offer a mix of tranquil forest routes and open mountain landscapes, perfect for all skill levels. **Finland's Lapland region,** especially around **Ylläs and Levi**, provides a magical experience with trails winding through snow-covered forests and past frozen lakes, often illuminated by the Northern Lights. **Austria's Seefeld** is another top destination, known for its world-class cross-country skiing facilities set against the backdrop of the Austrian Alps. **Sweden's Dalarna region**, home to the famous Vasaloppet race, offers extensive trail networks and breathtaking scenery for skiers looking to challenge themselves or enjoy a peaceful winter escape.

For a more leisurely experience, consider skiing on flat terrain at local golf courses or community parks, where you can take in the beauty of nature without the strain of hilly trails. Many parks and resorts offer rentals and lessons, making it easy to enjoy cross-country skiing with no need to invest in equipment right away.

3.12 Cooking for Health: Fun Workshops and Classes

Cooking is an art form that can significantly enhance your health as you advance in age. Learning healthy cooking techniques can revolutionize your diet and overall well-being. For instance, steaming a vibrant array of vegetables not only preserves their nutrients but also ensures your meal is light and flavorful. Opting to grill a piece of fish and season it with herbs and spices yields a dish that's both healthy and delicious. Adding herbs and spices like turmeric, ginger, and garlic infuses your meals with flavor while bringing many health benefits—such as anti-inflammatory properties and antioxidant support—transforming every dish into a mini wellness feast. These methods not only elevate the taste of your food but also bolster your health, providing both nutrition and enjoyment in every bite.

Understanding the specific nutritional needs of seniors is vital, as your body requires different nutrients with age. For example, increasing fiber intake, lowering cholesterol, and incorporating more vitamins and minerals are crucial for maintaining a healthy body and mind. Learning how to prepare meals that meet these needs can be transformative. Many cooking classes and resources focus specifically on seniors, helping you prepare recipes that are high in fiber, packed with vitamins, and low in cholesterol. Think of it as acquiring a culinary education tailored to your body's evolving requirements. Resources like **America's Test Kitchen Online Cooking School** and **Rouxbe** provide in-depth cooking lessons, including those focused on nutrition and healthy eating, guiding you step-by-step through creating meals that nourish both body and soul.

Cooking can also be a communal affair. Social cooking events turn the kitchen into a dynamic social space. In a cooking workshop, the experience goes beyond just learning a new recipe—it's about laughter, shared stories, and forging new friendships. These gatherings foster a sense of community, blending education with social interaction. Whether you're rolling dough alongside someone or debating the ideal mix of herbs, the connections formed are as enriching as the cuisine. **Meetup.com** is a great online resource for finding local cooking classes and events where you can bond with like-minded people while sharpening your culinary skills. Many local community centers, culinary institutes, and even supermarkets offer classes focused on both healthy cooking techniques and nutrition. For those who prefer to learn at their own pace, digital platforms like **MasterClass** and **Udemy** offer cooking courses taught by renowned chefs, allowing you to hone your skills from the comfort of home. You can explore a wide variety of cooking styles and cuisines, with lessons ranging from basic techniques to gourmet meals. With these resources at your fingertips, you're never too far from your next culinary adventure, whether you're cooking for health, for fun, or for community connection.

3.13 Relax, Renew, Rebalance: Spa and Hot Springs Escapes

Sinking into a warm, bubbling hot tub, the stresses of daily life melt away as you take in the serene surroundings. Spa retreats offer more than just a day of pampering; they provide a rejuvenating experience that can significantly improve your health and well-being. These retreats combine relaxation with health benefits, such as reducing stress, alleviating chronic pain, and enhancing your general sense of well-being through therapies like massages, hydrotherapy, and yoga. The word "spa" itself originates from the Belgian town of Spa, which became famous for its mineral-rich thermal springs as early as the 14th century. The healing properties of its waters attracted visitors from across Europe, and soon the term "spa" became synonymous with places offering water-based therapies. Today, spas worldwide incorporate a variety of treatments designed to relax the body and mind, from ancient mineral baths to modern luxury retreats.

Picture yourself enjoying a massage that loosens tight muscles or a hydrotherapy session that soothes arthritis pain, leaving you feeling refreshed and revitalized. There are plenty of spa retreats worldwide that offer a range of therapeutic treatments tailored to individual wellness needs. Please refer to the **Resources Chapter** for a list of renowned Spa Retreats.

Your luxurious spa experience doesn't have to be expensive. You don't need to travel far or break the bank to enjoy the benefits of a spa day. In fact, nearly every town has local spas, and many are located in hotels or wellness centers. Many local spas offer affordable services, especially if you take advantage of senior discounts or special packages designed for specific days like Mother's Day, Valentine's Day, or even "spa week" promotions that offer reduced rates. Hotel spas often have day passes that allow you to enjoy their facilities without booking an overnight stay. Some gyms and community centers even offer spa services like massages, facials, and saunas at much lower rates than high-end resorts. Planning ahead and taking advantage of these deals can allow you to pamper yourself regularly, without the high price tag of a luxury resort. Whether you're looking for a simple massage or a more comprehensive wellness package, there's likely an affordable option nearby that fits your needs.

One particularly powerful spa experience comes from **hot springs**. Bathing in natural hot springs has been practiced for centuries, revered for its therapeutic benefits. The warm waters naturally raise your body temperature, dilating blood vessels and improving circulation. This increased blood flow helps deliver oxygen and nutrients to tissues more efficiently, promoting healing and pain relief for conditions like arthritis and fibromyalgia. The buoyancy of the water also relieves pressure on joints, making it easier to move and stretch without discomfort. Meanwhile, the minerals in the water are absorbed through the skin, with elements like sulfur helping with skin conditions, calcium aiding in bone health, and magnesium easing muscle pain.

The calming environment of natural hot springs, often surrounded by stunning landscapes, also promotes mental well-being. The serene settings—whether nestled in the mountains, by a forest, or overlooking a coastal view—offer a break from the chaos of daily life, providing a moment of tranquility that can soothe the mind. Please refer to the **Resources Chapter** for a list of Hot Springs Retreats.

Preparing for your spa experience involves a bit of planning to maximize your comfort and enjoyment. Pack light, comfortable clothing, a swimsuit, and any personal items that make you feel at home. Communicate any specific health concerns to the staff before you arrive, so they can tailor treatments to your needs. Expect a mix of relaxation and gentle activity, and approach the experience with an open mind, ready to embrace the therapeutic benefits. Knowing what to expect can help you relax and fully immerse yourself in the experience.

Taking part in wellness programs offered by spa retreats can enhance the benefits of your stay. Many retreats include fitness classes, nutritional workshops, and mindfulness sessions as part of their programs. These activities provide a holistic approach to wellness, addressing both physical and mental health. Engaging in these programs can help you learn new skills and habits to take home, ensuring that the benefits of your spa retreat extend well beyond your stay.

By exploring spa and hot spring retreats, you're investing not just in your relaxation but in your overall well-being. Whether it's the soothing warmth of a natural hot spring or the calming energy of a luxurious spa, these experiences provide long-lasting physical and mental benefits that will enrich your retirement.

Taking care of your body and mind is essential for living your best life in retirement. But staying healthy is just one part of this exciting new chapter. Now that you're feeling rejuvenated, it's time to broaden your horizons and embrace all the world has to offer. Whether it's exploring new cultures or diving into global adventures, the next chapter will open doors to exciting travel opportunities, new experiences, and ways to engage with the world around you. Let's dive in and discover how your next adventure could be just a plane ride—or a short drive—away.

Chapter Four

The World at Your Fingertips: Senior-Friendly Destinations, Budgets, and Beyond

The world is more accessible than ever, and retirement opens up new possibilities for exploring it at your own pace. Are you dreaming of visiting famous historic destinations? Embarking on a group travel adventure? Enjoying the freedom of solo travel? Whatever it is, there's something for every kind of traveler. Even if you have physical limitations, the travel industry has adapted to make the globe more accessible than ever before. In this chapter, we'll dive into the best destinations, tips for group and solo travel, and practical advice for navigating the world with physical limitations, ensuring your adventures are safe, enjoyable, and, of course, unforgettable.

4.1 The Best Senior-Friendly Travel Destinations Worldwide

When selecting a destination for your next adventure, a few key considerations can make all the difference in ensuring a smooth and enjoyable trip. Start by thinking about healthcare facilities—having access to quality medical care offers peace of mind, particularly when traveling far from home. It's also important to assess the accessibility of the destination. Opt for places with well-maintained sidewalks, ramps, and accessible public transportation that cater to mobility needs, allowing you to explore comfortably and confidently.

Another crucial factor is senior-friendly transportation. Look for destinations with efficient systems, such as buses with low floors or areas where taxis are readily available. This will make getting around much easier and stress-free.

To streamline your planning, keep a simple checklist in mind: reliable healthcare, easy accessibility, safe and efficient transportation, and, of course, plenty of attractions that inspire your curiosity. With these essentials covered, you can focus on the excitement of your journey, knowing that both comfort and adventure await you at every turn.

Now, let's dive into some of the top destinations that cater specifically to seniors, offering a blend of accessibility, culture, and ease of exploration. **Florence, Italy**, with its rich art scene and relatively flat terrain, is ideal for leisurely strolls through centuries of history.

Explore iconic sites like the Uffizi Gallery and the Duomo without worrying about steep climbs. The city's compact layout means that many of its best attractions are within walking distance, and accessible transport options ensure a smooth visit.

Kyoto, Japan, is another perfect destination for those seeking serenity combined with accessibility. Its stunning temples and zen gardens, such as the Golden Pavilion and Fushimi Inari Shrine, offer peaceful escapes. The city's efficient public transport, including buses and subways with senior-friendly options, ensures you can move around with ease.

In **Barcelona, Spain**, you can enjoy world-class architecture with Gaudi's masterpieces, like the Sagrada Familia and Park Güell, and many senior discounts at major attractions. The city's wide boulevards, accessible public transportation, and plentiful benches in parks and along promenades make it a senior-friendly spot for exploring. Whether you're strolling down Las Ramblas or savoring tapas at a local café, Barcelona offers something for every taste, all with comfort in mind.

Vienna, Austria, is renowned for its grandeur and senior-friendly amenities. From the majestic Schönbrunn Palace to its opera houses, the city offers accessible transportation and discounted tickets for seniors at many of its iconic attractions. With its flat streets and easy access to parks and cafes, Vienna is ideal for leisurely exploring its rich heritage.

For those looking for hidden gems, **Ljubljana, Slovenia**, is a fantastic option. This small, compact city boasts a charming old town where you can easily explore its picturesque streets and bridges. Ljubljana also stands out for its excellent health facilities and affordable, accessible public transportation, making it a secure and tranquil place for senior travelers to enjoy.

For a fairy-tale vibe, head to **Bruges, Belgium**, a small, easily navigable city known for its winding canals and stunning medieval architecture. Whether you're taking a boat ride through the canals or wandering its picturesque streets, Bruges offers a relaxed pace perfect for senior travelers.

In **Stockholm, Sweden**, an efficient transport system makes it easy to get around, with many of the city's museums, parks, and attractions offering senior discounts. The city's blend of urban life and easy access to nature creates a perfect balance, with plenty of quiet spots to relax by the water or take a leisurely boat tour through its archipelago.

For those seeking bike-friendly cities, **Amsterdam and Copenhagen** offer extensive cycling paths, senior-friendly public transport, and easy access to cultural hotspots. With flat terrain and beautiful canals, these cities offer a scenic and enjoyable way to explore on two wheels.

Closer to home, **Charleston, South Carolina**, offers a slice of Southern charm with its cobblestone streets, historic plantations, and antebellum mansions. Charleston is known for its walkable downtown area and senior-friendly guided tours that bring history to life. Explore its gardens or indulge in Lowcountry cuisine, as Charleston delivers a warm and welcoming experience with ease of movement and plenty of relaxing spots to take a break.

In Canada, **Banff**, located in the heart of the Rocky Mountains, provides a stunning backdrop of snow-capped peaks and crystal-clear lakes. Banff offers both adventure and tranquility for nature lovers: take in the views from the Banff Gondola or enjoy a quiet hike on one of the area's many accessible trails. Senior discounts on park fees and accessible amenities in its hotels and restaurants make Banff an excellent choice for a stress-free retreat.

If you're looking for a city steeped in history, **Quebec City, Canada,** delivers cobblestone streets, historic architecture, and charming shops, all within a compact, walkable area. Senior discounts on public transport and at some of the city's main attractions make exploring Old Quebec a hassle-free experience. For added convenience and a touch of adventure, take the city's funicular, which connects the upper and lower parts of Old Quebec. This scenic ride offers easy access to different areas of the city and is an attraction in itself, giving you a unique view of the historic landscape as you travel between the two levels.

Across the globe in **Sydney, Australia,** seniors can enjoy scenic harbor views, world-class museums, and famous landmarks like the Sydney Opera House and Bondi Beach. The city's efficient public transport includes senior discounts, and many attractions are easily accessible. For those who enjoy the outdoors, the Botanical Gardens offer serene paths perfect for a relaxed walk by the water.

If a laid-back atmosphere with scenic harbor views is more your style, consider **Wellington, New Zealand**. With its excellent public transportation, waterfront promenades, and access to nature trails, Wellington provides a calm yet vibrant experience. Be sure to explore its art galleries and enjoy its famous coffee culture.

As you plan your travels, keep in mind that some developing nations might not have the same level of infrastructure for senior travelers. Doing research is essential, especially when it comes to accessibility, healthcare options, and reliable transportation. Always check if attractions offer senior discounts, guided tours in your language, and accessible facilities like ramps and elevators to ensure a smooth and enjoyable journey. With the right preparation, the world truly becomes an open invitation to explore at your own pace.

4.2 The Best Travel Times for an Unforgettable Experience

The timing of your trip can be the difference between a perfect getaway and a frustrating experience. One of the best ways to ensure smooth travel is to avoid extreme weather and peak tourist crowds by opting for shoulder seasons—the periods just before or after the high season in many destinations. Spring and fall typically offer mild weather, fewer tourists, and often lower prices, giving you the best of both worlds: pleasant conditions and a more relaxed atmosphere.

Take **Greece** as an example. Visiting in May means you'll experience comfortable temperatures ideal for exploring ancient ruins, wandering through charming villages, and enjoying the blooming wildflowers that blanket the countryside. Plus, you'll miss the sweltering heat and bustling crowds of summer, allowing for a more peaceful exploration of iconic sights like the Acropolis and Santorini cliffs.

For a scenic European trip, consider Italy's **Tuscany** in late September, when the weather is still warm but the summer crowds have thinned out. This is especially important because in August, Italy celebrates **Ferragosto**, a national holiday that marks the peak of summer. During this time, many Italians take extended vacations, and businesses in popular tourist areas may be closed. Crowds flock to the beaches and cities, making travel more hectic and accommodations harder to find. By late September, however, the bustle of Ferragosto has passed, and you can enjoy Tuscany's rolling hills, charming villages, and world-renowned vineyards in a more relaxed and peaceful setting.

Japan's breathtaking cherry blossom season in April is a beautiful time to visit. As delicate pink flowers blanket parks, temples, and city streets, the country comes alive with celebrations of sakura (cherry blossoms), offering a quintessentially Japanese experience. However, it's also one of the busiest times of the year, so booking early is essential to avoid overcrowded accommodations and ensure you get the best spots for viewing the blossoms.

If autumn colors captivate you, **Canada's Algonquin Park** in September and October is an ideal destination. The vibrant hues of red, orange, and gold set against the park's serene lakes and forests create a mesmerizing landscape, perfect for photographers and nature lovers alike. Hiking trails like the Lookout Trail or the Centennial Ridges Trail provide stunning panoramic views of the autumn foliage. Fall is the prime time for capturing the beauty of this Canadian gem, with fewer crowds than during the summer.

For a quieter Mediterranean escape, consider **Portugal's Algarve region** in October. While summer brings throngs of tourists to its golden beaches, by fall, the crowds have thinned, but the warm sun still graces the coastline. This is the perfect time to explore the Algarve's stunning cliffs, hidden coves, and quaint fishing villages at a more relaxed pace. The region is also home to incredible seafood, so you can enjoy freshly caught fare without the summer rush.

For those seeking a mix of urban sophistication and natural beauty, **Cape Town, South Africa,** in March is an excellent choice. With warm weather and fewer tourists, it's a great time to explore the city's vibrant cultural scene, climb Table Mountain, or visit the nearby Cape Winelands. March also marks the beginning of the whale-watching season along the coast. Head to Hermanus, a short drive from Cape Town, for one of the best shore-based whale-watching experiences in the world.

Always pack layers to accommodate temperature changes and comfortable shoes for all that exploring you'll be doing. Consider bringing a lightweight, waterproof jacket for unexpected rain, and a hat for sun protection. Compression socks can help with long flights, reducing swelling and keeping you comfortable. Don't forget essential medications, and pack an extra supply just in case of travel delays. A small first-aid kit with bandages, pain relievers, and any over-the-counter medications you may need can be a lifesaver. Finally, make sure you have a power adapter if traveling internationally and a photocopy of important documents like your passport. With a bit of planning, each trip can be as comfortable as it is memorable.

4.3 Group Travel: Finding Retirement Travel Clubs

Group travel is an increasingly popular option for retirees, offering many benefits that can make exploring the world both enjoyable and stress-free. One of the main advantages is cost savings—travel clubs often negotiate discounted rates for accommodations, transportation, and excursions, making group travel more affordable. Another significant benefit is enhanced safety. Traveling with a group provides a sense of security, knowing you have others around to navigate unfamiliar places, especially in more remote or challenging destinations. Beyond the practical aspects, group travel offers a unique sense of camaraderie. Shared experiences, from exploring historic landmarks to enjoying meals together, can create lasting friendships. These connections with fellow travelers often make the journey more memorable and enjoyable.

Choosing the right travel club is key to ensuring your trip matches your personal interests and travel style. Many travel clubs cater specifically to retirees, offering everything from luxury cruises to adventure trips and cultural tours. When selecting a travel club, consider the pace of the trips they offer—do they allow for leisurely exploration, or are they packed with a busy itinerary? It's also important to check the destinations they focus on and whether these align with your travel goals. Group size is another consideration; smaller groups often offer a more intimate experience, while larger groups may provide more social opportunities and diverse activities.

Please check the **Resources Chapter** for some reputable group travel companies for retirees.

You can also explore online platforms like **Meetup.com** or **Facebook Groups**, which allow travelers to connect with like-minded individuals and join organized trips or form their own. Websites like **Traveling Alone Together** and **Seniors Travel Club** are additional resources where you can find group travel options and join communities of retirees who love to explore.

Once you've chosen your travel club and destination, preparing for the trip is essential to ensure a smooth experience. Start by gathering all necessary paperwork, such as passports, visas, and travel insurance. Some travel clubs may assist with this process, but it's important to stay organized and double-check everything before you leave. Packing essentials will vary depending on the destination and the type of trip, but it's always a good idea to bring comfortable clothing and shoes for walking, layers for changing weather conditions, and any medications you may need. Consider bringing a small travel journal to jot down experiences along the way. It's also important to set expectations for group travel—while there may be structured activities, it's equally valuable to allow for flexibility and personal time, balancing socializing with relaxation.

4.4 Solo Travel: Exploring the World on Your Own Terms

Traveling solo offers a unique sense of freedom and empowerment, especially in retirement. One of the greatest benefits is complete control over your itinerary—you can explore destinations at your own pace, without having to accommodate the preferences of others. Whether you're an early riser looking to catch the sunrise, or someone who prefers leisurely afternoons exploring museums, solo travel lets you structure your day exactly how you like. Solo travel also encourages personal growth—navigating new environments on your own builds confidence. Plus, it offers a special opportunity for self-reflection and the chance to immerse yourself fully in the experience without distractions.

Another perk of solo travel is the ability to connect with new people. You'll often find that locals and fellow travelers are more likely to engage with you when you're alone, creating opportunities for spontaneous conversations and meaningful connections. Traveling alone doesn't mean you have to be lonely—solo travelers often form bonds with people they meet along the way, sharing meals, stories, and adventures.

Choosing the right destination is essential for ensuring a safe and enjoyable solo travel experience. Safety is a key factor, so look for places known for their traveler-friendly environments and low crime rates. Countries like **Japan, New Zealand,** and **Ireland** are recommended for solo travelers because of their safety, welcoming culture, and well-developed tourist infrastructure.

For those seeking a cultural experience, European cities like **Amsterdam, Vienna,** and **Barcelona** offer easy-to-navigate public transportation, plenty of solo-friendly attractions, and a variety of group tours you can join if you want some company. If nature is more your style, **Costa Rica** is ideal for solo travelers looking for adventure, with its accessible national parks and eco-lodges that provide a sense of community. In the U.S., cities like **Portland, Oregon**, or **Santa Fe, New Mexico**, are known for their solo-traveler-friendly vibe, with walkable streets, cultural experiences, and plenty of safe, social accommodations like boutique hotels or hostels.

Solo travel requires a bit more preparation to ensure a smooth and safe journey. First, always make sure you have adequate travel insurance—this is crucial for covering unexpected events, such as medical issues or cancellations. Having a detailed itinerary that you share with friends or family back home is another way to ensure your safety. It's also a good idea to familiarize yourself with local customs and basic phrases in the local language, especially if you're visiting a non-English-speaking country.

When it comes to packing, it's important to bring items that enhance your sense of safety and comfort. A money belt or hidden pouch can be useful for keeping your valuables secure, and carrying a small first-aid kit ensures you're prepared for any minor emergencies. Solo travelers should download travel apps like **Google Maps, TripIt**, and **Translate**, which can make navigating new destinations easier. Joining solo traveler forums or groups online can provide you with up-to-date travel advice and potential connections with other travelers along the way.

While solo travel is liberating, it's important to stay vigilant, especially when navigating unfamiliar places. Always be aware of your surroundings and trust your instincts. Researching neighborhoods ahead of time can help you avoid unsafe areas. If you're arriving in a new city late at night, consider arranging transportation in advance or staying at accommodations with a 24-hour front desk. Solo travelers should also avoid sharing too much information with strangers, such as your full itinerary or the fact that you're traveling alone.

Using apps like **Airbnb** or staying in hostels with high ratings from fellow solo travelers is a great way to ensure safe accommodations. In larger cities, walking tours and group excursions are excellent ways to explore while enjoying some company. When dining out, treat yourself to a nice restaurant or cafe—it's one of the joys of solo travel! Many solo travelers bring a book, journal, or tablet for company if they prefer quiet time, or strike up a conversation with fellow diners if they're feeling social.

Solo travel doesn't mean you have to go it alone the entire time. There's a thriving community of solo travelers around the world, and joining this community can enhance your experience. Websites and platforms like **Solo Traveler World**, **Women on the Road**, and **Traveling Alone Together** offer tips, advice, and even meetups for solo travelers. These forums are full of resources and support, with experienced travelers sharing insights on the best destinations, how to stay safe, and how to make the most of traveling alone.

You can also use platforms like **Meetup.com** or **Couchsurfing** to connect with locals or other travelers at your destination. Many cities offer solo traveler meetups, walking tours, or group dinners that provide opportunities to meet new people while maintaining the flexibility of traveling on your own.

Please refer to the Resources Section for a list of companies specializing in solo travel.

4.5 A Comprehensive Guide to Traveling with Physical Limitations

Traveling with disabilities or physical limitations doesn't have to mean limiting your experiences. Whether you're a cane user, a slow walker, or have hearing or vision impairments, some companies specialize in making travel accessible and enjoyable for everyone. For wheelchair users, travelers with complex health issues like dialysis, or those with developmental disabilities, specialized companies like **Easy Access Travel, Planet Abled, Wheel the World, Tapooz Travel**, and **Seable Holidays** provide tailored solutions to ensure a smooth journey. These organizations offer services such as arranging accessible tours, transportation, and accommodations that cater to specific needs. For example, **Easy Access Travel** focuses on cruises and vacations with mobility aids, while **Planet Abled** and **Wheel the World** design inclusive travel experiences across the globe. **Seable Holidays** and **Tapooz Travel** provide unique adventures with support for those who are vision or hearing-impaired. No matter your requirements, these companies are dedicated to helping you see the world comfortably and confidently, ensuring that your travel aspirations are not just possible but fulfilling.

Before packing your bags, a medical check-up is crucial. Your doctor can assess your fitness for travel and update the necessary medications. Discuss travel insurance that covers pre-existing conditions. This isn't just paperwork; it's your safety net. Imagine exploring new places with peace of mind, knowing you're covered if anything unexpected happens.

Choosing the right accommodations and transport options is like picking the perfect pair of shoes for walking—comfort and functionality are key. Look for hotels with wheelchair accessibility, elevators, and proximity to medical facilities. Many places offer accessible rooms with grab bars, roll-in showers, and lower beds. When it comes to getting around, prioritize transport options that cater to your needs, like accessible taxis and buses with low floors. Some destinations even offer specialized services for seniors or those with mobility issues.

Packing for accessibility might sound tedious, but it's the secret sauce to a hassle-free trip. Start with a collapsible cane and a portable seat cushion. Medication organizers ensure you never miss a dose, crucial when you're busy sightseeing. Think about comfort, too. Compression socks can prevent swelling on long flights, and a lightweight, easy-to-carry bag can hold all your essentials. The key is to be prepared without being overburdened.

On-the-ground support services can be your best friend. Before you go, research local healthcare services and accessibility equipment rentals. Many countries offer services that rent out wheelchairs, scooters, or even portable ramps. Knowing where to find these can save you from a lot of stress. Some destinations also have apps or services that connect you with local caregivers or medical professionals. Having a support system in place, ready to help at a moment's notice, is not a luxury, it's a necessity.

4.6 Seeing the World Without Breaking the Bank

Traveling the world doesn't have to be expensive. With a bit of research and flexibility, you can explore incredible destinations without blowing your budget. Whether you're drawn to the historic charm of Europe, the vibrant cultures of Southeast Asia, or the breathtaking landscapes of South America, there are countless budget-friendly options that offer unforgettable experiences. Let's take a look at some of the most affordable yet enriching destinations where you can stretch your travel dollars further.

Eastern Europe: Cities like **Budapest, Hungary, Prague, Czech Republic,** and **Krakow, Poland** offer rich cultural experiences, stunning architecture, and relatively low costs compared to Western Europe. You can explore medieval castles, take river cruises, and enjoy delicious local cuisine at a fraction of the price you'd pay in cities like Paris or Rome. Public transportation is affordable, and many museums and cultural sites offer senior discounts. In **Montenegro**, the coastal town of Kotor, nestled between the Adriatic Sea and rugged mountains, is a **UNESCO World Heritage Site** with affordable accommodations and dining. **Bulgaria** is another hidden gem. **Sofia**, the capital, offers a mix of ancient Roman ruins, Ottoman mosques, and Soviet-era architecture, all at a fraction of the cost of other European capitals. The city of **Plovdiv**, one of the oldest continuously inhabited cities in Europe, offers Roman amphitheaters, art galleries, and charming old town streets to explore.

Southeast Asia: Countries like **Thailand**, **Vietnam**, and **Cambodia** are known for their affordability and breathtaking beauty. In Thailand, you can lounge on white-sand beaches, explore ancient temples, and feast on street food for just a few dollars a day. Vietnam's bustling cities, lush countryside, and UNESCO World Heritage sites like Ha Long Bay offer a blend of adventure and relaxation, with low-cost accommodations and meals. Cambodia's **Angkor Wat** is a must-see, and the cost of living in the country is remarkably low, making it a dream destination for budget-conscious travelers.

South America: Head to **Cusco, Peru** or **Medellín, Colombia**, for vibrant culture, stunning landscapes, and affordable travel experiences. Cusco, the gateway to Machu Picchu, offers fascinating Incan history and beautiful architecture. Meanwhile, Medellín has transformed into a modern, thriving city with great public transportation, beautiful parks, and a lively cultural scene. Both cities offer affordable accommodations, delicious local food, and plenty of free or low-cost activities.

Portugal: **Lisbon** and **Porto** provide a blend of old-world charm and modern vibrancy. With beautiful tile-adorned buildings, scenic waterfronts, and delicious (yet affordable) cuisine, Portugal is an excellent budget-friendly European destination. Public transportation is efficient and cheap, and many attractions offer senior discounts.

Mexico: Beyond the popular resort areas, cities like **Oaxaca** and **Guanajuato** offer rich cultural experiences, local markets, and stunning historical sites at a fraction of the cost. Explore ancient ruins, colorful festivals, and enjoy authentic Mexican cuisine without straining your wallet.

United States: There are many budget-friendly options in the U.S. Cities like **Asheville, North Carolina**, and **Santa Fe, New Mexico**, offer a mix of natural beauty, art, and history. In **Texas**, **San Antonio** offers a scenic River Walk and rich historical sites like the Alamo. **New Orleans, Louisiana** is famous for its unique blend of cultures, vibrant music scene, and delicious Creole and Cajun cuisine. New Orleans offers plenty of free attractions like walking tours of the historic French Quarter, visiting St. Louis Cathedral, or simply soaking up the lively atmosphere on Bourbon Street. **Memphis, Tennessee, is k**nown for its role in American music history. Memphis offers budget-friendly experiences like visiting Beale Street for live blues performances, exploring Sun Studio, and paying respects at the National Civil Rights Museum. **Kansas City, Missouri,** famous for its barbecue and jazz scene, also boasts free attractions like the Nelson-Atkins Museum of Art and City Market. The city's affordable accommodations and public transportation make it an excellent choice for budget-conscious travelers. **St. Augustine, Florida** is the nation's oldest city; it offers plenty of affordable history and charm. Stroll through the cobblestone streets, explore Castillo de San Marcos, and visit the Fountain of Youth Archaeological Park without breaking the bank. **Salt Lake City, Utah,** is a gateway to the great outdoors with stunning views of the surrounding mountains, close to national parks Arches and Zion. The city itself has budget-friendly attractions like Temple Square and free outdoor concerts in the summer. **Albuquerque, New Mexico,** known for its annual Balloon Fiesta, is an affordable destination year-round. Visit Old Town for its historic charm, explore the Sandia Mountains, or check out the Petroglyph National Monument—all at reasonable prices.

Canada: For a taste of European charm without leaving North America, head to **Montreal**, where you'll find a blend of French and Canadian culture, beautiful old-town streets, and a vibrant art scene. **Halifax, Nova Scotia**, is another excellent choice, offering coastal beauty, maritime history, and affordable prices.

Morocco: For a more exotic yet affordable experience, **Marrakech** offers bustling souks, stunning palaces, and a rich cultural heritage. Accommodations range from budget-friendly riads (traditional guesthouses) to luxury resorts, and exploring the vibrant city streets doesn't cost a thing.

These destinations prove you don't need to spend a fortune to have rich, memorable travel experiences. By opting for less expensive countries and regions, you can immerse yourself in different cultures, enjoy unique attractions, and create lifelong memories—all while staying within your budget. No matter where your retirement adventures take you, the world is full of affordable gems waiting to be explored. Pack your bags and get ready for the journey of a lifetime—without breaking the bank.

Chapter Five

Epic Journeys of a Lifetime: Unforgettable Travel Experiences

The world is waiting for you. A quaint Parisian café invites you to sip wine with the Eiffel Tower in view. The vibrant markets of Marrakech beckon, rich with the scent of spices and adventure. The ancient stone circles of Avebury draw you in, offering a glimpse into millennia of history. Norway's majestic fjords welcome you to sail through serene waters, where towering cliffs meet the sky. Retirement grants you the freedom to explore at your own pace, without busy schedules. With so many incredible destinations, where will your journey begin? Let's explore how to turn your travel dreams into reality.

5.1 Eco-Tourism: Environmentally Conscious Travel

Eco-tourism is like combining your love for travel with a hearty dose of Mother Nature's TLC. It focuses on sustainable travel practices that minimize your environmental footprint while supporting conservation efforts. As a retiree, you have the chance to contribute to these efforts. Whether it's taking part in a beach cleanup or supporting local eco-friendly businesses, your actions can make a significant impact on preserving these natural wonders for future generations.

Choosing eco-friendly destinations is akin to picking a vacation spot that's as kind to the environment as it is to you. National parks, wildlife reserves, and conservation areas often lead the pack in eco-tourism. Consider the **Galápagos Islands**, where strict regulations protect the unique wildlife, or **Costa Rica's Monteverde Cloud Forest**, renowned for its biodiversity and eco-lodges. **The Serengeti National Park in Tanzania** offers sustainable safaris, while the **Great Barrier Reef in Australia** promotes coral conservation. **Patagonia in Chile** and **Argentina** is a haven for eco-conscious trekkers. For an off-the-beaten-path option, visit **Iceland**, where geothermal energy powers most of the country, and its dramatic landscapes are carefully protected. **Bhutan**, known for its commitment to environmental preservation, limits tourist numbers to protect its natural and cultural heritage. The fjords of **Norway** also offer sustainable tourism, with eco-friendly cruises and a deep respect for preserving the local environment. Other notable mentions include the **Azores in Portugal**, the **Białowieża Forest in Poland,** and **Canada's Banff**

National Park. These destinations offer stunning natural beauty and at the same time, prioritize environmental sustainability.

Taking part in conservation activities during your travels adds a layer of purpose to your adventures. You could join a wildlife habitat restoration project, where you help plant native species to restore ecosystems. Guided eco-tours often include educational programs that teach you about local flora and fauna and the importance of conservation. Imagine taking part in a turtle nesting project in **Mexico** or a reforestation effort in the **Amazon**. In **New Zealand,** you might contribute to penguin conservation efforts by maintaining nesting sites. In **Kenya**, some safaris offer opportunities to assist with anti-poaching initiatives or support local wildlife research. In **Iceland**, you could join glacier conservation tours that actively work to monitor and protect fragile ice formations. In the U.S., you could help restore coral reefs in **Florida** or join trail maintenance projects in national parks like **Yosemite** or the **Great Smoky Mountains.** Volunteers can also participate in beach cleanups along the **Pacific Coast** or help protect sea turtles in **North Carolina**. These activities enrich your travel experience and leave a positive mark on the environment. You become a guardian of nature, one trip at a time.

Minimizing your travel footprint is easier than you might think. Start by using public transportation, which reduces carbon emissions compared to private cars. Opt for eco-friendly accommodations—look for places that use renewable energy, reduce waste, and support local communities. Practicing 'Leave No Trace' principles is crucial; always clean up after yourself and avoid disturbing wildlife. Consider packing reusable items like water bottles, shopping bags, cutlery, and travel containers to cut down on single-use plastics. Be mindful of water usage, especially in areas where it's scarce, and try to reduce energy consumption by turning off lights and electronics when not in use. With these simple practices, you can enjoy your travels while keeping the planet green and healthy.

5.2 Voluntourism: Combining Travel with Volunteer Work

Exploring a new country while making a meaningful impact on the local community is what voluntourism is all about. It offers a unique blend of travel and volunteer work, allowing you to immerse yourself in a new culture while contributing to local projects. It's more than just sightseeing—it's about giving back and forming deeper connections with the people and places you visit. You might find yourself teaching English in a remote village, helping build homes, or assisting in wildlife conservation efforts. The benefits are immense: you gain a deeper understanding of the local way of life, make lasting friendships, and come home with a sense of accomplishment and purpose. However, it's not all sunshine and rainbows. The challenges include adjusting to different living conditions, facing cultural differences, and dealing with language barriers. But these hurdles make the experience even more rewarding.

Voluntourism offers countless opportunities across the globe, from rural villages to bustling cities, with each destination providing unique experiences and challenges. In **Costa Rica**, for example, you can contribute to wildlife conservation projects, helping to protect endangered species like sea turtles. If you're passionate about education, **Tanzania** offers chances to teach English in local schools or assist with community development initiatives. In **Nepal**, you might support rebuilding efforts in remote villages affected by natural disasters or working in orphanages to improve the lives of children. For those interested in environmental work, **Australia** offers conservation projects that help restore natural habitats and protect native wildlife.

Several organizations specialize in connecting travelers with voluntourism opportunities. Please refer to the **Resources Chapter** for the list of some of the reputable organizations.

Choosing the right program is crucial. Start by identifying your skills and interests. Are you a retired teacher who loves working with children? Look for programs focused on education. Maybe you're passionate about wildlife—there are plenty of conservation projects that could use your help. Research the organization thoroughly. Check reviews, ask about the nature of the work, and ensure they follow ethical practices. Some organizations might exploit local communities or volunteers, so it's essential to choose one that genuinely benefits both parties. Consider the duration of the stay, too. Some programs last a few weeks, while others can extend to several months. Pick one that fits your schedule and energy levels.

Proper preparation is important for a successful voluntourism experience. Start with the basics: make sure your passport is up to date, and research visa requirements for your destination. Vaccinations might be necessary depending on where you're going. Mental and physical preparation is equally important. You might be working in challenging environments, so it's essential to be in good health and have the right mindset. Training sessions provided by the organization can equip you with the necessary skills and knowledge. They might offer online courses or in-person workshops to prepare you for the work ahead. Packing the right gear, including comfortable clothing and any specific equipment needed for your tasks, ensures you're ready for the adventure.

Once you're on the ground, making the most of your experience involves fully engaging with the local community and culture. Start by learning some basic phrases in the local language—it's a gesture that's always appreciated and can help break the ice. Building genuine relationships with fellow volunteers and locals can enrich your experience immeasurably. Don't be shy—join in local activities, share meals, and listen to their stories. These interactions offer a deeper understanding of the culture and leave you with friendships that last long after you've returned home. Keep a journal to document your experiences, reflections, and the people you meet. This not only helps you process the experience but also creates a wonderful keepsake to look back on. If you enjoy sharing your adventures, your journal entries can serve as the foundation for a blog, vlog, or YouTube channel, allowing you to inspire others with your voluntourism journey. By turning your personal reflections into public content, you can connect with a broader audience and encourage more people to get involved in meaningful travel experiences.

5.3 Senior Safari Adventures: Planning the Trip of a Lifetime

Safaris offer an unforgettable way to experience wildlife and nature up close, with different types catering to various interests and travel styles. Whether you're interested in a traditional drive through sprawling savannahs, a walking safari that lets you explore on foot, or a boat safari along rivers and lakes, each option provides a unique perspective on the natural world. Many safaris also incorporate conservation efforts, giving you the chance to contribute to protecting these precious ecosystems. It's not just about witnessing wildlife—it's about being immersed in the rhythm of nature and supporting the environments that sustain it.

The first step in planning your safari is choosing the right type. Walking safaris offer an immersive experience where you can feel the earth beneath your feet and hear the subtle sounds of nature. However, they require a good level of fitness and stamina. **Zambia's South Luangwa National Park** is renowned for its expertly guided walking safaris, offering a chance to track wildlife while learning about the flora and fauna up close. In **Zimbabwe, Mana Pools National Park** also provides exceptional walking safari experiences along the Zambezi River.

If you prefer a more relaxed approach, vehicle-based tours provide comfort while still offering breathtaking views of wildlife. Destinations like **Kenya's Masai Mara, Tanzania's Serengeti, South Africa's Kruger National Park, and Namibia's Etosha National Park** are popular choices. Each offers unique landscapes and wildlife, ensuring an unforgettable adventure.

If a boating safari piques your interest, consider exploring the winding waterways of **Botswana's Okavango Delta**, where you can observe wildlife from a traditional mokoro (canoe). Another excellent option is a boat safari through **Sri Lanka's Gal Oya National Park**, where you can watch elephants swimming between islands in one of the country's largest reservoirs.

Preparation is key to a successful safari. Start with vaccinations—consult your doctor about necessary shots, such as those for yellow fever and typhoid. Some countries also require malaria prophylaxis. Check visa requirements well in advance; some destinations allow visas on arrival, while others require pre-approval. Pack smartly: lightweight, neutral-colored clothing is best for blending into the environment. Don't forget sturdy and comfortable walking shoes. Depending on the climate, you might need a warm jacket for chilly mornings and evenings. A good camera and binoculars are must-haves for capturing those once-in-a-lifetime moments.

Staying healthy and safe during your safari is paramount. Hydration is crucial, especially in hot climates, so carry a reusable water bottle and drink plenty of fluids. Equally important is protecting yourself from the sun—wear a broad-spectrum sunscreen, a wide-brimmed hat, and sunglasses, and seek shade during the hottest parts of the day. Use insect repellent to protect against bites, and wear long sleeves and pants during dawn and dusk when mosquitoes are most active. Ensure your travel insurance covers medical emergencies in remote areas; it's worth the peace of mind. Familiarize yourself with local health facilities and emergency contacts. Following these precautions will help you enjoy your safari without worrying about health issues.

To maximize your safari experience, consider hiring knowledgeable local guides. Their expertise can transform your trip, offering insights into animal behavior and local ecosystems. Engage in conservation efforts or community visits to deepen your connection with the area. Some tours offer opportunities to visit local schools or partake in wildlife preservation projects. These activities will enrich your experience and contribute positively to the communities you visit, making your safari more impactful and memorable.

5.4 Sea Voyages and River Cruises: Unlocking Unforgettable Adventures

Lounging on the deck of a cruise ship with the horizon stretching before you is the perfect start to a memorable journey. Cruises have become increasingly popular, especially with retirees, for good reason. They offer a convenient and stress-free way to explore multiple destinations without the hassle of packing and unpacking at every stop. With everything from gourmet dining to entertainment, fitness centers, and even medical facilities onboard, cruises cater to every need, allowing travelers to unwind and savor the experience. For retirees, cruises also provide a chance to meet like-minded travelers, join special interest groups, and take part in organized activities, adding a social and enriching dimension to the trip. Whether you prefer a smaller, more intimate ship or the wide range of amenities found on larger vessels, the options are endless, making it easy to find the perfect cruise for your interests and lifestyle.

Selecting the right cruise is crucial to making this dream a reality. Start by considering the size of the ship. Larger ships offer a plethora of activities and dining options but can be overwhelming. Smaller ships provide a more intimate experience and easier navigation.

Look for cruises that cater specifically to seniors, offering a wide range of activities like dance classes, lectures, and wellness programs, including yoga, meditation, and gentle exercise classes tailored to different fitness levels. You'll often find enrichment programs such as cooking demonstrations, wine tastings, and cultural workshops. For those seeking intellectual stimulation, cruises offer guest speakers, educational seminars, and destination-focused talks. There are often opportunities for card games, trivia competitions, and bridge tournaments, creating a sense of community onboard.

Medical facilities are a must—ensure the ship has a well-equipped medical center and staff. Special accommodations like accessible cabins and priority boarding can make your trip even more comfortable.

Ocean cruise destinations like the **Mediterranean, Caribbean,** and **Alaska** are popular for their stunning views and rich cultural experiences.

In the **Mediterranean**, you can explore historic cities like **Rome, Barcelona**, and **Athens**, each offering ancient landmarks and vibrant local culture. **Rome** is famous for its ancient ruins and art museums, while **Barcelona** dazzles with Gaudí's architecture, and **Athens** offers a glimpse into the cradle of Western civilization. **Santorini** enchants with its iconic white-washed buildings and stunning sunsets over the Aegean Sea, while **Mykonos** offers a lively atmosphere with beautiful beaches and vibrant nightlife. **Dubrovnik**, known as the "Pearl of the Adriatic," boasts medieval walls and breathtaking coastal views. **Istanbul**, where East meets West, is rich with Byzantine and Ottoman history, offering landmarks like the Hagia Sophia and Grand Bazaar. **Venice**, with its romantic canals, and **Cannes**, home to the famous film festival, bring their charm to the Mediterranean. Each destination is a gateway to the region's rich history, culture, and unforgettable landscapes.

The **Caribbean** offers tropical paradises such as **St. Lucia, the Bahamas,** and **Aruba**, known for their crystal-clear waters and beautiful beaches. **St. Lucia**, with its dramatic Piton mountains, lush rainforests, and natural hot springs, makes a perfect destination for both relaxation and adventure. **The Bahamas**, with its famous pink sand beaches and vibrant coral reefs, is a haven for snorkeling, diving, and wildlife enthusiasts, offering encounters with dolphins and sea turtles. **Aruba**, often called "One Happy Island," boasts year-round sunshine, stunning white-sand beaches, and colorful colonial architecture, blending Caribbean charm with Dutch influences. Each island offers a unique mix of natural beauty, culture, and activities, from exploring local markets to lounging in secluded coves.

For breathtaking natural beauty, cruises to **Alaska** often include stops in **Glacier Bay** and **Juneau,** where you can witness glaciers and wildlife up close. Other popular cruise destinations include **Norway's Shores & Fjords**, where dramatic cliffs and waterfalls line the coastline, and **New Zealand's Milford Sound**, offering awe-inspiring landscapes. The **Baltic Sea** is a cultural treasure trove, with stops in cities like **Helsinki** and **Oslo**, where you can delve into Viking history and explore Scandinavian heritage. Don't miss the chance to witness the Northern Lights on a cruise to **Norway** or **Iceland**, offering one of nature's most spectacular displays. **Tallinn, Stockholm**, and **Copenhagen** provide fascinating glimpses into the art, architecture, and history of **Northern Europe**.

River cruises offer a unique way to experience the culture and history of a destination. As you sail down iconic rivers like the **Danube, Rhine, or Seine**, the landscape unfolds before you—castles perched on hilltops, vineyards lining the banks, and charming villages with cobbled streets and vibrant markets. River cruising tends to be more immersive, with ports of call often located in the heart of cities, allowing for easy and quick access to local landmarks and attractions.

These cruises are also known for their inclusive excursions, with many offering guided tours of historical sites, UNESCO World Heritage landmarks, and local cultural experiences. You can visit historic castles along the **Rhine**, explore the art-filled museums of **Amsterdam**, or sip wine in the vineyards of **France's Bordeaux region**—all while enjoying the comforts of your floating hotel.

River cruises also offer the chance to attend onboard lectures and cultural performances, enhancing your understanding of the region you're visiting. On a **Mekong River** cruise, for instance, you might watch traditional Apsara dances or listen to local musicians. Cruises along the **Nile** provide access to ancient Egyptian temples and pyramids, with expert guides explaining the mysteries of the pharaohs.

Staying healthy and safe on a cruise starts with food safety. Stick to bottled water and be cautious with buffet-style dining. Motion sickness can put a damper on the party, but you can manage it with remedies like ginger tablets or acupressure wristbands. Navigating the ship safely is essential; wear non-slip shoes and use handrails when moving around. Many cruise lines offer mobility aids like wheelchairs and scooters for rent. These small precautions can ensure you enjoy your trip with no hiccups. Shore excursions can be thrilling but choose wisely. Opt for guided tours that offer a balance of adventure and relaxation. Safety is key, so stick with group tours and always have a map and local emergency numbers handy.

Budgeting for a cruise can be a balancing act. All-inclusive packages might seem pricey upfront but can save you money in the long run by covering meals, activities, and excursions. Look for senior discounts and special promotions. Booking during off-peak times can also score you significant savings. When choosing a cruise company, it's essential to do some research. Start by reading customer reviews on trusted travel websites like **CruiseCritic** or **TripAdvisor** to get a sense of other travelers' experiences. Pay attention to feedback on the quality of service, cleanliness, and onboard activities. Opt for companies with a strong reputation for safety and customer satisfaction like **Expedia, TripAdvisor, CruiseDirect, CruiseWatch**. Avoid cruise lines with frequent complaints about hidden fees, poor service, or overcrowding. Make sure the company is transparent about what's included in the price—watch out for extra charges for gratuities, Wi-Fi, or premium dining. If possible, talk to friends or family who have cruised with the company to get firsthand recommendations. Last, check for the cruise line's sustainability efforts; companies that prioritize eco-friendly practices often provide a more conscientious travel experience.

5.5 Top Historical Landmarks for Your Global Bucket List

Exploring the ruins of ancient civilizations is like taking a journey through time, where each destination offers a unique glimpse into humanity's rich and diverse history. The thrill of standing where empires once flourished, where ancient leaders ruled, and where age-old stories were born is something that can only be truly appreciated in person. History comes alive when you walk through these iconic sites, immersing yourself in the grandeur of past civilizations.

The **Pyramids of Giza**, rising majestically from the sands of Egypt, are a testament to the ingenuity and ambition of the pharaohs. In **Rome, the Colosseum**, still towering over the city, echoes with the legacy of gladiatorial combat and the roaring crowds of ancient times. High in the **Andes, Machu Picchu** invites you into the sophisticated world of the Inca Empire, with its intricately designed terraces and temples. The **Acropolis of Athens** remains a symbol of Greek democracy and culture, while the **Great Wall of China** stretches endlessly across the landscape, a marvel of ancient engineering and defense. In **England**, the mysterious **Stonehenge** continues to intrigue visitors with its ancient origins and purpose.

Other must-visit historical destinations include **Petra in Jordan**, an ancient city carved into rose-red cliffs that served as a vital crossroads of trade, and **Angkor Wat in Cambodia**, the largest religious monument in the world, showcasing the grandeur of the Khmer Empire. The ancient city of **Pompeii in Italy**, preserved under volcanic ash, provides an incredibly detailed snapshot of life in the Roman Empire. The temples of **Luxor in Egypt** reveal millennia of Egyptian history, while **Kyoto in Japan** offers a window into the country's imperial past with its centuries-old temples and palaces. Each of these places carries stories, legends, and an aura that can only be truly appreciated in person.

Planning visits to these historical sites involves a bit of strategizing to make the most of your experience. Early mornings or late afternoons are often the best times to visit to avoid the swarms of tourists and the midday heat. Many sites offer senior discounts on tickets, so don't forget to inquire or check online beforehand. Guided tours can enrich your visit with fascinating anecdotes and deeper insights, making the history come alive. Whether it's a small group tour or a private guide, having an expert by your side can transform your visit from a simple sightseeing trip into an educational adventure.

Navigating historical sites requires a bit of preparation, especially considering the physical demands they might pose. Uneven surfaces, steep climbs, and extensive walking are common. Look for sites that provide amenities like benches for resting, accessible pathways, and shuttle services. Comfortable, supportive footwear is a must. Carry a small, lightweight backpack with essentials like water, a hat, sunscreen, and any necessary medications. Taking breaks and pacing yourself ensures you can enjoy the experience without overexerting.

I remember our trip to Pompeii vividly. We hadn't anticipated just how enormous the site was, nor did we fully appreciate the challenges posed by its ancient sidewalks. I was wearing sandals that weren't particularly comfortable, and we hadn't packed any snacks or extra water. By the time we reached the end of our tour, we were completely exhausted. Though the experience of walking through this incredibly well-preserved Roman city was stunning, we weren't able to see as much as we had hoped because of our lack of preparation. The vast scale of Pompeii, combined with the uneven stone streets, made it far more physically demanding than expected. Next time, we'll definitely be better prepared with sturdy shoes and snacks so I can fully take in the wonder of such a remarkable place.

Preserving memories of these visits can be as enriching as the visits themselves. Photography is a fantastic way to capture the beauty and details of each site. Journaling adds another layer, allowing you to reflect on your experiences and emotions. Blogging or vlogging lets you document your travels in real-time, creating a dynamic way to capture memories and inspire others with your stories. Before you go, immerse yourself in documentaries, books, or online courses about the sites you'll visit. This pre-visit education can deepen your appreciation, making the trip even more fulfilling.

5.6 Cultural European Tours for the Curious Retiree

Imagine strolling through the cobbled streets of **Prague**, each corner revealing a new piece of history, or standing in awe before the masterpieces of the **Louvre in Paris**. Planning a cultural tour in Europe starts with choosing destinations rich in history and art. **Florence, Italy**, with its Renaissance treasures, and **Vienna, Austria**, known for its classical music heritage, are must-visits.

Don't overlook hidden gems like **Bruges in Belgium**, a medieval town that feels like stepping into a fairy tale, or **Porto in Portugal**, where vibrant culture and stunning architecture await. For a unique experience, head to **Munich, Germany**, during Oktoberfest, where you can enjoy lively beer halls, traditional Bavarian music, and hearty local cuisine. Other amazing destinations include the charming town of **Rothenburg ob der Tauber in Germany**, with its perfectly preserved medieval architecture, and **Dresden**, a city rich in baroque splendor.

For classical music lovers, **Salzburg, Austria**, the birthplace of Mozart, offers an enchanting atmosphere with its beautiful baroque architecture and the annual **Salzburg Festival** celebrating his legacy.

In cities like **Graz, Austria**, and **Girona, Spain**, you'll find fewer tourists and a more intimate feel, with stunning architecture and rich histories that rival more famous destinations.

Imagine wandering through the ancient streets of **Bath, England**, where Roman baths and Georgian architecture transport you back in time. England is rich in cultural sites like **Canterbury Cathedral**, a UNESCO World Heritage Site that showcases stunning Gothic architecture, and **Oxford**, home to the world-renowned university and charming historic buildings. In **Scotland**, a visit to **Edinburgh Castle** offers panoramic views of the city and a deep dive into Scotland's turbulent history. For something truly mystical, explore the **Isle of Skye**, where rugged landscapes and ancient clan traditions are still alive, while **Glasgow** boasts a vibrant arts scene and impressive Victorian architecture.

France is home to more than just the Louvre. In **Normandy**, visit the stunning **Mont Saint-Michel**, a medieval abbey perched on a tidal island. In the south, explore the **Palace of the Popes** in Avignon, a UNESCO site with fascinating papal history. **Strasbourg**, with its blend of French and German influences, offers a unique cultural experience. And don't forget the **Château de Chambord** in the Loire Valley, a true marvel of Renaissance architecture. While you're in the area, make sure to visit **Château de Chenonceau,** famously spanning the River Cher with its stunning arches, and **Château de Villandry**, known for its magnificent Renaissance gardens. Further along the Loire, you'll find **Château d'Amboise,** where Leonardo da Vinci spent his final years. Each of these castles offers a unique glimpse into France's regal past, with enchanting architecture, lush landscapes, and fascinating history waiting to be explored.

In Italy, beyond Florence's Renaissance treasures, explore the Amalfi Coast for breathtaking views of dramatic cliffs, sparkling seas, and charming seaside villages like Positano and Ravello. Ravello, in particular, is known not only for its stunning gardens and panoramic views but also for its annual Ravello Festival, a prestigious musical event held each summer that brings classical music performances to its open-air venues. For a quieter escape, head to Verona, the city of Romeo and Juliet, where you can visit Juliet's famous balcony and wander through Roman ruins, including a well-preserved amphitheater still used for operas today.

Siena offers a step back in time with its preserved medieval streets, impressive cathedral, and the thrilling Palio horse race held twice a year in the historic Piazza del Campo. Further south, Naples provides a gateway to ancient history with the nearby ruins of Pompeii and Herculaneum, frozen in time by the eruption of Mount Vesuvius. Don't miss Sicily, where Greek temples like those in Agrigento's Valley of the Temples blend seamlessly with Roman villas, Baroque architecture, and lively markets. In Sicily's capital, Palermo, you can explore a rich tapestry of cultural influences, from Norman palaces to bustling street food stalls. Whether you're drawn to Italy's art, architecture, or history, every region offers its own distinct and captivating experience.

For a different vibe, visit **Split**, **Croatia**, where the ancient **Diocletian's Palace** meets vibrant modern life, or **Zagreb**, a city full of Austro-Hungarian charm with bustling markets and beautiful parks. In **Hungary**, **Budapest** is a must-visit with its thermal baths, stunning **Parliament Building**, and the **Buda Castle** overlooking the Danube River. **Turkey** offers a captivating blend of ancient and modern worlds. In **Istanbul**, you'll be mesmerized by landmarks like the **Hagia Sophia**, **Topkapi Palace**, and the bustling **Grand Bazaar**. Don't miss the chance to visit **Ephesus**, one of the best-preserved ancient cities, showcasing the grandeur of Roman architecture. **Bulgaria**, with its hidden gems, is an underrated cultural destination.

The ancient capital, **Veliko Tarnovo**, offers a glimpse into medieval Bulgarian history, while the **Rila Monastery**, a UNESCO World Heritage Site, is a masterpiece of Bulgarian art and architecture.

In the Baltics, **Estonia** is a country where medieval charm meets cutting-edge technology. **Tallinn**, the capital, boasts one of the best-preserved medieval towns in Europe, with its cobblestone streets, historic towers, and Gothic spires. In the Netherlands, explore **Amsterdam**, where you can marvel at the masterpieces of **Van Gogh** and **Rembrandt** in the **Rijksmuseum**, or take a peaceful canal cruise through the city's scenic waterways. The **Keukenhof Gardens**, with their **world-famous tulip displays**, are a must-see in spring, offering a colorful and quintessentially Dutch experience.

For those who prefer a leisurely pace, senior-friendly tour options are abundant. Companies like **Road Scholar** and **Saga Holidays** offer packages tailored to seniors, focusing on slower-paced itineraries with ample rest periods. These tours often include skip-the-line tickets to major attractions, ensuring you spend more time enjoying and less time queuing. Group sizes are usually smaller, providing a more intimate and personalized experience. Whether it's a four-week grand tour of Europe or a quick getaway to a single city, these packages take the stress out of planning and allow you to immerse yourself fully in the cultural experience.

Engaging with local culture can turn a pleasant trip into an unforgettable one. Learn a few basic phrases in the local language—simple greetings and polite phrases go a long way. Familiarize yourself with local customs; for instance, in Spain, it's common to greet people with a kiss on each cheek, and in Germany, don't forget to clink your beer glasses and say "Prost!" at Oktoberfest. Try the local cuisine, whether it's sampling tapas in Barcelona, pierogi in Poland, gelato in Rome, or indulging in bratwurst and pretzels in Germany. Take part in local festivals or cultural events and don't be shy about interacting with locals. They can offer insights and recommendations that you won't find in any guidebook.

Maximizing the experience of your cultural tour involves a bit of strategic planning. Visit major sites early in the morning or late in the afternoon to avoid crowds. Guided tours can provide deeper insights and often include access to areas not open to the general public. Seek out hidden spots known only to locals—those charming cafes tucked away in alleys, or small museums that house incredible collections. Take your time to savor each moment, whether it's enjoying a leisurely lunch at a sidewalk café or sitting quietly in a centuries-old cathedral. Your golden years are the perfect time to explore the rich tapestry of Europe's cultural heritage.

Themed cultural tours

A few years ago, my husband and I decided to take a cultural tour focused on the life of Mozart, our favorite composer. We envisioned this trip as a way to immerse ourselves in the rich musical history of Europe while exploring some of its most beautiful cities. Our journey began in **Prague**, a city that, while not a primary residence of Mozart, held a special place in his heart. We attended a performance of *The Marriage of Figaro* at the **Estates Theatre**, where Mozart conducted the world premiere of his famous opera Don Giovanni in 1787. Sitting in the historic auditorium, we experienced the same venue where Mozart once captivated audiences with his genius. The performance was breathtaking, and knowing that scenes from the movie *Amadeus* were filmed in this theater added an extra layer of historical significance. Watching the opera in such a meaningful and beautiful setting made it one of the most memorable experiences of our trip. Another highlight of our visit to Prague was exploring **Bertramka**, a historic villa where Mozart stayed during his visits to the city. This charming estate, now a museum, was once the residence of the Dušek family, close friends of Mozart. Here, he reportedly completed *Don Giovanni* just days before its premiere.

From Prague, we rented a car and drove to **Vienna**, the true heart of our Mozart pilgrimage. Once in Vienna, we dove headfirst into the rich history of classical music. We visited the **Mozarthaus**, Mozart's former residence, which is now a museum dedicated to his life and works. The feeling of walking through the same rooms where Mozart composed some of his greatest masterpieces was simply awe-inspiring. We also attended a concert at the **Vienna State Opera**, and it was a mesmerizing experience. The city's blend of imperial grandeur, music, and art made every moment feel like stepping into a living museum.

From Vienna, we decided to take the scenic route rather than the bustling Autobahn, driving along the **Danube River** as we made our way to **Salzburg**, Mozart's birthplace. This slower pace allowed us to stop in charming towns like **Melk** and **Dürnstein**, each offering its own unique slice of Austrian history and culture. We spent time at the **Melk Abbey**, a baroque masterpiece perched above the Danube, and wandered through the picturesque vineyards surrounding the river, soaking in the tranquility of the countryside.

In **Salzburg**, we visited the **Mozart Residence** and his birthplace on **Getreidegasse**, both now museums, offering a deeper understanding of his early life. We also explored the **Salzburg Cathedral**, where Mozart was baptized, and **St. Peter's Abbey**, where he composed some of his early works. The **Hohensalzburg Fortress**, towering over the city, provided us with breathtaking views of the surrounding Alps and a chance to immerse ourselves in centuries of history. The fortress, with its medieval architecture and panoramic views, was awe-inspiring on its own, but our experience there was made even more special by attending an intimate chamber orchestra concert within its historic halls. The music, echoing through the fortress, created an unforgettable atmosphere, transporting us back to the times when Salzburg was alive with the sound of classical compositions. To top off the evening, we indulged in a romantic dinner at the fortress, dining on Austrian cuisine as the city below sparkled with lights. The combination of history, music, and a beautifully prepared meal created one of the most enchanting nights of our trip, blending the past and present in a truly magical way.

Of course, we couldn't miss exploring the sites where ***The Sound of Music*** was filmed. Wandering through the **Mirabell Gardens**, where the famous "Do-Re-Mi" scene was shot, brought back memories of the beloved musical. Walking along the same paths, surrounded by vibrant flowers and framed by the fortress in the background, gave us a sense of nostalgia and connection to Salzburg's cinematic legacy. The film's iconic settings, scattered throughout the city, added another layer of charm and history to our visit, making our journey through Salzburg a delightful blend of music, film, and history.

Though not directly tied to Mozart, we couldn't resist making a stop in the medieval town of **Český Krumlov** on our way back to **Prague**. Nestled in the Czech countryside, this UNESCO World Heritage Site, with its winding streets and fairy-tale castle, was like stepping into another time. Wandering through its streets, we were reminded of how much history and culture Europe has to offer at every turn.

This journey not only deepened our appreciation for Mozart and classical music but also enriched our understanding of European history and culture. The opportunity to explore these cities at our own pace, venturing off the beaten path and connecting with local traditions, was an unforgettable experience. If you're considering a cultural tour of Europe, I highly recommend planning around the figures and places that resonate with you—whether it's music, art, history, or food—and taking the time to savor each stop along the way.

While my husband and I planned our Mozart-inspired cultural tour at our own pace, there are countless other themed cultural tours in Europe that cater to a wide range of interests. If you prefer to have your itinerary set, or just want the convenience of a guided experience, many companies specialize in themed cultural tours that allow you to explore Europe's rich history, art, and traditions. Here are a few themed cultural tours you might want to consider:

Shakespeare's England: Literary Tour of the UK

If you are a lover of literature, a tour of Shakespeare's England is a must. Starting in **Stratford-upon-Avon**, the birthplace of William Shakespeare, you can visit his childhood home, the school where he studied, and the **Royal Shakespeare Theatre**, where his works are still performed. The tour can take you to **London**, where you can experience the **Globe Theatre**, a replica of Shakespeare's original theater. Nearby, **Oxford** offers its own literary charm, home to great authors like J.R.R. Tolkien and Lewis Carroll. For those wanting an immersive literary journey, many companies offer guided tours that include stops at Shakespeare's haunts, as well as performances of his plays.

Impressionist Art in France

Art lovers can take a trip through the heart of **France**, visiting key locations that inspired the great Impressionist painters. Start in **Paris**, where you can explore the **Musée d'Orsay**, home to masterpieces by **Monet, Degas, and Renoir**. Travel to **Giverny**, where you can visit **Monet's house and gardens**, immortalized in his famous water lily series. A stop in **Rouen**, known for its beautiful cathedral often painted by **Monet**, can round out this art-lovers pilgrimage.

The Viking Trail: Scandinavia's Rich Heritage

For those fascinated by ancient history and mythology, a tour tracing the Viking legacy through **Norway, Denmark,** and **Sweden** offers a deep dive into the Norse culture. Visit **Oslo's Viking Ship Museum**, tour **Roskilde** in Denmark where Viking ships were built, and explore the ancient trading town of **Birka** in Sweden. Companies like **Viking River Cruises** often combine these historical experiences with scenic voyages along the fjords and rivers that Vikings once traversed, making it both an educational and visually stunning journey.

Music Lovers' Vienna to Leipzig Tour

If classical music is your passion, a tour from **Vienna, Austria,** to **Leipzig, Germany,** offers an opportunity to explore the lives and works of some of the greatest composers. **Vienna**, with its rich musical heritage, is home to museums dedicated to **Beethoven and Schubert**, as well as the legendary **Vienna State Opera**. It's also the city where **Johann Strauss**, the "Waltz King," composed many of his most famous works. You can visit the **Strauss Residence**, now a museum, where he lived and composed the iconic *Blue Danube* waltz. From there, travel to **Leipzig**, where **Bach** spent much of his life. You can visit **St. Thomas Church,** where Bach was choirmaster, and the **Bach Museum.** Along the way, you might also explore **Salzburg**, Mozart's birthplace, and **Bayreuth,** where Wagner's famous opera festival takes place. This journey through Europe's musical history offers a harmonious blend of cultural discovery and melodic inspiration.

Ancient Civilizations Tour: Greece and Italy

History buffs can embark on a journey through the cradle of Western civilization by visiting the ruins of ancient **Greece** and **Italy**. Begin in **Athens**, exploring the **Acropolis**, the **Parthenon**, and ancient theaters, before heading to the island of **Delphi**, home of the Oracle. Then make your way to **Rome**, where you'll walk through history at the **Colosseum**, the **Roman Forum**, and the awe-inspiring **Pantheon**. Don't miss the lesser-known, but equally remarkable, site of **Paestum** in **Southern Italy**. This ancient city, originally founded by the Greeks, boasts some of the best-preserved Greek temples in the world. The three colossal temples dedicated to Hera and Athena rival the grandeur of those in Athens, and the site offers a quieter, more reflective atmosphere. For a more immersive experience, companies such as **Road Scholar** or **Odyssey Traveller** offer small group tours, complete with expert historians to guide you through ancient relics and architecture.

5.7 Learning While Traveling: Cultural Exchange Programs

Cultural exchange programs offer a unique and enriching way to travel, allowing you to deeply immerse yourself in a new culture while gaining firsthand experience in local traditions. Unlike typical sightseeing trips, cultural exchanges provide opportunities for language immersion, culinary lessons, art workshops, and homestays, giving you a deeper, more personal understanding of the culture you're visiting. Whether you're learning to cook authentic local dishes, participating in traditional festivals, or engaging in daily life with a host family, these experiences provide a rich, personal connection to the people and customs of a foreign country. For retirees, cultural exchange programs are an excellent way to combine travel with learning, offering not only new skills and knowledge but also meaningful connections that often lead to lifelong friendships.

Selecting the right cultural exchange program requires careful research, especially when looking for options tailored to older adults. Start by considering your interests and goals—do you want to focus on learning languages, history, arts, or something else entirely? Once you've narrowed down your interests, look for reputable programs through established organizations. Programs like **Road Scholar, GoAbroad,** and **Global Volunteers** offer a variety of cultural exchange opportunities specifically designed for older adults. It's important to consider factors like the duration of the program (whether it's a short-term stay or an extended cultural immersion), the level of support services provided (such as language assistance or emergency contacts), and the reviews of past participants. Many exchange programs provide accommodations like homestays or local apartments, so you'll also want to look into the housing options and see if they fit your comfort level. Reading participant testimonials can give you a clearer idea of the experience and ensure the program is trustworthy and well-run.

Proper preparation is essential to make the most of your cultural exchange experience. Start by learning some basic phrases in the local language to help with daily communication—simple greetings, polite phrases, and common questions go a long way in showing respect for the culture you're entering. You can use apps like **Duolingo** or **Babbel** to get a head start. Conducting some cultural research ahead of time is also helpful. Familiarize yourself with the country's customs, etiquette, and traditions to avoid cultural faux pas and better appreciate your experiences. Planning the logistics for an extended stay is another important step. This includes securing the proper visas, ensuring your passport is up to date, and obtaining travel insurance. Make sure to pack thoughtfully, considering the climate, local dress codes, and any specialized items you might need for your cultural activities. Preparing mentally for an extended stay abroad—being open to new experiences and flexible with any challenges—will also help ensure a rewarding experience.

Please refer to the **Resources Chapter** for a list of reputable organizations offering cultural exchange programs.

5.8 Savoring the World Through Food and Wine Adventures

Food and wine travel offers a rich, sensory way to experience the world, allowing you to immerse yourself in local culture through its cuisine and regional wines. This type of travel provides a perfect blend of indulgence and education, whether you're strolling through vineyards, taking part in cooking classes, or dining at local restaurants. The joy of tasting authentic dishes paired with locally produced wines gives you a deep appreciation for the history and traditions behind them. For retirees, food and wine travel is an ideal way to engage your senses, expand your culinary knowledge, and enjoy new destinations in a relaxing yet enriching way.

There are countless destinations around the world where food and wine lovers can indulge in culinary delights. **Italy** is a classic choice for both food and wine enthusiasts, offering experiences such as tasting Chianti in **Tuscany**, enjoying pasta in **Bologna**, or learning to make traditional pizza in **Naples**. In the picturesque countryside, you can explore vineyards, enjoy truffle hunts, and participate in pasta-making classes with local chefs. **France** is another premier destination, famous for its rich culinary traditions and world-renowned wines. In regions like **Bordeaux and Burgundy**, you can tour vineyards, sip fine wine, and enjoy gourmet meals that showcase local flavors. **Paris** is a haven for food lovers, offering Michelin-starred dining, bustling markets, and intimate patisseries.

For those seeking more exotic flavors, **Spain** offers a blend of vibrant cuisine and outstanding wines. Tapas tours through cities like **Seville or Barcelona** are a fantastic way to sample regional specialties, while a trip to the **La Rioja** wine region lets you savor some of Spain's best wines.

Argentina is another excellent destination for food and wine travel, particularly for those who love steak and Malbec. In **Mendoza**, you can tour vineyards set against the backdrop of the Andes and enjoy world-class wines paired with traditional Argentine dishes.

In the USA, **Napa Valley in California** is an iconic wine region known for its exquisite wines and farm-to-table dining experiences. Pairing locally sourced meals with Napa's famous Cabernet Sauvignon is a quintessential American food and wine experience. **Sonoma** offers a slightly more relaxed vibe but with equally high-quality wines. For a different kind of food and wine experience, **New Orleans** blends Creole and Cajun flavors with a lively atmosphere and some of the best food festivals in the country. In **Oregon**, you'll find excellent Pinot Noir wines in the **Willamette Valley**, paired with fresh seafood and locally grown produce.

South Africa's food and wine scene is a hidden gem waiting to be explored. The **Western Cape**, particularly **Stellenbosch** and **Franschhoek**, offers world-class vineyards set against breathtaking mountain backdrops. Here, you can indulge in award-winning wines like Pinotage and Chenin Blanc, paired with farm-to-table cuisine that highlights the region's fresh, local produce. Wine estates often offer guided tours, tastings, and gourmet meals, allowing visitors to immerse themselves in the rich culinary heritage of South Africa. **Cape Town** is another must-visit, with its vibrant food markets, top-tier restaurants, and coastal views that make every dining experience unforgettable.

Australia's food and wine regions are as vast and diverse as its landscapes. The **Barossa Valley**, just outside **Adelaide**, is renowned for its bold Shiraz and other robust red wines. In addition to its acclaimed wineries, the region offers culinary tours where you can sample artisanal cheeses, olive oils, and fresh produce straight from the farm. For those seeking a coastal wine experience, the **Margaret River** in **Western Australia** provides both world-class vineyards and stunning beaches. **Melbourne** and **Sydney** are home to vibrant food scenes with markets, award-winning restaurants, and cultural diversity that bring a wide array of global flavors to the table.

In Canada, the **Naramata Bench** wine region in British Columbia's Okanagan Valley is a hidden gem that rivals some of the world's best wine destinations. Nestled along the eastern shores of **Okanagan Lake**, this area boasts not only award-winning wines but also stunning landscapes, perfect for a relaxing and scenic getaway. Known for its small boutique wineries, Naramata offers a laid-back atmosphere where you can chat with winemakers, sip exceptional Pinot Gris or Syrah, and take in breathtaking lake views all at once. The region is also a paradise for food lovers, with farm-to-table restaurants serving fresh, local produce that pairs beautifully with the region's wines. Living in British Columbia, my husband and I have spent several vacations exploring the Naramata region, and even after multiple visits, we feel like we've only scratched the surface of what this magical place has to offer. We'd spend our days cycling between vineyards, and our evenings unwinding by the lake, watching the sunset over the Okanagan. Beyond the wine, the area offers great opportunities for hiking, swimming, and enjoying the pristine beauty of the Okanagan Valley.

When planning a food and wine travel experience, it's important to find the right combination that matches your preferences. Some travelers prefer guided culinary and wine tours, where local experts take you through the best vineyards, restaurants, and markets, explaining the history and nuances behind every dish and glass of wine. Others might enjoy a more hands-on experience, such as cooking classes paired with wine tastings, where you learn to prepare local dishes and understand how different wines enhance the flavors. Wine and food festivals are another excellent way to immerse yourself in the local wine culture—events like the **Sonoma Wine Country Weekend** or **Italy's Alba White Truffle Festival** provide the perfect combination of food, wine, and festivity.

If you're seeking something more intimate, vineyard stays offer the chance to live in the heart of a wine region, surrounded by grapevines, where you can meet winemakers and experience the winemaking process firsthand. Many luxury travel companies and specialized food and wine tour operators, such as **Zicasso, Butterfield & Robinson,** and **Culinary Backstreets**, offer customized itineraries that combine the best experiences.

Researching the local cuisine and regional wines before your trip will help you appreciate what you're about to experience. Learning a few basic phrases in the local language can enhance your interactions with chefs, winemakers, and restaurant staff. It's also helpful to pack with food and wine tours in mind—comfortable shoes are essential for walking through vineyards, markets, or cobblestone streets. Consider bringing a wine carrier if you plan to purchase bottles to bring home, or look into shipping services offered by many wineries. Also, don't forget to research customs regulations if you plan on bringing wine or food items home. Ensure you make reservations at highly rated restaurants and popular wineries in advance, especially if you're traveling to renowned food and wine regions during peak seasons. Planning your itinerary to include visits to farmers' markets and local food festivals can offer a chance to taste seasonal ingredients and get a feel for the local food culture.

While indulging in the finest wines during your travels, it's essential to remember that moderation is key, especially for seniors. Many studies suggest that moderate alcohol consumption, particularly red wine, can offer health benefits such as improved cardiovascular health, reduced risk of certain types of heart disease, and increased levels of HDL, the "good" cholesterol. The Mediterranean diet, which includes moderate wine consumption, is often cited for its health benefits, including longevity and reduced inflammation.

For seniors, however, it's important to balance these potential benefits with the risks of overconsumption. While traditional guidelines suggest that moderation means one glass of wine per day for women and up to two for men, recent studies are challenging the idea that even this amount is entirely risk-free. Research now shows that alcohol, even in moderate amounts, may increase the risk of certain diseases, including breast, liver, colon, and esophageal cancer. Alcohol can interfere with the body's ability to absorb essential nutrients, weaken the immune system, and exacerbate chronic conditions like high blood pressure and diabetes. For older adults, it's especially important to consider these risks, as alcohol can interact negatively with medications, impair balance, and contribute to dehydration, increasing the risk of falls and other health complications. When enjoying food and wine travel, it's essential to stay informed about these emerging findings and consider personal health risks when deciding how much alcohol to consume. Savor each sip, but be mindful of your limits to ensure you're maximizing the health benefits without risking adverse effects.

As we conclude our exploration of unforgettable travel destinations and once-in-a-lifetime experiences, it's time to turn up the excitement volume and dive into a world of thrilling adventure. While wandering through ancient cities and relaxing on scenic river cruises can satisfy your soul, some of us, retirees, crave the rush of adrenaline and the challenge of more extreme activities. In the next chapter, we'll explore heart-pounding adventures like hot air ballooning over stunning landscapes, scuba diving into the depths of the ocean, skydiving from dizzying heights, and much more. So, if you're ready to take your retirement to new heights—literally—let's jump into the exhilarating world of adventure and excitement!

Chapter Six

Sky High & Deep Dive: Adventure-Fueled Experiences

As the ground drops away beneath you, the world stretches out in a stunning panorama, and your heart races—not from fear, but from the thrill of adventure. Welcome to the world of extreme sports, where retirement is just the beginning of new, exhilarating experiences. Whether it's skydiving, paragliding, zip-lining through dense forests, or taking on white-water rapids, these adrenaline-pumping activities can inject excitement into your golden years. Embracing these challenges isn't just about pushing your physical limits—it's about embracing life to the fullest, proving that age is no barrier to adventure.

6.1 Skydiving and Paragliding: Thrills in the Sky

Let's start by understanding the basics. Skydiving and paragliding both offer the thrill of flight, but they're as different as night and day. Skydiving is like jumping straight into an adrenaline rush. You strap on a parachute, board a plane, and at a dizzying height, you leap into the sky. The first few seconds are a free fall, with the wind roaring in your ears, then you pull the cord, and the parachute opens, slowing your descent for a peaceful float down to earth. Paragliding, on the other hand, is gliding gracefully through the air. You take off from a hill or cliff, with a wing-like parachute catching the wind, allowing you to soar gently for miles, enjoying a bird's-eye view of the landscape below. Both require specific equipment: skydiving needs a parachute rig and an altimeter, while paragliding involves a paraglider, harness, and helmet. Beginners in both sports can expect thorough training sessions, usually starting with tandem flights where an instructor handles the technicalities, letting you savor the experience.

Safety first, always! When it comes to skydiving and paragliding, choosing certified and reputable operators is crucial. Look for companies with excellent safety records, glowing reviews, and certifications from recognized bodies like the **United States Parachute Association (USPA)** for skydiving or the **United States Hang Gliding and Paragliding Association (USHPA)** for paragliding. If you're traveling internationally, be sure to research the equivalent certifications in other countries. These certifications will give you peace of mind knowing you're in safe hands, no matter where you are. The operators provide thorough safety briefings, quality equipment, and certified instructors who can guide you through every step of the process. Imagine being paired with an instructor who's logged thousands of jumps or flights—talk about peace of mind! They'll ensure you understand the procedures, from how to handle the equipment to what to do in case of an emergency. Rest assured, reputable companies maintain and inspect their gear rigorously, so you're flying with the best.

Please refer to the **Resources Chapter** for a list of reputable organizations for skydiving and paragliding, along with their websites.

Before you take to the skies, it's essential to consider the physical and health requirements for these activities. Skydiving and paragliding aren't as physically demanding as running a marathon, but they do require a certain level of fitness. Weight limits are in place to ensure safety—typically around 220-240 pounds, though this can vary by operator. If you have heart conditions, severe back issues, or mobility constraints, it's wise to consult your doctor beforehand. Both sports involve short bursts of physical effort and can be exhilarating, which might not be suitable for everyone. But if you're in good health and your doctor gives you the green light, the sky's the limit!

If you're ready to take the plunge or glide through the skies, there's no shortage of breathtaking destinations to choose from. Picture yourself in **Interlaken, Switzerland**, where the snow-capped peaks of the Swiss Alps and stunning views of crystal-clear lakes serve as the backdrop for both skydiving and paragliding. For those seeking adventure at the far edge of the world, **Queenstown, New Zealand,** offers an equally exhilarating experience combining adrenaline-pumping activities with awe-inspiring scenery. If tropical landscapes are more your style, in places like **Maui** and **Oahu**, the lush valleys, volcanic craters, and endless coastline provide a spectacular setting as you leap or glide with the vast Pacific Ocean beneath you. In **Chamonix,**

France, you can soar over Europe's highest peaks with Mont Blanc towering in the distance. For an unforgettable mix of city and nature, **Cape Town, South Africa,** offers the best of both worlds. Skydiving here gives you unparalleled views of **Table Mountain**, **Robben Island**, and the ocean. Or, if you prefer a more leisurely adventure, paragliding from **Lion's Head** or **Signal Hill** allows you to take in the iconic scenery with a gentle descent over the stunning landscape. Even urban environments offer their own unique thrill, and **Dubai** is a prime example offering a one-of-a-kind view of the archipelago of artificial islands of **Palm Jumeirah** and the glittering skyline of the city. For those seeking serenity alongside their adventure, the peaceful **Phewa Lake Pokhara in Nepal** is an idyllic destination for paragliding, creating a surreal experience that blends tranquility with exhilaration.

No matter which destination you choose, these iconic locations guarantee that your skydiving or paragliding adventure will be nothing short of spectacular, leaving you with unforgettable memories and stories to tell.

Capturing the moment is a big part of the thrill. Most adventure companies offer video or photo packages that document your experience from start to finish. Imagine showing your grandkids a video of you free-falling through the sky or gliding serenely over a mountain range—they'll think you're the coolest grandparent ever! These packages often include a video of the entire experience, from the nervous anticipation before the jump to the triumphant landing. Some even offer GoPros attached to your helmet, giving you a first-person perspective on your adventure. It's not just about the bragging rights (though that's a perk); it's about reliving the thrill and sharing it with family and friends. So, get ready to strike a pose and let the wind ruffle your hair—a picture-perfect moment awaits.

6.2 Scuba Diving: Exploring Underwater Worlds

Floating weightlessly in a vibrant underwater wonderland, surrounded by colorful fish and intricate coral formations, feels like stepping into another realm. If this sounds like a dream come true, then scuba diving is your ticket to this magical world. To get started, you'll need to obtain a scuba diving certification. Two popular beginner-friendly courses are the **PADI Open Water Diver** and the **NAUI Scuba Diver**. These courses typically involve a mix of classroom study, pool sessions, and open-water dives. You'll learn the fundamental skills, safety procedures, and equipment handling needed for a safe and enjoyable dive. The courses are structured to build your confidence gradually, ensuring that by the time you take your first open water dive, you'll feel like a fish in water.

Selecting the right dive spots is crucial, especially for beginners and older divers. You want locations with calm waters and abundant marine life. Some top destinations include the **Great Barrier Reef in Australia**, known for its breathtaking biodiversity, and **Cozumel in Mexico**, famous for its crystal-clear waters and vibrant coral reefs. The Bahamas offers excellent beginner sites with shallow, calm conditions, while **Bonaire in the Caribbean** is a diver's paradise with easy shore entries and protected marine parks. Other notable spots are the **Maldives, the Red Sea in Egypt, and the Florida Keys**. Each of these locations promises a unique underwater adventure, filled with colorful coral gardens, playful dolphins, and friendly sea turtles.

Investing in scuba gear can be a bit like shopping for a new wardrobe—exciting but overwhelming. The basic gear includes a mask, snorkel, fins, wetsuit, buoyancy control device (BCD), regulator, and tank. As a beginner, you might want to start by renting gear to get a feel for what you like. However, owning your equipment can be more comfortable and sanitary. When buying, focus on fit and comfort—nothing ruins a dive faster than an ill-fitting mask or a wetsuit that feels like a straitjacket. Maintenance is key to longevity; always rinse your gear with fresh water after dives and store it in a cool, dry place to prevent mold and damage.

Conservation awareness is a big part of diving responsibly. The underwater world is fragile, and it's our job to protect it. Always practice respectful diving by not touching or disturbing marine life and never collecting souvenirs. Participate in underwater clean-ups and spread the word about marine conservation. Educate yourself on the local ecosystems before each dive and choose operators committed to sustainable practices.

6.3 Motorcycle Road Trips: On the Open Road with Confidence

There's nothing quite like the thrill of the open road, the rushing wind, and the sense of freedom that comes with a motorcycle road trip. Whether you're cruising along scenic coastal highways or winding through rugged mountain passes, motorcycle travel offers a unique connection to the journey. It's not just about the destination, but the adventure of the ride itself—the ability to explore at your own pace, discover hidden gems off the beaten path, and experience the landscape in an entirely new way. For beginners, this section will guide you through the essentials of planning your first motorcycle road trip, from selecting the right bike to ensuring your safety and comfort on the road.

Before you hit the highways, select the right motorcycle. Think of it as choosing a dance partner; you want someone who moves with you effortlessly. Comfort, handling, and reliability are key. For long-distance touring, consider a touring bike like the **Honda Gold Wing**, known for its plush seats and smooth ride, or the **BMW R 1250 RT**, which offers excellent handling and advanced features. If you prefer something lighter, a cruiser like the **Harley-Davidson Softail** might be more your style. These bikes are designed for comfort over long distances, with ergonomic seating and ample storage for your gear.

Speaking of gear, let's talk about the essentials. A high-quality helmet is non-negotiable; it's your best defense against the unexpected. Full-face helmets offer the most protection, but if you prefer something less confining, modular helmets are a great compromise. Protective clothing is also a must—think sturdy jackets with armor, gloves, and boots that cover your ankles. Weather can be unpredictable, so pack gear for various conditions: a breathable rain suit, thermal layers for chilly mornings, and ventilated jackets for hot afternoons. Don't forget a basic repair kit, including tire repair tools, a multi-tool, and spare fuses. These can save the day if you encounter minor issues on the road.

Planning your route is where the adventure truly begins. Instead of focusing on the fastest way from point A to point B, look for scenic roads and interesting stops. For those new to road trips or looking for a leisurely experience, start with routes that offer scenic beauty without the stress of challenging driving conditions. **The Great River Road** along the Mississippi River is an excellent choice for beginners, providing beautiful river views and easy-to-navigate roads through quaint Midwestern towns. Another beginner-friendly option is **Route 66**, particularly the stretch between Chicago and St. Louis. This iconic road trip offers wide, well-maintained highways and charming roadside stops, making it perfect for those easing into long-distance travel. It is also a classic ride that delivers a taste of history and culture.

The **Pacific Coast Highway in California** offers stunning ocean views, while the **Blue Ridge Parkway in Virginia** winds through picturesque mountains. For a more rugged experience, consider the **Beartooth Highway in Montana and Wyoming**, which takes you through some of the most dramatic alpine landscapes in the U.S., or the **Tail of the Dragon in Tennessee**, famous for its 318 curves over 11 miles, making it a thrilling ride for experienced motorcyclists.

If you're up for an international adventure, the **Great Ocean Road in Australia** is a breathtaking ride along the coastline, offering iconic views of the Twelve Apostles. In Europe, the **Stelvio Pass in Italy** is one of the highest and most challenging roads in the Alps, perfect for those seeking adventure and incredible mountain vistas. **Canada's Icefields Parkway**, which connects Jasper and Banff National Parks, offers jaw-dropping views of glaciers, turquoise lakes, and wildlife.

Each route you take should include regular rest stops, not just for refueling but to stretch your legs and take in the sights. Points of interest, like national parks, historic landmarks, and quirky roadside attractions, add flavor to your trip, making each day a new adventure. Whether you prefer scenic coastal drives, mountainous terrain, or cultural explorations, choosing the right route will elevate your motorcycle road trip to an unforgettable experience.

Joining motorcycle clubs or groups can enrich your road-tripping experience. These communities are treasure troves of knowledge, offering tips and advice from seasoned riders. Clubs often organize group rides, providing a safe and social way to explore new routes. You'll find camaraderie and support, whether you're navigating a tricky mountain pass or just looking for the best diner in town. Plus, riding with a group adds an extra layer of safety, as there's always someone watching your back.

Popular groups like the **Harley Owners Group (H.O.G.)**, one of the largest motorcycle communities globally, offer local chapters that organize rides and events year-round. For women riders, groups like **Women on Wheels (WOW)** or the **Motor Maids** provide a welcoming community focused on empowering female motorcyclists. If you're looking for long-distance travel tips or global routes, **Adventure Riders** is an online forum and group for adventure touring enthusiasts. The **American Motorcyclist Association (AMA)** also connects riders through organized events, rides, and races across the U.S., while the **Iron Butt Association** caters to those interested in extreme long-distance riding. Whether you're riding with a large club or a small local group, these communities bring a new dimension to your motorcycle adventures. Gear up, plan your route, and get ready to experience the thrill of the open road in a whole new way! Are you ready?

6.4 Hot Air Balloon Rides: Seeing the World from Above

There's something truly magical about the serene silence of floating above the earth, with the landscape unfolding beneath you like a patchwork quilt. Hot air ballooning offers this breathtaking experience, where the world seems to slow down, and you feel completely at peace, drifting gently in the breeze.

For me, hot air ballooning holds an especially dear place in my heart. Over twenty-five years ago, my husband proposed to me at a beautiful balloon festival in Ontario, Canada. The sky was filled with vibrant colors as dozens of balloons took flight, creating a mesmerizing scene. As we floated above the rolling hills and forests, he got down on one knee—an unforgettable moment set against the backdrop of the sky and earth coming together. That magical day remains one of the most cherished memories of our lives.

Hot air ballooning is an experience that offers both adventure and tranquility. Whether you're looking for a romantic moment, or want to enjoy panoramic views from above, it's a journey you won't forget.

Choosing a reliable operator is crucial for a safe and enjoyable flight. Look for companies with strong safety records and certified pilots. Customer reviews can also provide insights into the experience. Operators with a good reputation will offer comprehensive safety briefings and well-maintained equipment. Certified pilots, often with thousands of hours of flying experience, ensure that you're in safe hands. They'll guide you through the process, from takeoff to landing, making sure you're comfortable and informed throughout the journey.

Before you take off, expect a brief orientation where you'll learn about the balloon, the basket, and safety protocols. The preparation includes inflating the balloon, which is a spectacle in itself. As you ascend, the noise from the burners fades, replaced by the gentle whisper of the wind. The ride typically lasts an hour, giving you ample time to soak in panoramic views.

Destinations like **Cappadocia in Turkey** offer surreal landscapes dotted with fairy chimneys, while the **Loire Valley in France** presents châteaux and vineyards. Other fantastic spots include the **Serengeti in Tanzania,** where you might spot wildlife below, and **Napa Valley in California**, with its rolling vineyards. You can also float above the ancient temples of **Bagan in Myanmar**, or experience the stunning red rock formations in **Sedona, Arizona**. The **Masai Mara in Kenya** offers the chance to see the Great Migration from the air, while **Queenstown in New Zealand** provides an unforgettable backdrop of snow-capped mountains and shimmering lakes. For a more unique experience, try drifting over the mesmerizing desert dunes in **Dubai,** where the vast, golden landscape stretches endlessly beneath you.

Weather plays a significant role in ballooning. Ideal conditions include clear skies and calm winds. The best times of year for ballooning are typically spring and fall when the weather is stable and temperatures are mild. However, Mother Nature can be unpredictable, so flexibility is key. Flights are often scheduled for early morning or late afternoon when winds are typically calmer. If the weather doesn't cooperate, rescheduling might be necessary. While this can be disappointing, it's essential for safety. Keep an eye on the forecast and stay in touch with your operator for updates.

To ensure a comfortable and enjoyable experience, consider a few accessibility and comfort tips. Dress in layers, as temperatures can vary from ground level to higher altitudes. Wear comfortable shoes, as you'll be standing for the duration of the flight. Bringing a camera is a must, but make sure it has a strap to keep it secure. If you have mobility concerns, discuss them with the operator beforehand. Many companies offer accommodations, such as sturdy baskets with doors for easier access. With these preparations, you can fully enjoy the breathtaking views and the unique sensation of floating peacefully above the world.

6.5 White Water Rafting: Riding the Waves of Adventure

Navigating the twists and turns of a roaring river, feeling the spray of water on your face as you paddle through surging rapids, is an experience like no other. White water rafting delivers an exhilarating rush of adrenaline while immersing you in the beauty of nature. Let's start with the basics. Understanding river classifications is key to a safe and enjoyable experience. Rivers are rated from Class I to Class V, with Class I being gentle, easy waters suitable for beginners, and Class V reserved for experts who thrive on intense, turbulent rapids.

If you're new to the sport, start with Class I or II rivers, such as the **Nantahala River in North Carolina** or the **Kicking Horse River in Canada**. The **Rogue River in Oregon** offers a mix of calm and exciting sections, making it perfect for a varied experience. For those looking to venture further, the **Soca River in Slovenia** provides stunning scenery and manageable rapids, while the **Rio Grande in Texas** offers a unique blend of natural beauty and adventure.

The **Chattooga River** on the border of **Georgia and South Carolina** is another great option for beginners, with sections offering both peaceful paddling and thrilling rapids. The **Lower New River in West Virginia** also features calm stretches that are ideal for newcomers to whitewater rafting.

The **Snake River in Wyoming** offers scenic Class I and II sections through Grand Teton National Park, where you can enjoy wildlife sightings and incredible mountain views. The **Middle Fork of the American River in California** is another great option for beginners, with plenty of gentle rapids and stunning canyon landscapes.

For more experienced rafters, **the Colorado River through the Grand Canyon** delivers an epic adventure, offering a combination of heart-pounding Class IV and V rapids along with jaw-dropping canyon views. **Costa Rica's Pacuare River** is a must-visit for those seeking both thrilling rapids and lush, tropical surroundings, often touted as one of the most beautiful rivers in the world. The **Zambezi River in Zambia,** with its world-class Class V rapids near Victoria Falls, and the **Futaleufú River in Chile,** set against the dramatic Patagonian landscape, are also prime destinations for seasoned adventurers. For an exotic experience, consider the **Ayung River in Bali,** where you'll navigate rapids while surrounded by vibrant jungles and ancient temples.

Safety and training are non-negotiable when it comes to white water rafting. Always go with guided tours led by professional rafting companies. These experts provide not just the equipment but also the knowledge and skills to ensure a safe trip. Before you even dip a toe in the water, you'll receive a safety briefing covering everything from paddling techniques to what to do if you fall in. Experienced guides lead the way, directing the raft and ensuring everyone works together. They keep a vigilant eye on the river's conditions, adjusting the plan as needed to keep you safe. Remember, the best adventures are those you can relive with joy, not regret.

White water rafting demands a good level of physical fitness and a willingness to work as a team. Paddling through rapids requires strength and coordination, and you'll need to follow the guide's commands precisely to navigate the river successfully. This isn't just a solo endeavor; teamwork is crucial. Each person in the raft plays a vital role, whether it's paddling in sync or leaning the right way to balance the raft. Think of it as a group dance, where everyone's movements must align. It's a fantastic way to bond with friends or family, turning a thrilling adventure into a shared triumph.

While you're having the time of your life, it's important to remember that these waterways are delicate ecosystems. Promoting environmental awareness is part of the adventure. Follow 'Leave No Trace' principles—pack out everything you bring in and avoid disturbing wildlife. Participate in river clean-up initiatives if you can. Many rafting companies support these efforts and welcome volunteers. By respecting the natural beauty of these rivers, you ensure they remain pristine for future adventurers. Think of it as giving back to the places that give you so much joy.

6.6 Mountain Biking for the Energetic Retiree

The thrill of riding through lush forests, over rolling hills, and along scenic trails, all while getting a fantastic workout, is what makes mountain biking so appealing. It's not just for the young and reckless; it's a fantastic fit for retirees looking to add a dash of adventure to their fitness routine. This sport combines cardiovascular exercise, strength training, and mental challenges, making it a triple benefit to your health. Pedaling up hills gets your heart pumping, navigating rocky paths improves your balance and coordination, and the sheer joy of being outdoors boosts your mental well-being. It's like a gym session, a nature hike, and a meditation retreat all rolled into one.

While I'm not into mountain biking myself, my husband is an avid mountain biker and has explored some of the most scenic and challenging trails out there. He's tackled routes in places like **Mont-Sainte-Anne in Quebec, Canada** - the home to the UCI Mountain Bike World Cup, **Cortina d'Ampezzo in Italy, Mount Snow in Vermont**, and the epic **Continental Divide Trail in Colorado**, to name a few. While I usually hike during his rides, through his adventures, I've come to appreciate the beauty and excitement that mountain biking offers. For those seeking an adventurous way to stay fit, it's hard to beat the thrill of the ride.

Choosing the right equipment is crucial for a safe and enjoyable mountain biking experience. Start with the bike itself. Look for a model that offers good suspension to absorb shocks and a comfortable seat to save your backside on long rides. Brands like **Trek, Specialized, and Giant** offer excellent options tailored for all skill levels. A well-fitting helmet is your first line of defense, and don't skimp on quality. Pads for your knees and elbows can save you from scrapes and bruises. Consider investing in a good pair of gloves to improve your grip and reduce hand fatigue. A hydration pack, like a CamelBak, ensures you stay hydrated without having to stop frequently. Additional equipment like a small first aid kit, a multi-tool for quick repairs, and a portable pump can make your rides more enjoyable and trouble-free.

Starting safely with mountain biking involves easing into the sport. Don't rush to tackle the most challenging trails right away. Begin with flat, easy trails to build your confidence and skills. Learn to read trail ratings, which indicate the difficulty level. Green trails are beginner-friendly, blue are intermediate, and black diamond trails are for advanced riders. Stick to green trails initially, focusing on basic skills like shifting gears, braking, and maintaining balance. Gradual skill-building is essential. As you get more comfortable, try trails with slight inclines and gentle descents. Remember, it's not about speed; it's about enjoying the ride and staying safe.

British Columbia, where we live, is home to some of the world's best mountain biking destinations. **Whistler** is a globally renowned hotspot with trails for all levels, while **Vancouver's North Shore** offers excellent beginner and intermediate paths. Don't miss **Silver Star Mountain in Vernon**, BC, known for its variety of trails and breathtaking views. In the U.S., iconic spots like **Moab, Utah**, provide stunning red rock landscapes, while **Sedona, Arizona**, features scenic desert routes. For lush, forested adventures, **Pisgah National Forest in North Carolina** is a great option.

In Europe, **Cortina d'Ampezzo in Italy** delivers stunning rides through the Dolomites, and **Les Gets in France** is a favorite for alpine biking. **Austria's Saalbach-Hinterglemm** offers an extensive network of trails with views of the Austrian Alps. In **Spain, the Pyrenees** offer challenging trails with rewarding views, while **Slovenia's** bike parks, especially in **Kranjska Gora**, provide both thrilling descents and beautiful alpine scenery.

Joining mountain biking clubs or community groups can enhance your experience. These clubs offer structured rides, providing a safe environment for beginners to learn. They often organize group rides, where experienced riders share tips and advice. This camaraderie makes the sport more enjoyable and helps you push your limits safely. Clubs also offer social events, workshops, and even trips to famous biking trails. Whether you're a solo rider looking to make new friends or someone who enjoys group activities, these communities can provide the support and motivation you need to keep riding.

6.7 Soaring Through the Skies with Zip-Lining

Zip-lining is one of those heart-pumping adventures that can make you feel like a kid again, no matter your age. Gliding through the treetops or across expansive valleys, feeling the wind in your face as you speed through the air, is a thrilling experience that gives you a unique perspective of nature. Best of all, zip-lining can be a fantastic option for retirees looking for an adventurous activity that's both exhilarating and accessible.

Safety is always the top priority, and the good news is that zip-lining is designed with rigorous safety protocols in place. Reputable zip-lining companies provide professional guides who ensure that you're harnessed securely and thoroughly briefed on how to zip-line safely. The equipment used—harnesses, helmets, carabiners, and zip-line cables—undergoes regular safety checks to meet industry standards. Always choose zip-lining operators who are certified by recognized safety organizations, such as the **Association for Challenge Course Technology (ACCT)** or other local governing bodies. Don't hesitate to ask questions about the safety record of the company before booking, and look for glowing reviews from other participants.

Zip-lining doesn't require extensive physical training, but it's important to ensure you're comfortable with the idea of heights and short bursts of physical activity. Some courses involve hiking between zip lines, so a moderate level of fitness is recommended. Be sure to dress appropriately—closed-toe shoes with a good grip are essential, and wearing comfortable, weather-appropriate clothing will keep you at ease during the experience. If you have any health concerns, such as heart conditions or mobility limitations, check with your doctor beforehand to ensure zip-lining is safe for you.

The beauty of zip-lining is that it can be found in some of the world's most scenic destinations. In the U.S., **Haleakalā National Park in Maui, Hawaii,** offers an unforgettable zip-lining experience where you can glide over lush forests with views of volcanic craters. The **Great Smoky Mountains in Tennessee and North Carolina** feature treetop zip-line courses with incredible views of the rolling mountains and valleys below. **Hunter Mountain in New York's Catskills** region offers a long and thrilling zip-line ride that's perfect for adventure-seekers of all ages.

For those looking to explore beyond the U.S., **Costa Rica** is a zip-lining paradise, with courses through the dense canopies of tropical rainforests, where you might spot exotic wildlife from above. The **Arenal Volcano** area, in particular, is known for its breathtaking zip-lining tours over waterfalls and lush greenery. In Canada, **Whistler in British Columbia** is famous for its stunning zip-lining courses that allow you to soar over alpine forests and crystal-clear lakes. Europe has its own share of thrills, with **Interlaken in Switzerland** offering scenic zip-lining experiences through the majestic Swiss Alps, and **Madeira, Portugal,** providing coastal and mountainous views as you zip through nature reserves.

One of the best things about zip-lining is its accessibility. It's not an overly physically demanding activity, making it suitable for retirees who want an adventurous experience without the intensity of high-impact sports. Plus, zip-lining companies usually cater to all fitness levels, and guides are always on hand to ensure you feel safe and comfortable. Whether you're zipping through a forest canopy or across a mountain range, the thrill is unforgettable, but so is the sense of accomplishment. It's an exciting, yet manageable, adventure that leaves you feeling energized and connected to the great outdoors.

As with any adventure, don't forget to capture the memories. Many zip-lining companies offer helmet-mounted GoPro rentals or photo packages that document your entire experience. Whether it's the breathtaking landscapes or the joy on your face, these memories will be ones to cherish for years to come.

Adventure is the spice of life, and your golden years are the perfect time to savor it. From thrilling skydives to serene hot-air balloon rides, to heart-pounding white-water rafting, the opportunities for excitement are endless.

As we descend from the thrilling heights of skydiving and the depths of scuba diving, it's time to reconnect with the serenity of nature in all its beauty. For those who find joy in quieter, yet equally rewarding pursuits, the great outdoors offers endless possibilities. In the next chapter, we'll explore how to fully embrace the outdoors, offering activities that blend excitement with the calming presence of nature.

Chapter Seven

The Great Outdoors: Exploring Nature's Wonders

The beauty of the natural world is that it caters to everyone as outdoor activities provide a space for reflection, physical fitness, and a little adventure. There's something truly special about stepping outside and feeling the gentle warmth of the sun or the cool shade of a forest canopy. Whether you're strolling through a quiet woodland trail, exploring scenic mountain paths, or simply sitting by a tranquil lake, nature has a way of grounding us and reminding us of life's simple pleasures. Spending time outdoors is not just a pastime—it's a chance to reconnect with the world around us, stay active, and find joy in exploration.

7.1 Bird-Watching: Connecting with Nature's Winged Wonders

Bird-watching opens up a world of quiet excitement and connection with nature. From the delicate flutter of a hummingbird to the graceful glide of an eagle, each moment spent observing birds is an opportunity to witness the beauty of the natural world. The thrill lies in the unpredictability—whether you're in your own backyard or exploring a nature reserve, you never know which species will cross your path. Bird-watching is not only a relaxing and fulfilling pastime but also a chance to sharpen your observation skills, stay active, and appreciate the wonders of nature. It's a perfect way to enjoy the outdoors while engaging in a lifelong learning experience.

Choosing the right equipment is the first step in becoming a bird-watching aficionado. You don't need to break the bank to get started, but a good pair of binoculars can make all the difference. Look for binoculars with a magnification of 8x or 10x and ensure they are lightweight and easy to handle. Brands like **Nikon** and **Bushnell** offer reliable options at various price points. A field guide is also essential; it's the birdwatcher's bible. Guides like the **Sibley Field Guide to Birds**, the **Peterson Field Guide to Birds of North America**, and **The Golden Guide's Birds of North America**, which is portable and accessible for beginners, are excellent choices. These books offer detailed illustrations and descriptions, making it easier to identify the feathered friends you encounter.

Best bird-watching practices are crucial for a rewarding experience. Start by choosing the best times of day for bird-watching, typically early morning or late afternoon when birds are most active. Remain quiet and unobtrusive; sudden movements or loud noises easily startle birds. Wear neutral-colored clothing to blend into the environment.

Learn to use your binoculars efficiently by practicing at home, focusing on stationary objects before moving targets. The more you practice, the better you'll become at spotting and identifying birds. Familiarize yourself with common species in your area, and gradually expand your knowledge to include rarer finds. Websites like **eBird** can be invaluable for tracking bird sightings and learning about local species.

Local bird-watching spots can turn an ordinary day into an extraordinary adventure. National parks and nature reserves are often teeming with bird life. Places like the **Everglades National Park in Florida** or **Point Reyes National Seashore in California** are renowned for their avian diversity. Even local parks and green spaces can be treasure troves of bird activity. Many nature reserves offer guided bird-watching tours tailored to seniors, providing an opportunity to learn from experienced guides and meet fellow bird enthusiasts. These tours often reveal hidden gems and secret spots that you might miss on your own.

In addition to these U.S. hotspots, you can find other incredible destinations for bird-watching around the world. The **Amazon Rainforest in Brazil** offers the chance to spot hundreds of exotic species, including colorful toucans and macaws. In Europe, the wetlands of **Doñana National Park in Spain** provide a haven for flamingos and other migratory birds. If you're seeking something more remote, **New Zealand's Stewart Island** is home to rare species like the kiwi and yellow-eyed penguin. **Canada's Point Pelee National Park in Ontario** is famous for its spring migration, attracting bird enthusiasts from around the globe. **In Africa, the Okavango Delta in Botswana** offers an unparalleled bird-watching experience, with species like the African fish eagle soaring above its pristine waters.

Join bird-watching clubs to enrich your experience and enhance your skills. Local clubs provide a platform to meet fellow enthusiasts, exchange information, and take part in organized outings. Clubs often host events like bird counts, workshops, and lectures, offering both social and educational benefits. Websites like **Audubon** or **Birding-Pal** can help you find clubs in your area.

Always take a moment to reflect on your bird-watching journey. What are your favorite bird-watching spots? Have you had any memorable encounters with rare birds? How has bird-watching enriched your connection with nature? Jot down your thoughts and experiences in a journal. This reflection can deepen your appreciation for this delightful pastime and inspire new adventures in the great outdoors.

7.2 Fishing and Boating: Relaxing by the Water

Imagine casting a line into a serene lake, the sun gently warming your back, and the anticipation of that first bite. Getting started with fishing is easier than you might think. Freshwater fishing is perfect for beginners, whether you're at a local pond or a lazy river. A simple rod and reel combo, a tackle box with hooks, weights, and a variety of bait can get you started. If you prefer the thrill of the ocean, saltwater fishing might be your calling. Here, you'll need sturdier gear to handle bigger fish and the salty environment. Fly-fishing, on the other hand, is an art form of gracefully casting a delicate fly to land just right in a stream, enticing a trout. It requires a bit more finesse and specialized equipment like a fly rod, reel, and flies that mimic insects.

Safety on the water is paramount, especially as we get older. Always wear a life jacket. It's not just a safety precaution—it's literally a lifesaver. Understanding boat operation basics is crucial too. If you're new to boating, consider taking a boating safety course. These courses cover everything from navigation rules to emergency procedures. Knowing local boating laws and regulations can save you from fines and ensure a safe outing. For instance, some areas require specific permits or have speed limits to protect wildlife and other boaters. Make sure your boat is equipped with safety gear like flares, a first-aid kit, and a whistle. And remember, never boat alone—having a buddy ensures someone's there to help if something goes wrong.

Finding accessible fishing and boating locations that cater to seniors can make your experience even more enjoyable. Look for places with amenities like piers, ramps, and rental facilities that offer senior assistance. State parks often have accessible fishing spots with flat, stable surfaces and handrails. Marinas sometimes offer boat rentals with easy boarding options and staff to assist you. For example, **Lake Tahoe** has several marinas that rent out boats and provide assistance to ensure a smooth and enjoyable day on the water. The **Florida Keys** offer many fishing charters that cater to seniors, providing everything from equipment to bait.

Local fishing clubs are fantastic for learning from more experienced anglers. These clubs often organize group fishing trips, providing a chance to explore new spots and techniques. It's also a great way to make new friends who share your passion. Clubs often host events, workshops, and tournaments, making it easy to stay engaged and motivated. Websites like **Meetup** and local community boards are good places to find these clubs.

7.3 Exploring the Wonders of National Parks

There's something awe-inspiring about stepping into a national park, where the beauty of nature stretches as far as the eye can see and history is etched into every landscape. Whether you're gazing over the vast expanse of the Grand Canyon, walking beneath towering redwoods, or listening to the gentle rustle of leaves in the breeze, national parks offer a unique opportunity to reconnect with the natural world. These protected spaces are not just for the adventurous—they provide a sanctuary for retirees seeking both tranquility and adventure. From accessible trails to educational programs, exploring national parks can turn your retirement years into a journey of discovery, filled with breathtaking views, wildlife encounters, and moments of quiet reflection in nature's grandest settings.

Selecting the right national park can elevate your retirement adventures to new heights. Look for parks that are senior-friendly, with accessible trails, well-equipped visitor centers, and educational programs. **Yellowstone National Park** offers stunning geysers and wildlife viewing, with accessible boardwalks and shuttle services. **Acadia National Park in Maine** provides beautiful coastal views and wheelchair-accessible trails like the Ocean Path. Other notable mentions include **Zion National Park** with its easily navigable Pa'rus Trail, and the **Everglades National Park**, where you can explore the unique ecosystem via accessible trails and boat tours. Don't overlook the **Great Smoky Mountains, Shenandoah National Park, or the Blue Ridge Parkway**, all of which offer a mix of accessibility and breathtaking scenery.

My husband and I have had some unforgettable experiences exploring many of these majestic parks, and our visits have been nothing short of incredible. From the jaw-dropping vistas of **Yosemite's** granite cliffs to the deep blue waters of **Crater Lake**, each destination offered its own unique charm. **Canyonlands** took us into a desert wonderland of rock formations where gods got really serious about architecture and design. And **Olympic National Park** treated us to a blend of lush rainforests and rugged coastlines. Each park gave us the chance to immerse ourselves in nature's beauty, leaving us with treasured memories of adventure and awe.

Maximizing park benefits extends beyond just the physical experience. Research has shown that spending time in nature can significantly boost your mental well-being, lower stress levels, and even improve your immune system. Participating in ranger-led tours and nature workshops can deepen your appreciation for these natural wonders. Imagine learning about the geology of the Grand Canyon from an expert or understanding the delicate ecosystems of the Everglades through a hands-on workshop. These programs not only educate but also provide opportunities to meet fellow nature enthusiasts and make new friends. The psychological benefits of immersing yourself in nature are profound, offering a sense of peace and fulfillment that's hard to replicate elsewhere.

Safety and accessibility features are crucial for ensuring a comfortable and enjoyable experience. Many parks offer shuttle services that can take you to key viewpoints and trailheads, reducing the need for extensive walking. Accessible trail ratings help you choose paths that match your fitness level and mobility. Accommodations within or near the parks often provide accessible rooms equipped with features like grab bars in the bathrooms, roll-in showers, and wider doorways. For instance, **Yosemite National Park** has accommodations ranging from accessible campsites to fully equipped lodges. Always check the park's website or contact the visitor center for up-to-date information on accessibility features and safety guidelines.

Conservation and etiquette play a significant role in preserving these natural treasures for future generations. Simple practices like packing out all your trash, staying on designated trails, and respecting wildlife can make a big difference. Many parks have volunteer programs where you can contribute to conservation efforts, such as trail maintenance or habitat restoration. Seniors often bring a wealth of knowledge and experience to these initiatives, making them invaluable advocates for conservation. Imagine the satisfaction of knowing you've played a part in preserving the beauty of Yellowstone or the biodiversity of the Everglades. Your efforts ensure these parks remain pristine and accessible for years to come, allowing future generations to enjoy the same breathtaking landscapes and experiences.

7.4 Hidden Treasures: The Exciting World of Treasure Hunting

The thrill of a treasure hunt combined with the joy of exploring new places. That's geocaching—a real-world, outdoor adventure game that uses GPS-enabled devices to find hidden containers, or "caches," scattered around the world. It's like a modern-day treasure hunt, perfect for adding a dash of excitement to your retirement. Each cache contains a logbook to sign and sometimes trinkets to trade. The beauty of geocaching is that it can be done anywhere, from your local park to exotic destinations, making it an ideal hobby for both homebodies and globetrotters alike.

To get started, you'll need to set up a geocaching account. Head over to the **Geocaching.com** website or download the app on your smartphone. Sign up for a free account, though premium memberships offer additional features. Once you're logged in, you can search for caches nearby. Caches are rated by difficulty and terrain, so choose one that matches your comfort level. The app provides coordinates and clues to guide you. Input the coordinates into your GPS device or use your smartphone's built-in GPS to start your hunt. It's that simple! Just think of it as a high-tech scavenger hunt that takes you to interesting nooks and crannies you might never have discovered otherwise.

The health benefits of geocaching are a fantastic bonus. This activity encourages walking and mild physical exertion, which can improve cardiovascular health and overall fitness. Navigating to caches also involves a bit of problem-solving and mental stimulation, keeping your brain engaged. The excitement of finding a cache can be a great motivator for spending time outdoors and exploring new locations. Imagine the joy of discovering a hidden gem in your neighborhood or stumbling upon a breathtaking view you never knew existed. It's a fun way to stay active and curious, turning every outing into an adventure.

While on your geocaching quests, it's important to follow some basic etiquette and safety rules. Always leave the cache as you found it, ensuring it's well-hidden for the next adventurer. Respect the environment—don't disturb plants or wildlife, and stick to marked paths. Carry a small bag to pick up any litter you come across; it's a small act that contributes to the beauty and cleanliness of the area. Safety-wise, always let someone know where you're going and when you expect to return, especially if you're venturing into remote areas. Wear appropriate clothing and footwear for the terrain, and bring essentials like water, snacks, and a first-aid kit. With these precautions, you can enjoy the thrill of the hunt safely and responsibly.

7.5 Camping and Glamping: Relaxing Outdoor Retreats

Camping is a fantastic way to immerse yourself in nature, with the crackle of a campfire, the scent of pine trees, and the starry sky above. But let's be honest—not everyone is thrilled at the idea of sleeping on an air mattress or braving the elements. This is where glamping, or glamorous camping, comes in. Traditional camping involves pitching a tent, cooking over an open fire, and sleeping on a sleeping mat. It's rugged and adventurous. Glamping, on the other hand, offers the same connection with nature but with a touch of luxury. Think cozy tents with proper beds, gourmet meals, kitchenettes, and private bathrooms. If you love the idea of being outdoors but crave comfort, glamping might just be your perfect match.

When it comes to gear, both camping and glamping require some preparation. For traditional camping, invest in a high-quality tent that's easy to set up and offers good ventilation. Comfortable sleeping mats or air mattresses are a must; your back will thank you. Ergonomic chairs can make sitting around the campfire more enjoyable. Don't forget a reliable cooler to keep your food fresh and a portable stove for cooking.

Glamping requires less gear than traditional camping, but it's always worth adding personal touches like soft blankets, fairy lights for ambiance, and perhaps a portable fan or heater depending on the season. However, before packing, it's important to check what is provided by the glamping facility. Some glam sites offer nearly everything, from towels and toiletries to cooking equipment, while others may require you to bring essentials like towels, a first aid kit, insect repellent, or even pots and pans. Cutlery, dishes, and cooking utensils might also be necessary depending on the site, so it's always a good idea to confirm what's included ahead of time. Having the right gear can make all the difference in ensuring a comfortable and enjoyable experience, whether you're roughing it or indulging in a luxurious stay.

Finding senior-friendly campgrounds can enhance your outdoor experience. Look for campgrounds that offer easy access to medical facilities. Many state parks and private campgrounds cater to seniors, providing level campsites with easy access to facilities. Some even offer cabins, yurts, safari-style lodges, and treehouses for those who prefer a bit more comfort or adventure. Websites like **Recreation.gov** and **KOA** can help you find campgrounds with the amenities you need. These sites often feature reviews from other campers, so you can get an idea of what to expect before you go, such as clean restrooms and hot showers.

Activities in campgrounds are varied and can be tailored to your interests and energy levels. Nature walks are a fantastic way to explore your surroundings; many campgrounds have well-marked trails that range from easy to challenging. Photography can capture the beauty of your adventure, whether it's a stunning sunrise or a curious squirrel. Relaxing in nature, reading a book, or listening to the sounds of the forest can be incredibly rejuvenating. Safety should always be a priority. Always inform someone of your plans, carry a first-aid kit, and be aware of local wildlife. Make sure your campsite is free of food scraps to avoid attracting animals. And always follow fire safety guidelines if you're enjoying a campfire.

7.6 Charting the Course: Planning Your Dream RV Adventure

There's nothing quite like the freedom of hitting the open road in an RV, where your home travels with you, offering the flexibility to explore new destinations at your own pace. Whether you're parked by a serene lake, nestled in a forest, or overlooking a breathtaking mountain range, the possibilities for adventure and discovery are endless. RV travel allows you to embrace spontaneity, wake up to a new view each morning, and enjoy the comforts of home wherever you go.

Choosing the right RV is crucial for comfort and ease. For retirees, think about a Class B or C motorhome. These are smaller and more maneuverable compared to the larger Class A rigs, making them perfect for navigating both highways and scenic byways. Look for features that prioritize comfort, such as a spacious sleeping area, a well-equipped kitchen, and a bathroom with a decent-sized shower. Maintenance shouldn't be a headache, so opt for models known for reliability and ease of upkeep. Brands like **Winnebago** and **Airstream** are often praised for their quality and durability.

Mapping out your journey is where the fun begins. Picture cruising along the **Pacific Coast Highway** with the ocean on one side and towering cliffs on the other. Or perhaps winding through the **Blue Ridge Parkway,** surrounded by the vibrant hues of autumn leaves. When planning your route, consider destinations that offer both scenic beauty and accessibility. National parks like **Yellowstone, Acadia**, and the **Grand Canyon** are fantastic choices, with plenty of RV-friendly facilities. The **Outer Banks in North Carolina** or **Florida's Everglades National Park** also make for memorable stops, blending natural beauty with accessible campgrounds. Canada offers stunning options, like **Banff and Jasper National Parks in Alberta**, where you can park your RV amid towering peaks and turquoise lakes. For a coastal adventure, head to the **Cabot Trail in Nova Scotia**, where you can drive along dramatic cliffs, explore quaint fishing villages, and camp with breathtaking ocean views. In **British Columbia, Vancouver Island's Pacific Rim National Park Reserve** offers lush rainforests, sandy beaches, and endless opportunities for wildlife spotting right from your RV. For a more remote experience, venture to **Gros Morne National Park in Newfoundland,** where the rugged landscape and fjords create a true sense of wilderness adventure. **On-**

tario's **Algonquin Provincial Park** offers serene lakes and endless opportunities for wildlife viewing.

Apps like **RV Parky** or **AllStays** can help you find campgrounds, rest stops, and points of interest along the way. Don't forget to include some quirky stops, like the world's largest ball of twine or a local food festival. Consider visiting odd roadside attractions like the **Cadillac Ranch in Texas**, where vintage cars are half-buried in the desert, or the giant **Paul Bunyan statue in Minnesota.** For a touch of nostalgia, stop by classic diners or vintage gas stations along **Route 66**. You could even visit niche museums, like the **Spam Museum in Minnesota** or the **UFO Museum in Roswell, New Mexico.** Seeking something unique? How about checking out the colorful street art of **Wynwood Walls in Miami** or the **Enchanted Highway in North Dakota**, where oversized metal sculptures dot the landscape? Each quirky stop adds character to your journey and creates memories that go beyond the typical travel itinerary.

Safety and maintenance are non-negotiable for a worry-free trip. Before hitting the road, conduct a thorough pre-trip inspection. Check tire pressure, fluid levels, and ensure all lights are functioning. Make a checklist to cover everything from securing loose items inside the RV to testing the brakes. Keep a basic toolkit and spare parts handy; you never know when you might need to tighten a bolt or replace a fuse. Safety extends to driving practices as well. Take your time, especially on unfamiliar roads, and always be mindful of the RV's size, especially when maneuvering through tight spaces or parking.

Community and resources can elevate your RV experience. Joining RV clubs like the **Good Sam Club** or **Escapees RV Club** connects you with a network of fellow enthusiasts who share tips, advice, and stories. Online forums and social media groups are treasure troves of information, from the best campgrounds, to the ones you need to avoid, to must-see hidden gems. These communities offer support and camaraderie, turning solo adventures into shared experiences.

7.7 Horseback Riding: Essentials for a Safe and Enjoyable Experience

Horseback riding is a timeless activity that offers a unique way to enjoy the outdoors while staying active. Whether you're trotting through open meadows, winding along forest trails, or taking in the serene beauty of a mountain vista, horseback riding combines adventure, relaxation, and a connection to nature. Beyond the sheer joy of it, riding a horse improves your balance and core strength. As you adjust to the horse's movements, your muscles engage in a workout that's both gentle and effective. It's like having a fitness class in nature. And let's not forget the stress reduction. There's something incredibly soothing about the steady, rhythmic motion of horseback riding. It's a perfect way to clear your mind and find a sense of calm amidst life's hustle and bustle.

Selecting a riding school that caters to beginners, particularly older adults, is crucial for a safe and enjoyable experience. Look for schools that provide gentle, well-trained horses. These horses are usually calm and accustomed to novice riders, making them the perfect companions for your equestrian adventure. Ask about the instructors' qualifications and experience with older riders. A good instructor will be patient, understanding, and capable of teaching at a pace that suits you. Visit the school beforehand to get a feel for the environment and the horses.

Safety gear and techniques are top priorities for horseback riding. Always wear a helmet; it's your first line of defense against head injuries. Proper footwear is also important—opt for boots with a small heel to prevent your feet from slipping through the stirrups. Comfortable, breathable clothing that allows freedom of movement is ideal.

Learning basic riding techniques can enhance your experience and safety. Start with mastering the mounting and dismounting process. Learn how to hold the reins, guide the horse, and use basic commands like "walk," "trot," and "stop." Understanding these fundamentals can boost your confidence and ensure a smoother ride.

One of the most rewarding aspects of horseback riding is the connection with nature. Riding through a forest trail or across a meadow provides a unique perspective on the natural world. You're not just observing nature; you're a part of it. The horse becomes your guide, leading you through landscapes you might never have explored on foot. This connection with nature is invigorating and tranquil at the same time. But equally special is the bond you form with the horse itself. Horses, with their gentle strength, grace, and intelligence, have a way of sensing their rider's emotions and adapting accordingly. As you ride, you develop a sense of trust and communication with your horse, working together to navigate the terrain. It's a partnership that brings a deeper level of awareness and connection to your surroundings. The horse's beauty, with its flowing mane and powerful, elegant stride, adds to the experience, making it not just a physical journey but an emotional one as well. Whether you're riding along a beach, through a mountain trail, or in a serene park, the experience is bound to leave you refreshed and rejuvenated, both from the beauty of nature and the unique bond with your horse.

7.8. Exploring the Night Sky: Stargazing and Astronomy Clubs

I think everyone agrees that there's something absolutely magical about standing under a clear night sky, with the stars twinkling above you, far from the hustle and bustle of everyday life. For people looking to reconnect with nature and find a sense of awe in the great outdoors, stargazing offers the perfect escape. It's a peaceful yet invigorating activity that you can enjoy from your own backyard or while traveling to some of the world's best dark-sky locations. The beauty of this hobby is that you can start simple—no need for a telescope just yet. Begin by learning to identify some of the major constellations, such as Orion, Ursa Major, and Cassiopeia. Apps like **SkyView** or **Star Walk** can help guide you as you explore the night sky, pointing out planets, stars, and constellations as you go. All you need is a comfortable chair, a blanket, and a clear night.

Once you're hooked, you might want to invest in a telescope for a closer look at the planets, moons, and star clusters that fill the night sky. Telescopes range from beginner-friendly models to more advanced equipment, so start with one that fits your needs. For beginners, a simple refractor telescope with a 60-80mm aperture is a great starting point. This type of telescope is easy to use and portable, making it ideal for casual stargazing. If you're more serious about the hobby, consider a Dobsonian or reflector telescope, which provides more power and allows you to see deep-sky objects like galaxies, nebulae, and distant planets. Don't forget about essential accessories, such as a star map and a red flashlight (which helps preserve your night vision). Binoculars are also a great alternative for beginners and are portable for easy stargazing on the go. Look for features such as adjustable magnification, sturdy tripods, and portability if you plan to take your stargazing adventures to remote locations.

One of the best ways to deepen your appreciation of the night sky is by joining an astronomy club. These groups often organize star-gazing events, where members gather in open areas away from city lights for the best views. Sharing the experience with others can make it even more enjoyable, and experienced astronomers are always happy to share their knowledge and equipment. Whether you're spotting a shooting star or marveling at a lunar eclipse, an astronomy club offers a great way to meet like-minded people and discover new celestial wonders.

Stargazing is about more than just looking up—it's about immersing yourself in nature and appreciating the tranquility of the great outdoors. You may stargaze from a remote mountain lodge, a national park, or even during a camping trip under a vast, starry sky. Many national parks, such as **Bryce Canyon** and **Big Bend** in the **U.S.**, or **Jasper National Park in Canada**, offer designated dark sky preserves, making them perfect for stargazing enthusiasts. As the sun sets and the stars emerge, you'll find stargazing to be a meditative outdoor activity, helping you to slow down, breathe deeply, and reconnect with nature in a peaceful, awe-inspiring way.

The outdoor element of astronomy adds a whole new dimension to this activity. Whether you're attending a stargazing event at a nearby observatory or camping under the stars in a remote wilderness area, this hobby lets you explore the world in a different light—literally. You might plan trips to renowned dark sky reserves or attend stargazing festivals, combining travel with your new passion for the night sky.

Please refer to the **Resources Chapter** for a list of some popular stargazing festivals.

The connection between the beauty of the cosmos and the great outdoors makes stargazing an enriching adventure for your retirement years.

As we wrap up this chapter on the Great Outdoors, it's clear that nature offers endless opportunities for joy, adventure, and connection.

Whether you're bird-watching, hiking, fishing, or horseback riding, each activity brings its own unique benefits.

Chapter Eight

Conclusion

So here we are, at the end of this book and at the beginning of your journey. Remember that moment when I realized retirement wasn't just some distant concept, but a reality staring me in the face? Friends around me were retiring, and I thought, "Hey, I want to retire—but what then?" That moment of clarity sent me on a deep dive into exploring what retirement could be—a phase of life filled with opportunities, growth, and excitement. This book was born from that journey, designed to help you embrace retirement with confidence and enthusiasm.

We've covered a wide range of exciting possibilities together. From the importance of health and fitness in keeping your body and mind sharp, to planning unforgettable travel adventures that span serene outdoor escapes, cultural tours through Europe, and adrenaline-pumping sports like skydiving and scuba diving. Whether you're hiking through national parks, bird-watching in scenic reserves, or exploring ancient ruins in far-off lands, the aim has been to inspire you to fully embrace life in retirement, pursuing activities that fuel both your passion and your well-being. We've explored how to maximize these exciting experiences while staying mindful of your health, safety, and budget. You've seen that you can fill your retirement years with travel, excitement, and wellness without sacrificing financial peace of mind.

The key takeaway? Stay open to new experiences, prioritize health and wellness, and remember that this chapter of your life is a thrilling new beginning. It's a time to explore fun, adventure, and personal growth like never before.

Now, here's your call to action: pick at least one new activity or destination that excites you and start planning for it. Trust me, stepping out of your comfort zone will be the best decision you make. Whether it's booking that river cruise you've always dreamed of, or simply taking a leisurely walk through a local nature trail, every small step counts.

Reflecting on my own journey, I've seen firsthand how these activities can transform your life into a richer, more fulfilling experience. I'm confident that with the right mindset, your retirement years can truly be your best years yet.

Resources

Chapter 2.

Cost-Saving Tips for Retirees

These organizations provide resources, advocacy, and often discounts and services tailored to the needs of older adults.

1. **United States:** AARP (American Association of Retired Persons) (www.aarp.org) is the nation's largest nonprofit, nonpartisan organization dedicated to empowering Americans 50 and older to choose how they live as they age.

2. **United Kingdom: Age UK**(www.ageuk.org.uk). Age UK offers support, advice, and services to older people in the UK. They provide resources on health, financial advice, and offer discounts on products and services through partnerships.

3. **Canada: CARP (Canadian Association of Retired Persons)**(www.carp.ca). CARP is a national, non-profit organization that advocates for financial security, improved healthcare, and rights for older Canadians. They offer discounts on

insurance, travel, and various services for members.

4. **Australia: National Seniors Australia**(www.nationalseniors.com.au). National Seniors Australia is a leading advocacy group for older Australians, providing information on pensions, healthcare, and financial planning. They also offer discounts on travel, insurance, and other services.

5. **New Zealand: Grey Power**(www.greypower.co.nz). Grey Power is an advocacy organization representing senior citizens in New Zealand. It offers members discounts on a wide range of services and lobbies the government on issues like healthcare, pensions, and seniors' rights.

Medical Insurance:

1. **Medicare**(www.medicare.gov). For U.S. retirees, Medicare is an essential resource for medical coverage. Be sure to understand what is covered and consider supplemental plans like **Medigap** or **Medicare Advantage** to ensure you're fully protected, especially if you're traveling abroad where Medicare may not cover certain medical needs.

2. **Private Health Insurance Marketplaces**(www.healthcare.gov for U.S. residents). If Medicare doesn't fully meet your needs, private health insurance or supplemental plans might fill the gaps, especially for expats or retirees traveling internationally. Websites like **Healthcare.gov** help you compare private plans.

3. **Cigna Global Health Insurance**(www.cignaglobal.com).

Ideal for retirees living abroad, Cigna offers international medical coverage, including access to global healthcare networks and coverage for both routine and emergency medical needs.

Insurance and Legal Considerations:

1. **International Driver's Permit (IDP)** (www.aaa.com or www.idpapp.com). If you plan on driving in a foreign country, an International Driver's Permit is often required. It's easy to obtain and valid in over 150 countries. Check the requirements for the countries you plan to visit to avoid legal complications while driving abroad.

2. **LegalZoom**(www.legalzoom.com). Offers online legal services for a variety of needs, including wills, estate planning, and legal advice related to international travel. It's a great resource for making sure your legal matters are in order before you head off on any adventures.

3. **U.S. Department of State – Travel Advisories**(www.travel.state.gov). Stay up-to-date with the latest travel advisories and legal considerations for U.S. travelers abroad, including information on international driving laws, visas, and health requirements in specific countries.

4. **Foreign Embassies and Consulates**(www.embassy.org or your country's government website). If you're traveling or living abroad, knowing how to contact your country's embassy or consulate is crucial. They can help with legal issues,

lost passports, and emergency assistance.

Chapter 3.

Mindfulness and Meditation Retreats

1. **Spirit Rock Meditation Center (California, USA).** A renowned mindfulness retreat center nestled in the hills of Northern California. Spirit Rock offers a variety of retreats, from beginner mindfulness weekends to in-depth meditation immersions. The center is known for its highly qualified instructors and peaceful, nature-filled environment.

2. **The Art of Living Retreat Center (North Carolina, USA).** Located in the scenic Blue Ridge Mountains, this retreat offers a blend of mindfulness, yoga, and Ayurveda. It focuses on stress reduction and self-care through guided meditation, breathing exercises, and holistic wellness practices. They offer programs ranging from weekends to week-long retreats.

3. **Shambhala Mountain Center (Colorado, USA).** Offering meditation and mindfulness retreats at an altitude of over 8,000 feet, this retreat provides deep spiritual teachings in a stunning, secluded mountain setting. Shambhala is known for its Buddhist-centered mindfulness practices and also offers yoga and tai chi.

4. **Plum Village (France).** Founded by Thich Nhat Hanh,

Plum Village is one of the most respected mindfulness centers in the world. Retreats here focus on mindful living and peaceful, slow-paced meditation practices. Retreat participants experience silence, community life, and teachings that inspire mindfulness in everyday actions.

5. **Kamalaya Wellness Sanctuary (Thailand).** Set on the tropical island of Koh Samui, Kamalaya is a luxurious retreat offering a blend of mindfulness, yoga, and wellness treatments. It's perfect for those looking to combine meditation with relaxation and self-care in a stunning resort environment.

6. **Vipassana Meditation Centers (Worldwide).** Vipassana retreats are widely respected for their deep and immersive silent meditation programs. Typically lasting 10 days, these retreats are donation-based and focus on the traditional Buddhist practice of Vipassana, or insight meditation. They are perfect for those seeking to dive deeply into meditation with no distractions.

7. **Esalen Institute (California, USA).** A unique retreat center on the California coast, Esalen offers mindfulness and meditation programs in combination with creative arts, personal growth, and bodywork. The stunning cliff side location and hot springs make it a perfect retreat for those looking to rejuvenate both body and mind.

8. **Gaia House (United Kingdom).** A silent meditation retreat center, Gaia House is set in the English countryside and offers mindfulness and insight meditation retreats. Their

programs are led by experienced teachers and cater to both beginners and experienced meditators.

9. **Kadampa Meditation Centers (Various Locations).** Offering meditation and mindfulness retreats worldwide, Kadampa centers focus on Buddhist teachings and offer both silent and guided retreats. They're an excellent option if you're looking for a retreat closer to home with structured teachings and community involvement.

10. **Sivananda Ashram Yoga Retreat (Bahamas).** While primarily focused on yoga, Sivananda also offers mindfulness and meditation programs. This retreat allows you to combine your mindfulness practice with daily yoga, healthy meals, and time for beach relaxation.

Floating into Wellness: The Sensory Deprivation Experience

1. **Float On** – Portland, Oregon, USA https://floathq.com/

2. **London Float** Therapy – London, ON, Canada http://www.londonfloattherapy.com/

3. **Float House** – Vancouver, Canada https://floathouse.ca/

4. **Pause Float Studio** – Los Angeles, CA https://pausestudio.com

5. **Urban Float** – Multiple locations in the USA https://www.urbanfloat.com/

6. **Floatation Locations** – multiple locations in North America https://floatationlocations.com/where-to-float/

7. **Floatworks** – multiple locations in the **UK https://floatworks.com/**

Famous Hot Springs Spa Resorts

1. **Banff Upper Hot Springs (Canada).** Located in Banff National Park, this iconic hot springs resort offers stunning mountain views while you soak in mineral-rich waters. The temperature of the water remains around 98–104°F year-round, providing a perfect place to relax and relieve muscle tension.

2. **Blue Lagoon (Iceland).** One of the most famous hot spring spas in the world, the Blue Lagoon offers geothermal seawater rich in minerals like silica and sulfur, known for its skin-rejuvenating properties. The spa offers in-water massages and treatments in a serene, otherworldly setting surrounded by volcanic landscapes.

3. **Tabacón Thermal Resort & Spa (Costa Rica).** Nestled near the base of the Arenal Volcano, this luxurious hot spring resort features natural thermal springs that flow through lush gardens. With multiple hot spring pools and waterfalls, it's a beautiful location to immerse yourself in mineral-rich waters, known to ease joint pain and muscle tension.

4. **Onsens in Hakone (Japan).** Japan is famous for its **onsens** (natural hot spring baths), and the Hakone region is one of

the most popular spots. Surrounded by beautiful views of Mt. Fuji and natural landscapes, Hakone's onsens are known for their therapeutic properties, including reducing stress and improving skin conditions.

5. **Chena Hot Springs Resort (Alaska, USA).** For a unique hot spring experience, visit Chena Hot Springs Resort near Fairbanks, Alaska. The natural geothermal springs are famous for their healing properties, and on a clear night, you can even soak under the Northern Lights, making this a magical retreat.

Spa Retreats Worldwide

1. **Aman Spa at Amanpuri (Thailand).** Located in Phuket, this luxury spa retreat offers a wide range of treatments, including Thai massage, Ayurvedic therapies, and holistic wellness programs. It's an ideal destination for those looking to combine spa relaxation with cultural experiences.

2. **Rancho La Puerta (Mexico).** Situated just across the U.S. border in Baja California, Rancho La Puerta is a wellness-focused resort offering a mix of spa treatments, fitness classes, and mindfulness workshops. Their spa offers a range of treatments tailored to seniors, including massages and hydrotherapy designed to reduce arthritis pain and increase mobility.

3. **Ananda in the Himalayas (India).** Nestled in the Himalayan foothills, Ananda offers luxurious spa treatments

based on Ayurveda, yoga, and meditation practices. The spa focuses on restoring balance to both mind and body with therapies aimed at rejuvenation and anti-aging.

4. **Canyon Ranch (Arizona, USA).** One of the most well-known wellness retreats in the U.S., Canyon Ranch offers a full range of spa treatments, wellness programs, and fitness activities. It's particularly renowned for its integrative approach, offering not just physical treatments but also health consultations, workshops, and classes to enhance well-being.

5. **Thermes Marins Monte-Carlo (Monaco).** Known for its cutting-edge anti-aging treatments, this luxurious spa is set on the French Riviera and offers a range of hydrotherapy treatments using seawater. Guests can enjoy thalassotherapy pools, steam baths, and saunas, all designed to detoxify and rejuvenate the body.

6. **Calistoga Ranch (California, USA).** Located in the heart of Napa Valley, Calistoga Ranch offers natural geothermal mineral pools combined with luxurious spa treatments, including mud baths and vinotherapy, which uses grape seeds and extracts to rejuvenate the skin.

7. **The Greenbrier (West Virginia, USA).** This historic spa offers a wide variety of treatments, including hydrotherapy, hot stone massages, and detox programs. The Greenbrier also features mineral baths sourced from local springs, known for their healing properties.

8. **Ojo Caliente Mineral Springs Resort & Spa (New Mex-

ico, USA).** Ojo Caliente is one of the oldest natural health resorts in the U.S., offering sulfur-free, geothermal mineral waters in a peaceful desert setting. The spa includes yoga classes, hot stone massages, and private outdoor soaking tubs.

9. **Terme di Saturnia (Tuscany, Italy).** This luxurious spa and thermal resort is known for its healing thermal springs, rich in sulfur and other minerals that are great for the skin and joints. The resort offers a wide range of wellness treatments, including thermal mud wraps and hydrotherapy sessions.

10. **Grand Resort Bad Ragaz (Switzerland).** Set in the Swiss Alps, this world-class resort offers thermal spa treatments using mineral-rich water from the Tamina Gorge. The spa specializes in health and wellness, offering personalized programs for rejuvenation and anti-aging.

11. **Thermae Bath Spa (Bath, England).** Located in the historic city of Bath, this spa uses natural hot spring water that has been used for healing since Roman times. The spa offers a combination of traditional treatments and contemporary spa therapies, all within a stunning rooftop pool setting.

12. **Lanserhof Tegernsee (Germany).** Nestled in the Bavarian Alps, Lanserhof is renowned for its cutting-edge medical spa treatments and detox programs. The spa offers everything from personalized wellness programs to relaxing massages, all within a scenic alpine environment.

13. **Brenners Park-Hotel & Spa (Baden-Baden, Germany).**

Baden-Baden is famous for its therapeutic waters, and Brenners Park-Hotel & Spa makes the most of this natural resource. With its luxurious setting, this spa focuses on well-being, offering a range of hydrotherapy treatments, medical wellness programs, and relaxing massages.

Chapter 4.

Group Travel: Finding Retirement Travel Clubs

1. **ElderTreks (https://www.eldertreks.com/).** This company provides adventure travel specifically for people over 50. They offer small-group trips to off-the-beaten-path destinations for those seeking a more adventurous experience.

2. **Traveling Professor (https://travelingprofessor.com/).** A travel company that offers small group tours with a focus on cultural immersion, often including history, art, and culinary experiences.

3. **Overseas Adventure Travel (O.A.T.) (https://www.oattravel.com/).** Known for small group tours, O.A.T. offers immersive experiences in less-traveled destinations with a focus on cultural engagement.

4. **Grand Circle Travel (https://www.gct.com/).** Specializes in small group trips, cruises, and river cruises designed for seniors. They offer a range of itineraries across the world, including in-depth tours of Europe, Asia, and South Amer-

ica.

Solo Travel: Exploring the World on Your Own Terms

1. Road Scholar (www.roadscholar.org). Specializes in educational travel, offering a wide range of solo-friendly tours around the world, including immersive experiences in art, history, and culture. Road Scholar also offers solo travel resources, scholarships, and assistance in finding travel companions if desired.

2. ElderTreks (www.eldertreks.com). An adventure travel company exclusively for people aged 50 and older, offering small-group adventures and destinations worldwide. Solo travelers can easily join these groups, and ElderTreks offers options with no single supplements, making it budget-friendly for solo explorers.

3. Overseas Adventure Travel (O.A.T.) (www.oattravel.com) . Specializes in small-group adventures and welcomes solo travelers, offering many trips with free or low-cost single supplements. The company focuses on immersive cultural experiences and includes both off-the-beaten-path and classic destinations.

4. Intrepid Travel (www.intrepidtravel.com). Offers small-group, adventure-focused tours worldwide. They welcome solo travelers on all trips, with many designed to encourage solo adventurers to connect with like-minded travelers. Intrepid also provides various itineraries suited for different physical abilities.

5. Solo Traveler Blog (www.solotravelerworld.com). A comprehensive online resource for solo travelers of all ages, featuring destination guides, safety tips, budget advice, and inspiring stories from other solo adventurers. It's especially useful for seniors seeking solo travel advice and inspiration.

6. Women Traveling Together (WTT) (www.women-traveling.com). WTT is a travel company specializing in small-group travel for solo women, particularly older women. It's perfect for female solo travelers looking for safety and companionship while still maintaining independence. They offer a variety of destinations worldwide.

7. Solo Traveler (National Geographic) (www.nationalgeographic.com/travel/solo-travel). National Geographic's travel site offers useful tips and inspiration for solo travelers, featuring everything from expert safety advice to recommendations on the best destinations for independent exploration.

8. Flash Pack (www.flashpack.com). Specializes in small-group adventures designed specifically for solo travelers in their 30s and beyond, with an emphasis on unique, off-the-beaten-path experiences. Ideal for seniors looking for adventure with a social element but also the independence of solo travel.

9. Traveling Alone Together (www.travelingalonetogether.com). A travel service that specializes in creating unique travel experiences for solo travelers, particularly women, with an emphasis on safety and community. Their trips foster a supportive and friendly environment, making it ideal for older solo travelers.

10. TripAdvisor Solo Travel Forum (www.tripadvisor.com/ShowForum-g1-i12357-Solo_Travel.html). An active online forum where solo travelers from all over the world share advice, ask questions, and offer tips. It's a valuable resource for gaining firsthand insight into solo travel destinations, safety concerns, and practical tips from fellow solo explorers.

Chapter 5.

Voluntourism

1. **Projects Abroad**: Offers a wide range of volunteer programs, including education, conservation, healthcare, and community development across various countries. (www.projects-abroad.org)

2. **GoEco**: Specializes in ecological and wildlife conservation projects, as well as community development and teaching .(www.goeco.org)

3. **Global Vision International (GVI)**: Provides ethical and sustainable volunteer programs focused on conservation, education, and community development. (www.gvi.co.uk)

4. **WWOOF (World Wide Opportunities on Organic Farms)**: Connects volunteers with organic farms worldwide, focusing on sustainable living and farming. (www.wwoof.net)

5. **Volunteer World**: A comprehensive platform offering volunteer projects in conservation, education, and social work, with reviews and detailed program information. (www.volunteerworld.com)

6. **Idealist**: Lists volunteer opportunities globally, including community development, healthcare, education, and more. (www.idealist.org)

7. **International Volunteer HQ (IVHQ)**: Offers affordable and responsible volunteer programs in over 50 countries, from teaching to wildlife conservation. (www.volunteerhq

THE ULTIMATE COLLECTION OF FUN THINGS TO... 153

.org)

8. **Earthwatch**: Focuses on scientific research and conservation projects worldwide, allowing volunteers to contribute to meaningful environmental work. (www.earthwatch.org)

9. **Habitat for Humanity**: Provides opportunities to help build homes for families in need in communities across the globe.(www.habitat.org)

10. **Global Volunteers**: Focuses on long-term sustainable development through education, health, and community-based programs. (www.globalvolunteers.org)

Cultural Exchange Tourism

1. **Cultural Homestay International (CHI):** Offers cultural exchange programs that include homestays, work and travel, and au pair experiences, providing immersive cultural engagement worldwide.(www.chinet.org)

2. **Global Citizen Year:** Focuses on cultural exchange through immersion in different countries, offering opportunities to engage in local communities through volunteer work and homestays.(www.globalcitizenyear.org)

3. **Friendship Force International:** Specializes in cultural exchange homestay experiences, allowing participants to live with host families and engage in meaningful cultural activities. (www.friendshipforce.org)

4. **Workaway:** Offers opportunities for cultural exchange by

connecting travelers with hosts who need help in exchange for accommodation, with options ranging from farm work to language exchange and artistic projects. (www.workaway.info)

5. **WWOOF (World Wide Opportunities on Organic Farms):** Not only a great way to learn about sustainable farming but also an excellent cultural exchange experience where you live and work with local families. (www.wwoof.net)

6. **GoAbroad:** Provides a wide range of cultural exchange opportunities, including internships, volunteer programs, and language immersion, in destinations around the world. (www.goabroad.com)

7. **InterNations:** A global community that offers cultural exchange meetups, networking events, and opportunities to connect with locals and expatriates in cities around the world. (www.internations.org)

8. **Road Scholar:** Known for its educational travel, Road Scholar offers cultural immersion programs specifically designed for older adults, allowing travelers to engage deeply with local customs and traditions. (www.roadscholar.org)

9. **The Experiment in International Living:** Offers immersive homestay and cultural exchange programs, including hands-on workshops in art, language, and local traditions. (www.experiment.org)

10. **Servas International:** A global peace and hospitality net-

work that connects travelers with hosts around the world, fostering cultural understanding and meaningful connections through homestays. (www.servas.org)

Chapter 6.

Skydiving and Paragliding: Thrills in the Sky

Skydiving Organizations:

1. **United States Parachute Association (USPA)** www.uspa.org

2. **British Parachute Association (BPA)** www.bpa.org.uk

3. **Australian Parachute Federation (APF)** www.apf.com.au

4. **European Parachuting Union (EPU)** www.epc.pt

5. **Fédération Française de Parachutisme (FFP)** www.ffp.asso.fr

Paragliding and Hang Gliding Organizations:

1. **United States Hang Gliding and Paragliding Association (USHPA)** www.ushpa.org

2. **Paragliding and Hang Gliding Federation of Australia (SAFA)** www.safa.asn.au

3. **British Hang Gliding and Paragliding Association (BHPA)** www.bhpa.co.uk

4. **Fédération Aéronautique Internationale (FAI)** www.fai.org

5. **Swiss Hang Gliding and Paragliding Association (SHPA)** www.shv-fsvl.ch

Chapter 7.

Stargazing and Astronomy Clubs

1. **Dark Sky Festival (Utah, USA)**: Held in Bryce Canyon National Park, this festival offers some of the best night sky views in the U.S. Attendees enjoy ranger-led stargazing sessions, telescope viewing, and presentations from astronomers. The park's natural dark skies make it an ideal location for spotting planets, distant galaxies, and meteor showers.

2. **Texas Star Party (Texas, USA)**: One of the largest stargazing events in the U.S., the Texas Star Party takes place in the remote Davis Mountains. This week-long festival attracts amateur and professional astronomers alike and offers nightly star parties, workshops, and telescope viewings.

3. **Jasper Dark Sky Festival (Alberta, Canada)**: Held in Jasper National Park, a designated Dark Sky Preserve, this festival offers stunning views of the night sky paired with expert-led stargazing tours, workshops, and even photography lessons. It's a fantastic way to combine outdoor adventure with celestial exploration.

4. **South Downs Dark Skies Festival (England, UK)**: Located in South Downs National Park, this festival celebrates the beauty of the dark night sky. The event includes stargazing sessions, astronomy talks, and opportunities to observe celestial events like meteor showers, all while enjoying the peaceful British countryside.

5. **Starmus Festival (Worldwide)**: Though not exclusively about stargazing, Starmus is an international festival that combines science, art, and music. With talks from leading astronomers and astronauts, stargazing sessions, and cultural events, it offers a broad exploration of the cosmos in various scenic locations around the world.

References

1. 200+ Bucket List Ideas for Retirement https://www.annuity.org/retirement/lifestyle/retirement-bucket-list/

2. How to Create a Retirement Budget https://www.ramseysolutions.com/retirement/how-much-money-will-you-need-in-retirement

3. Essential Digital Skills Evaluation Framework for Seniors https://officeforseniors.govt.nz/assets/documents/our-work/digital-inclusion/Essential-Digital-Skills-Evaluation-Framework-for-Seniors.pdf

4. Top 14 Travel Tips for Seniors [The Complete Travel Guide] https://blakeford.com/top-14-travel-tips-for-seniors-complete-travel-guide/

5. Outdoor Activities for Seniors with Limited Mobility https://www.seniorhelpers.com/mo/kansas-city-south/resources/blogs/best-springtime-outdoor-activities-for-seniors-with-limited-mobility/

6. The Health Benefits of Tai Chi for Seniors Aegis Living https://www.aegisliving.com/resource-center/the-heal

th-benefits-of-tai-chi-for-seniors/

7. Mindfulness for Your Health: The Benefits of Living Moment by Moment https://newsinhealth.nih.gov/2021/06/mindfulness-your-health

8. Effects of Aqua Aerobic Therapy Exercise for Older Adults https://www.ncbi.nlm.nih.gov/pmc/articles/PMC3820233/

9. Senior Exercise Programs & Classes https://tools.silversneakers.com/Classes

10. Try Float Therapy at These Hotels and Spas Around the World https://businesstravelerusa.com/wellness/try-float-therapy-at-these-hotels-and-spas-around-the-world/

11. Learning To Play Golf At 60 https://www.golf-madness.com/blog/learning-to-play-golf-at-60

12. Reasons Why Skiing is Vital for Seniors https://snowvision.net/blogs/winter-sports-guide/reasons-why-skiing-is-vital-for-seniors

13. Positive aging benefits of home and community gardening https://www.ncbi.nlm.nih.gov/pmc/articles/PMC6977207/

14. 8 Best American Road Trips For Seniors https://www.roadscholar.org/blog/8-best-american-road-trips-for-seniors/

15. 2024 Best Travel Discounts For Seniors https://www.theseniorlist.com/senior-discounts/travel/

16. 9 Bucket List Cruises for Seniors and Retirees https://travel.usnews.com/features/bucket-list-cruises-for-seniors-and-retirees

17. Savvy Senior Travelers https://www.ricksteves.com/travel-tips/trip-planning/savvy-senior-travelers

18. Travel Insurance for Pre-Existing Conditions https://www.nerdwallet.com/article/travel/travel-insurance-pre-existing-medical-conditions

19. Binoculars and Beyond: Nine Tips for Beginning Bird Watchers https://www.allaboutbirds.org/news/binoculars-and-beyond-nine-tips-for-beginning-bird-watchers/

20. The Benefits of Hiking For Seniors https://www.hearthstoneseniorliving.com/blog/benefits-hiking-seniors/

21. Benefits of Nordic Pole Walking for Seniors https://seasonsretirement.com/nordic-walking-for-seniors/

22. The Blissful Benefits of Hot Springs https://www.theearthandi.org/post/the-benefits-of-hot-springs

23. A Senior's Guide to Geocaching: What Is It, Why Do It and Tips for Getting Started https://www.thegardensmo.com/blog/a-seniors-to-geocaching-what-is-it-why-do-it-and-tips-for-getting-started

24. The Ultimate Guide to Planning Your First RV Trip https://explore.bookoutdoors.com/guides/the-ultimate-guide-to-planning-your-first-rv-trip/

25. 9 Glamping Destinations Throughout the U.S. * https://www.aarp.org/travel/vacation-ideas/outdoors/info-2021/glamping-destinations.html

26. Participating in Activities You Enjoy As You Age https://www.nia.nih.gov/health/healthy-aging/participating-activities-you-enjoy-you-age

27. Online cooking classes with international chefs https://www.thetablelesstraveled.com/cooking-classes

28. How to Build a Home Gym on the Cheap https://www.artofmanliness.com/health-fitness/fitness/how-to-build-a-home-gym-on-the-cheap/

29. World's 9 Best Places to Go Skydiving https://www.travelchannel.com/interests/outdoors-and-adventure/photos/best-places-to-go-skydiving-in-the-world

30. Age is just a number: Becoming a Scuba Diver after 60 https://www.richcoastdiving.com/post/scuba-certification-for-seniors

31. Motorcycle Touring for Beginners https://www.madornomad.com/motorcycle-touring-for-beginners/

32. Mountain Biking for Seniors: 5 Questions to Ask Before You Begin https://metalbladecycles.com/mountain-biking-for-seniors-5-questions-to-ask-before-you-begin/

33. How Safe Are Hot Air Balloons? (Solved) - Napa Valley Aloft https://nvaloft.com/2023/05/03/heres-what-you-need-to-know-about-hot-air-balloon-safety/

34. 13 White Water Rafting Tips for Beginners https://southeasternexpeditions.com/13-white-water-rafting-tips-beginners/

35. Your Best Ride is Ahead: Horseback Riding for Senior Citizens https://horserookie.com/horseback-riding-senior-citizens/

36. The 29 Best Glamping Resorts in the U.S. https://travel.usnews.com/features/top-glamping-resorts-in-the-us

37. The Top 16 Historical Sites in the World https://www.nomadicmatt.com/travel-blogs/ten-historical-sites/

38. 16 of the Best Ziplines Around the World https://backpackertravel.org/wanderlist/best-ziplines-around-the-world/

39. 20 Best Places for Wine Tasting Trips & Cruises for 2024-2025 https://www.adventure-life.com/activity/wine-tasting

40. Europe Themed or Special Events Tours 2024/2025 https://www.affordabletours.com/r/europe/spec/theme

41. 10 Best U.S. National Parks for Seniors to Visit https://travelingtulls.com/best-national-parks-senior-pass/

Retirement Reinvented

Your Inspiring Guide to Creative
Expression, Intellectual Growth,
Entrepreneurial Ventures, and Leaving
a Legacy for a Fulfilling and Meaningful
Life After Work

Lara West

Chapter One

Introduction

The day has arrived: retirement is no longer a distant concept but a new reality, filled with endless possibilities. This isn't the time to retreat from life; instead, it's the perfect moment to reimagine and reinvent it, exploring new intellectual, social, and creative avenues you might not have had time for earlier in life. If the thoughts of engaging in meaningful work, learning new skills, making a difference in your community, unleashing your creativity, and building lasting connections excite you, you're exactly where you need to be.

Let me take you back to when retirement first started to loom on the horizon for me. I wasn't content with the idea of "clocking out" of work and spending my days in idle leisure. I knew I wanted more in life—something vibrant, fulfilling, and challenging. I dove into researching and planning, uncovering countless ways to make retirement the most dynamic phase of my life. With each new discovery, I realized that retirement wasn't a conclusion, but an exhilarating new chapter—one filled with endless possibilities ahead. This revelation sparked the desire to write a book about reinventing life in retirement, which soon evolved into two volumes packed with exciting ideas.

If you've read the first book, *The Great Retirement Escape: Your Guide to Journeys Across the Globe, Adventures Close to Home, Inspiring Outdoor Activities, and Fun Active Lifestyle for Your Best Years Yet*, you may have already embarked on new adventures, explored exciting travel destinations, or rekindled your passion for the outdoors. If not, let me tell you about it.

I crafted this guide to help retirees and soon-to-be retirees unlock the secrets to a healthy and adventurous life. It covers everything from planning affordable global travel and immersing yourself in cultural and historical tours to finding thrilling activities like safaris, zip-lining, and a hot-air balloon ride, to name a few. It's also packed with travel tips for seniors, focusing on budget-friendly destinations, maximizing discounts, and balancing safety and adventure. Even if you have physical limitations, it's got you covered.

Beyond travel, *The Great Retirement Escape* dives into outdoor hobbies that can enrich your retirement, like bird-watching, kayaking, or more exhilarating pursuits like scuba diving. The book also emphasizes wellness, offering advice on fitness routines, mindfulness practices, and retreat ideas to help you stay active and stress-free in your golden years. If you enjoy motivational guides that combine actionable advice with inspiration for both physical and mental well-being, this book serves as an essential roadmap for crafting an adventurous, healthy, and joy-filled retirement. I invite you to pick up a copy and let it inspire your retirement adventures.

But retirement isn't one-size-fits-all. While passions like traveling and outdoor explorations energize and excite many retirees, I know that's not everyone's ideal vision of retirement. Perhaps you're someone who prefers intellectual journeys and introspective pursuits, or maybe you're looking for new ways to engage your mind, express your creativity, or build meaningful connections in your community. And that's exactly what *Retirement Reinvented* is about—exploring the many ways you can thrive in retirement without booking a flight or packing a backpack. I want to offer you a roadmap for exploring the areas of life beyond travels and outdoor activities and help you engage with the world in different but equally fulfilling ways. Whether you've already read my first book and are looking for more diversity in your retirement activities, or this is your first introduction to my work, I'm excited to help guide you through these new possibilities.

Retirement is an incredible opportunity to redefine who you are and what you want from life. It's not simply about stopping work but creating a new chapter filled with growth, creativity, and connection. But to get the most out of this time, it's essential to have a plan. Without one, it's easy to drift, feeling unmoored and unsure of what to do next. This book is here to help you map out that plan, providing inspiration and practical steps to bring your post-work life to full bloom. It will be a companion on your journey, with an uplifting, motivational tone to keep you excited about what lies ahead. I want you to see retirement as an adventure, a time to explore new passions, take risks, and grow in ways you may never have imagined. With each chapter, you'll find inspiration and ideas for crafting the retirement that suits your interests, talents, and dreams. Whether it's volunteering, launching a new business venture, or learning a new language, the possibilities are limitless.

In this book, we'll explore several key areas vital to leading a rich and rewarding retirement:

- **Rebranding Your Identity and Planning for an Active Retirement**—This chapter is about embracing your post-career life with enthusiasm and purpose. I'll guide you through the process of rediscovering who you are outside your job title, rebranding yourself in a way that aligns with your passions, and setting clear, achievable goals for an adventurous, active retirement. You'll learn how to create a balanced, fulfilling lifestyle that reflects your values and dreams.

- **Intellectual Pursuits**—For those who thrive on learning, we'll delve into ways to keep your mind sharp and engaged. From lifelong learning programs to mastering new gadgets, you'll find a wealth of ideas to stimulate your intellectual curiosity. Whether you want to study history, learn a new language, or delve into scientific discoveries, there's a world of knowledge waiting for you.

- **Creative Expression**—Retirement is the perfect time to explore your creative side, whether you've always been a creator at heart or are just beginning to discover your artistic potential. We'll discuss various creative outlets, such as painting, writing, music, and more. You'll learn to tap into your imagination and find joy in making things with your hands, heart, and mind.

- **Socializing and Building New Connections**—Retirement means stepping away from workplace social structures, but it doesn't have to mean isolation. In this chapter, I'll guide you through ways to cultivate and maintain meaningful relationships. From joining social clubs to hobby groups, I'll show you how to stay connected with others who share your interests. From making new friends to nurturing existing relationships, building a vibrant social life is key to enjoying a happy and fulfilling retirement. I'll also offer tips on staying socially active through virtual communities and online platforms if physical proximity is a challenge.

- **Community Engagement and Leadership**—Creating a sense of belonging and contribution is a vital part of retirement. In this chapter, we'll explore actively building and strengthening your community ties. There are countless ways to become a vital part of the community around you: volunteering for local causes, organizing community events, and participating in neighborhood improvement initiatives, to name just a few. We'll discuss how to take on leadership roles in your local clubs or organizations and the impact you can have by sharing your time and skills for the betterment of your community.

- **Home-Based Hobbies**—For those who prefer staying closer to home, this chapter offers a wide variety of engaging hobbies and activities you can enjoy from the comfort of your own space. Whether you're drawn to gardening, decorating, or winemaking, I'll provide suggestions for creative and fulfilling ways to spend your time. These activities are perfect for maintaining mental and physical health while enjoying the serenity of home life.

- **Entrepreneurial Endeavors and Part-Time Work**—Retirement doesn't mean stepping away from ambition or work altogether. Many retirees are eager to start new business ventures to pursue a passion, make extra income, or simply stay engaged. We'll explore how to turn your hobbies or skills into small businesses through consulting, online ventures, selling handcrafted goods, and more.

- **Leaving a Legacy**—Many retirees want to ensure they leave a lasting impact on their families, communities, or broader society. In this chapter, we'll explore meaningful ways to give back and create a legacy that resonates with future generations. From building your family tree to contributing to causes you care about, I'll provide guidance on how to leave behind something that matters.

As you dive into these chapters, remember that retirement is not a winding down, but a gearing up for the best years of your life. The freedom you now have can be channeled into exploring new passions, building deeper connections, and leaving a lasting legacy. So take a deep breath, open your mind to new possibilities, and get ready to create the retirement you've always dreamed of. The best is truly yet to come, and I can't wait to see where this journey takes you!

Chapter Two

From Worker to Creator: Crafting Your New Retirement Identity and Rhythm

Retirement marks the start of an exciting new phase of life, filled with opportunities to redefine who you are and how you spend your days. For decades, your identity may have been closely intertwined with your profession, but now is the time to evolve. Rebrand yourself not just as a retiree, but as someone who is continuously learning, embracing new passions, and expanding in ways that bring personal fulfillment and growth. This chapter will help you explore ways to rebrand your identity, create a new daily rhythm, master time management, and develop a morning routine that sets the tone for an energized, fulfilling day.

2.1 Overcoming the Fear of the Unknown

Many retirees face the fear of losing the structure and identity that their careers used to provide. Without the daily rhythm of work, it's easy to feel adrift or uncertain about what comes next. Similarly, the fear of isolation can creep in, as you may no longer have the built-in social network your workplace offered. Concerns about physical or cognitive decline can also create anxiety, as aging presents challenges that were once easier to ignore. Please understand that feeling uncertain or anxious is simply part of the process. By acknowledging these fears, you validate them as a natural part of the retirement transition.

One of the most effective ways to combat fear is to take action. Start by setting small, achievable goals to help build a sense of purpose and direction. For example, if you're concerned about isolation, make a goal to join one new social or community group, even if it feels outside your comfort zone. The key is to ease yourself into new routines and experiences, gradually expanding your horizons while building confidence in this new phase of life. Exploring new hobbies, volunteering, taking an online course, or engaging in part-time work can offer a renewed sense of purpose. These activities fill your days with meaningful tasks and provide an opportunity to meet new people and establish social connections. Remember, overcoming fear isn't about making drastic changes overnight—it's about steady, deliberate steps toward something new.

Adopting a growth mindset can be incredibly empowering as it shifts your focus from the limitations of aging to the possibilities that lie ahead. Instead of seeing retirement as a period of decline, view it as a time to pursue passions you may have set aside, deepen your knowledge in areas of interest, and explore creative endeavors that excite you. A growth mindset encourages you to see challenges not as obstacles, but as opportunities to learn and grow. By starting a new hobby, adjusting to a more flexible schedule, or stepping into community leadership roles, this growth mindset keeps you engaged, curious, and active.

Staying mentally, socially, and physically active is crucial in overcoming the fear of a decline in retirement. By continuing to engage in stimulating activities, learning new skills, mentoring others, or taking part in community events, you create a sense of purpose and vitality. Physical activity also helps to combat the fear of physical decline by keeping you strong, mobile, and energized.

Above all, remember that fear often dissipates when you take meaningful action. By staying active, following your plan, and embracing a growth mindset, you can turn your retirement fears into opportunities for discovery and fulfillment. You just need to take the first step and trust that the rest will follow.

2.2 Rebranding Your Identity in Retirement

For many years, your professional title and achievements had been central to your identity. Whether you were an executive, teacher, or skilled craftsman, your career likely defined much of who you were. But now, retirement offers a unique opportunity to step away from that career-based identity and embrace a new one, shaped by your passions, values, and aspirations. This is the perfect time to redefine yourself in ways that resonate with who you are today. Maybe that means becoming an artist, a community leader, a volunteer, or simply a lifelong learner. The goal is to choose roles that reflect your evolving interests.

Start by reflecting on what you enjoyed most during your working years. Did you love mentoring, managing complex projects, or solving intricate problems? Those skills don't need to fade in retirement. Instead, you can redirect them into new, meaningful pursuits. Perhaps you could mentor younger professionals, offer consulting services, or finally pursue a creative venture you've always dreamed of. This is also a great time to revisit hobbies or passions you may have put on hold during your career. Did you dream about painting, writing, gardening, or learning a foreign language? These activities can offer personal fulfillment right now and start shaping your new identity.

Embrace these roles with confidence and pride. When introducing yourself in social situations, feel free to use titles that reflect your new passions. Instead of a "retired accountant" or "former account manager," lead with your current passions. Perhaps you'll introduce yourself as a painter at a local gallery, a volunteer leading community initiatives, or a business owner if you've embarked on an entrepreneurial journey. Just as you cultivated a professional brand during your career, now is the time to craft a personal brand that aligns with your retirement goals.

Your personal brand in retirement should reflect the person you are now and the person you want to become. Whether you're a passionate photographer, a community organizer bringing people together, or an entrepreneur exploring new ventures, your personal brand is how others will come to know you in this exciting new phase of life. By actively connecting with social circles that align with your new identity—through clubs, groups, or online communities—you'll reinforce your personal brand and meet like-minded people who share your interests.

Rebranding your identity in retirement is a significant milestone, and like any major life transition, it deserves to be celebrated. While many people focus on career achievements during their retirement party, why not turn the spotlight on the future? Host a symbolic event or ritual that honors not only your past but also the exciting new adventures and roles you're stepping into. This celebration can take any form you like. Maybe it's a small gathering of close friends and family where you share your plans for this new chapter. You could create a vision board during the event, where everyone contributes ideas and inspiration for your retirement goals. What fun is that? Alternatively, you could plan a personal retreat, a few days spent reflecting on the transition, and setting your intentions for the future. The important thing is to mark the occasion in a way that feels meaningful to you. Retirement is the beginning of a fulfilling, creative, and purpose-driven new identity. So why not celebrate the freedom to reinvent yourself?

2.3 Embracing a New Rhythm: Crafting Your Retirement Week

One of the biggest adjustments in retirement is transitioning from a structured, work-driven schedule to one where you have full control over how you spend your time. Without the rigidity of a 9-to-5 job, scheduled meetings, and tight deadlines, ironically, you can easily feel overwhelmed by the sheer amount of freedom. The key to navigating this new reality is to establish a balanced rhythm that allows for a mix of activity, rest, and spontaneity.

The first step to creating a fulfilling schedule is identifying activities that genuinely excite you. These can be hobbies you've always loved but didn't have time for, or new interests you've wanted to explore. Are there creative pursuits like painting or photography that you've always wanted to try? Or perhaps you want to deepen your connection with your community by volunteering or mentoring? Rank these activities based on your level of passion and how accessible they are. For example, you might place weekly pottery classes at the top of your list if they're available nearby while traveling to new countries could be a long-term goal. By clearly identifying your interests, you'll know exactly how to fill your time with activities that bring you joy.

Now that you know what you want to do, it's time to create a flexible schedule that includes a wide variety of different activities. You don't have to plan every minute, but having a loose framework for your week will ensure you stay engaged without feeling overwhelmed. A balanced weekly schedule that includes both structured and unstructured time ensures that you stay engaged without overloading yourself with commitments.

- **Structured Time**: These are activities with set schedules, like attending a yoga class every Monday at 8 am or joining a book club every other Thursday at 7 pm. These structured events provide routine and a sense of purpose.

- **Unstructured Time**: Set aside time for rest and spontaneity. This could mean having free afternoons for reading, gardening, going for a leisurely walk, or doing something impromptu. Unstructured time allows you to relax and recharge.

To maintain a healthy and balanced lifestyle, aim for a mix of physical, intellectual, and social activities each week.

- **Physical activities** like walking, cycling, or gardening to keep your body strong and healthy.

- **Intellectual pursuits** like attending lectures, learning a new language, or playing chess to keep your mind sharp.

- **Social engagements** like joining clubs, volunteering, or spending time with friends to stay connected and engaged with your community.

Once you've listed your interests in each category, plan your week to create a healthy balance between active pursuits and downtime. Use a flexible weekly planner to allocate time for both structured activities and unstructured time for rest and spontaneity, as well as physical, intellectual, and social engagements. A typical week might look like this:

- **Monday**: Morning walk, painting class, and social lunch with friends.

- **Tuesday**: Yoga session, volunteer work at a local charity, and downtime for reading or gardening in the afternoon.

- **Wednesday**: Attend a lecture or cultural event, followed by a relaxing afternoon at home.

- **Thursday**: Cycling or bird-watching in the morning, then a hobby like photography or woodworking in the afternoon.

- **Friday**: A quiet morning at home, chores or shopping in the afternoon, and an evening out with friends or family.

A balanced schedule keeps you energized and prevents your days from feeling either too empty or too overwhelming.

And just because you're no longer working doesn't mean you should fill every day to the brim with activities or start a bunch of new hobbies. Rest is crucial to maintaining a healthy and fulfilling retirement, just like it was when you were working. Build downtime into your schedule, whether it's through afternoon naps, quiet reading, or spending time outdoors. This rest is necessary to avoid fatigue and ensure you remain energized for the people you love and activities you enjoy.

2.4 Time Management Tips for an Unstructured Day

As I mentioned earlier, without the structure of a traditional workday, managing your time in retirement can feel challenging. While you may have fewer obligations, creating a plan for your day helps maintain a sense of purpose and prevents time from slipping away unnoticed. Here's how you can do it.

Set Daily Goals. In retirement, just like in working life, setting goals gives your day structure. Start each day by identifying two or three key activities or tasks you'd like to accomplish. These goals don't need to be monumental—they could be as simple as writing five hundred words of your book, going for a ride, or trying out a new recipe. What's important is that you give yourself a sense of purpose for the day. Using tools like a paper planner, a digital calendar, or to-do list apps like **Todoist** can help you organize your tasks and track progress throughout the day. Having small, achievable goals will keep you motivated and help you end the day with a sense of accomplishment.

Prioritize. With so much freedom in retirement, it's easy to feel overwhelmed by the sheer number of things you could be doing. But just as you likely honed your ability to prioritize tasks during your career or in managing a business, you can apply those same skills to this new chapter of life. One effective tool to consider is the **Eisenhower Matrix**, which helps you categorize tasks by urgency and importance. By focusing first on activities that are both important and urgent, you can ensure that you spend your time on what you truly enjoy. This method also helps you balance high-energy activities and more relaxing ones. For example, you might prioritize a morning spent painting, followed by a slower afternoon of reading or gardening, making sure each day is both productive and fulfilling.

Overcome Procrastination. Even in retirement, procrastination can sneak in and prevent you from doing the things you love. One way to combat this is by breaking down large tasks into smaller, more manageable steps. If you've been wanting to compile your favorite recipes or family traditions into a scrapbook or cookbook for future generations, begin by setting aside 10 minutes to organize just a few handwritten notes, photos, or recipe cards. If you've been putting off organizing your travel memorabilia from past adventures, start by dedicating 20 minutes to sorting through a single album or box. Once you get started, momentum will often carry you through the rest of the task. Rewarding yourself after completing a task—whether with a treat or an exciting activity—can also be a powerful motivator.

Create Time Blocks for Better Focus. The time-blocking method involves dividing your day into blocks of time dedicated to specific activities. For instance, you could dedicate the morning to physical activity, the afternoon to creative work, and the evening to socializing with friends. Scheduling your time in blocks ensures you balance productivity and leisure each day, preventing time from slipping away aimlessly.

I don't know about you, but in my 60s, I'm more conscious than ever of how precious each minute is. I want to be intentional with my time, making sure every moment counts toward the things that truly matter and bring me joy.

2.5 Setting Up Your Morning Routine for an Energized Start

How you start your morning sets the tone for the rest of the day. Establishing a morning routine helps you feel energized, focused, and ready to tackle the day ahead. A well-structured morning reduces decision fatigue, sets a positive tone for the day, and provides you with a sense of accomplishment early on. By starting each day with purpose, you're more likely to stay engaged and active throughout the day.

To craft a morning routine that works for you, consider including the following elements:

- **Physical Movement.** Whether it's a jog around the neighborhood, yoga, or stretching, getting your body moving in the morning boosts your energy levels and improves your mood.

- **Healthy Breakfast.** Fuel your body with a nutritious breakfast to kick-start your metabolism. Whole grains, fruits, and protein provide the nutrients you need to stay energized.

- **Reflection or Meditation.** Dedicate a few minutes to mindfulness or reflection. This could involve meditation, journaling, or simply enjoying a quiet cup of coffee while thinking about the day ahead.

Everyone's morning routine will look different depending on their preferences and energy levels. If you're someone who loves to jump right into action, start your day with a burst of physical activity. If you prefer a slower start, ease into your day with quiet reflection or a leisurely breakfast. The key is to design a routine that fits your lifestyle and makes you feel good. What type of morning person are you?

- **Active Starter**: Wakes up at 6:00 a.m., spends 30 minutes on a brisk walk or yoga, enjoys a healthy smoothie, and spends a few minutes journaling before starting the day.

- **Slow and Reflective**: Wakes up at 8:30 a.m., enjoys a quiet cup of coffee on the porch, spends 20 minutes reading or journaling, followed by a light breakfast and a walk later in the morning.

- **Creative Burst**: Wakes up at 7:00 a.m., spends an hour working on a creative project such as writing or painting, enjoys a hearty breakfast, and follows it with a short walk.

By crafting a morning routine that aligns with your personal preferences and lifestyle, you can set yourself up for a day filled with energy, focus, and enjoyment. Your morning is the launchpad for how your entire day unfolds, so give yourself the gift of starting it off right.

In retirement, the balance between activity and relaxation, structure and flexibility, is the key to a fulfilling lifestyle. No longer tied to the demands of a career, you have the freedom to rebrand yourself, define your days, design your routines, and pursue passions that may have taken a back seat during your working years.

By embracing this new rhythm, you can explore roles beyond your professional identity, structure your days in ways that balance engagement with rest, and approach time with both intention and flexibility. Remember that this chapter of your life is a fresh start—a time for rediscovery, creativity, and growth. With thoughtful time management, a morning routine that sets the right tone, and a balanced schedule, you can thrive in your retirement and truly make it the most rewarding phase of your life.

The next chapter will explore how to deepen your intellectual pursuits in retirement, challenging your mind and building new neural connections. By engaging in continuous learning and stimulating mental activities, you'll keep your brain sharp and foster personal growth, opening the door to new ideas and possibilities. Stay open to what it can bring—the best is yet to come!

Chapter Three

Intellectual Pursuits: Mindful Exploration and Lifelong Learning

I magine sitting in a charming café in Rome, sipping a perfectly brewed espresso, when you casually start a conversation with the person next to you—in Italian. It's not just a scene from a movie; it's your life, brimming with new experiences. Retirement opens up a world of intellectual pursuits, and this is the perfect time to explore them. It could be taking courses in subjects you've always been curious about, sharpening your chess skills, diving into the world of video games to challenge your reflexes, or enjoying a friendly game of bridge with new friends—the possibilities are endless. These activities keep your brain sharp and provide the satisfaction of continued growth and discovery, proving that retirement is the beginning of a new intellectual journey.

3.1 Fluency on Your Terms: Exploring New Languages

So, you've always dreamed of chatting with locals in your favorite travel destinations, and now you finally have the time to make it happen by learning their language. Choosing the right language-learning tools is crucial for making this journey enjoyable and effective. For the tech-savvy, apps like **Duolingo** and **Babbel** offer interactive lessons that feel more like games than studying. They break down the language into bite-sized pieces, making it easy to fit learning into your daily routine. If you prefer a more structured approach, online platforms such as **Rosetta Stone** and **Coursera** provide comprehensive courses that dive deep into grammar, vocabulary, and pronunciation. And for those who cherish face-to-face interaction, local community centers and colleges often offer language classes tailored to beginners. These classes not only teach the language but also provide a social setting where you can meet fellow learners.

    Personally, I've always been drawn to live learning. After my trip to Italy a few years ago, I fell in love with the culture and the beautiful language, so I found an Italian Cultural Centre in my city and joined the beginner classes. It was an enriching experience, not just for the language, but for the cultural connection I felt every time I attended. Unfortunately, I couldn't continue because of my business schedule, but I look forward to rejoining those classes once I retire. I can't wait to immerse myself in the language again, this time with more freedom and focus.

Setting achievable goals is the next step in your language-learning adventure. Start small and build your confidence. A realistic goal could be holding a five-minute conversation with a native speaker or understanding a newspaper article. If you're planning a trip, aim to learn essential phrases that will help you navigate daily interactions, such as ordering food, asking for directions, or making small talk. Setting these manageable milestones keeps you motivated and gives you a sense of accomplishment as you progress. Remember, language learning is a marathon, not a sprint, so celebrate each small victory along the way.

Integrating language practice into your daily life can make learning feel less like a chore and more like an exciting part of your routine. Start by labeling household items with their foreign names; this constant visual reminder helps reinforce vocabulary. Listening to music or podcasts in the language you're learning can also be incredibly beneficial. Sing along to your favorite songs or follow a podcast while you're cooking or exercising. Watching films with subtitles is another effective method. Not only does it improve your listening skills, but it also gives you a cultural context that makes the language more relatable and fun.

Language exchange and social interaction can significantly enhance your learning experience. Taking part in language exchange meetups, either in person or online, provides practical speaking practice and the opportunity to interact with native speakers. Websites like **ConversationExchange.com** or **Tandem** are excellent platforms for finding language partners from around the world. These exchanges are mutually beneficial—you help someone learn English while they help you learn their language. Joining online forums or social media groups dedicated to language learning can also provide support, resources, and motivation. Engaging with a community of learners keeps you inspired and accountable, making the process more enjoyable and less isolating.

3.2 Expand Your Horizons with Online Learning

Learning new things at your own pace is incredibly rewarding, and today's technology makes it easier than ever. Whether you're interested in ancient civilizations, mastering a new hobby, or diving deep into scientific discoveries, online courses offer a world of knowledge right at your fingertips. Choosing the right platform is your first step toward this enjoyable and enriching experience. Platforms like **Coursera, Udemy, edX**, and **Khan Academy** offer a smorgasbord of courses that cater to every interest. **Coursera** collaborates with top universities to provide high-quality courses on anything from art history to data science. **Udemy** is more of a marketplace where experts offer courses on everything you can imagine—cooking, photography, personal finance, you name it. **Khan Academy** is fantastic for those who prefer a more structured academic style of learning, with a focus on subjects like math, science, and economics. Each of these platforms is user-friendly and designed to make learning accessible and enjoyable for people of all ages.

Identifying your interests and goals is crucial for making the most of your online learning experience. What sparks your curiosity? Are you fascinated by astronomy, or do you have a passion for culinary arts? Defining your learning goals can help you choose courses that are both enjoyable and beneficial. Perhaps you want to learn about digital photography to capture beautiful moments on your travels, or maybe you've always wanted to understand the complexities of financial markets. Setting these goals not only enhances your sense of fulfillment but also provides a clear direction for your learning journey. And remember, it's never too late to explore new interests or deepen existing ones. Retirement is the perfect time to indulge your intellectual curiosity without the constraints of a busy work schedule.

Now, let's talk about the technical setup and support you'll need to get started. First, ensure you have a reliable internet connection. This might sound obvious, but a strong and stable connection is key to uninterrupted learning. Next, you'll need a device—whether it's a computer, tablet, or even a smartphone. Most courses are designed to be accessible on various devices, so choose what you're most comfortable with. If you're not particularly tech-savvy, or never took online courses, don't worry. Many platforms offer step-by-step guides to help you get set up, from creating an account to navigating the course interface. If you run into issues, technical support is usually just a click away. Most platforms have excellent customer service teams ready to assist you with any hiccups you might encounter. Think of it as having your personal tech support team, always on standby to help you get the most out of your learning experience.

Engaging with course communities can significantly enhance your online learning experience. Most platforms offer forums or discussion boards where you can interact with fellow learners. This isn't just about making friends, though that's a lovely bonus; it's about deepening your understanding of the subject through shared insights and discussions. Participate in these forums, ask questions, and don't be shy to share your thoughts. Group discussions can provide diverse perspectives that enrich your learning. You'll find that engaging with a community of learners from around the globe adds a dynamic layer to your education. It's being part of a virtual classroom where everyone is just as eager to learn as you are.

Course Selection Checklist

Before diving into your first course, use this checklist to ensure you've chosen the right one:

- Interest: Does the course cover a topic you're passionate about?

- Difficulty Level: Is it suitable for your current knowledge level?

- Format: Do you prefer video lectures, text-based lessons, or interactive exercises?

- Time Commitment: Can you comfortably fit the course into your weekly schedule?

- Reviews: Have you checked reviews from other learners to gauge the course quality?

- Support: Does the platform offer adequate technical support and community engagement options?

3.3 Tech Savvy Seniors: Mastering New Gadgets

Mastering new gadgets can open up a world of convenience and excitement in your retirement. From wearable fitness trackers to tablets and smartphones, today's technology offers endless possibilities for staying connected, entertained, and informed. Whether it's learning to navigate the latest apps, using smart devices to make everyday tasks easier, controlling your home environment with ease, or exploring the world of virtual reality, embracing modern gadgets allows you to enhance your lifestyle in ways you never imagined. Understanding and mastering these tools can transform your retirement into an adventure of innovation and discovery.

Smart home devices like **Amazon Echo** or **Google Home** can transform your living space into a responsive, intelligent environment. Just say, "*Alexa, play my favorite jazz playlist,*" and your home is instantly filled with smooth tunes. Voice commands can handle everything from setting timers to streaming music, adjusting the thermostat, turning lights on and off, locking doors, and checking your calendar. These devices can also control smart home appliances like vacuum cleaners, coffeemakers, and security cameras, allowing you to manage household tasks with simple voice prompts. You can ask for weather updates, news briefings, or a recipe while cooking, and the hub can guide you through step-by-step instructions hands-free. They can serve as a personal assistant, setting reminders, sending messages, or making calls, all while keeping you effortlessly connected to your daily life.

But smart devices don't stop there. Smart light bulbs like **Philips Hue** allow you to adjust lighting with a simple voice command or through an app—dim the lights for movie night or brighten the room for reading. Smart thermostats like the **Nest** learn your schedule and preferences, optimizing energy use while keeping your home comfortable. Even your kitchen can get a high-tech boost. Smart appliances such as the **Instant Pot Smart Wi-Fi** or **GE Smart Ovens** let you control cooking settings from your smartphone, perfect for busy days or hands-free meal prep. And for coffee lovers, devices like the **Breville Smart Coffee Maker** allow you to brew your morning cup before you get out of bed.

Fitness trackers, like the **Fitbit, Oura Ring,** or **Apple Watch**, are another fantastic addition to your gadget lineup. They not only monitor your heart rate and track your steps but also remind you to move, helping you stay active and healthy. Some models go even further by monitoring sleep patterns, measuring oxygen levels, and even performing an electrocardiogram (ECG) right from your wrist. If you're looking to keep a closer eye on your health, smart scales such as the **Withings Body+** can sync your weight, BMI, and body composition with your smartphone, providing detailed reports to help you track your progress.

Leveraging smart technology for lifelong learning is another exciting opportunity. Devices like **Amazon Kindle, Google Play Books, Apple Books, Kobo, Nook, and Libby** make it easy to access thousands of books in an instant, and smart speakers can play educational podcasts on any topic you desire. Apps like **TED** or **Coursera** offer endless lectures and courses, while **YouTube** provides tutorials and documentaries.

Virtual reality (VR) devices are revolutionizing how we experience the world, offering an immersive way to explore new environments without leaving home. With a VR headset, you can walk through ancient ruins, visit art galleries, or even explore outer space, all from the comfort of your living room. It can be used for virtual travel, interactive fitness routines, or learning new skills in a fully immersive environment. Some VR platforms offer social experiences, allowing you to connect with friends or meet new people in virtual spaces, making it a unique way to stay engaged and active.

Virtual reality devices like the **Oculus Quest 2** and **PlayStation VR** are leading the charge in immersive experiences. The **Oculus Quest 2** is a standalone device that doesn't require a computer or console, making it user-friendly and perfect for everything from virtual travel to fitness games like **Beat Saber** or **Supernatural**, which turn exercise into a fun and interactive experience. The **PlayStation VR**, on the other hand, connects to the **PlayStation console** and offers access to a wide variety of VR games and experiences, including virtual museum tours and explorations of ancient cities.

For those looking to explore the world, apps like **Google Earth VR** let you virtually "fly" anywhere in the world, and platforms like **AltspaceVR** or **Rec Room** offer social VR spaces where you can meet others, attend live events, or play games together. These devices and platforms make VR an exciting tool for exploration, learning, and staying socially connected in retirement. And if you're curious about exploring video games, we'll dive deeper into their benefits in a later section of this chapter.

Customizing these gadgets to fit your personal needs is key to making them more user-friendly. Start by adjusting the text size on your tablet or smartphone to improve readability, especially when reading e-books or checking emails. Boost the sound settings on smart devices to ensure you never miss an important notification or call. Whether you're using your smart speaker to make grocery lists, control your TV with a device like **Amazon Fire TV Stick**, or even ask it for weather updates, these tweaks make tech more accessible and fun to use.

While these gadgets offer incredible convenience, online safety is crucial. Stay vigilant when managing emails, texts, or social media interactions. If you receive an email asking you to verify personal details, don't act hastily—it could be a phishing attempt. Always check the sender's email address and avoid clicking suspicious links. Use strong, unique passwords for each account, and consider a password manager like **LastPass** to keep track of them. Keep all your devices and software updated to protect against the latest security threats, and be cautious of unsolicited calls or messages asking for sensitive information. Following these steps will safeguard your online activities and give you peace of mind while exploring the digital world.

Mastering new gadgets in retirement isn't just about convenience—it's an excellent way to keep your brain sharp and engaged. Learning how to use smart devices like tablets, fitness trackers, or smart home assistants challenges your cognitive skills in exciting ways. Navigating new technology requires problem-solving, memory, and attention to detail, all of which contribute to keeping your brain active. Every time you figure out how to program a smart thermostat or ask your voice assistant to turn on the lights, you're reinforcing neural pathways that help maintain cognitive flexibility. By engaging with these gadgets, you are essentially exercising your mind in the same way you would by tackling a crossword puzzle or learning a new language. The more you use these devices, the more comfortable you become, and this process of ongoing learning strengthens your ability to absorb and apply new information.

Mastering smart technology can also help improve your multitasking abilities. For instance, you might use a tablet to browse recipes while a smart oven cooks your meal or adjust the lighting while you listen to an audiobook through your smart speaker. These small but dynamic tasks push your brain to handle multiple inputs, enhancing coordination. Engaging with technology helps maintain cognitive function and provides a fun, stimulating way to continue learning throughout retirement.

Incorporating smart devices into your life can turn every day into an opportunity for efficiency, health, learning, and fun. Embrace the potential of technology and make your retirement smarter, easier, and more enjoyable.

3.4 Brain Games and Puzzles for Daily Mental Exercise

Engaging in a challenging crossword puzzle or tackling a Sudoku grid is more than just a way to fill your day—it's an excellent way to keep your brain sharp and active. Every word you piece together or number you place strengthens your cognitive abilities, turning what seems like a leisurely activity into a powerful mental workout. **Crosswords** help sharpen your vocabulary and memory recall by challenging your knowledge of word associations. **Sudoku**, with its numerical grid, is excellent for improving logic and pattern recognition. Logical puzzles stimulate critical thinking and problem-solving, pushing your mind to think outside the box. Even jigsaw puzzles, with their focus on visual-spatial reasoning, engage different parts of your brain, helping you see patterns and complete tasks with focus. These activities keep your mind agile and provide a satisfying sense of accomplishment.

Establishing a daily brain exercise routine can be a fun and effective way to keep your cognitive abilities in top shape. You might start your morning with a crossword before breakfast, tackle a Sudoku puzzle after lunch, and spend some time on a challenging jigsaw puzzle in the evening. The key is to keep variety in your routine to ensure your brain is consistently challenged in different ways. Mixing various types of puzzles prevents your brain from getting stuck in a routine and keeps your mental workouts engaging and enjoyable. Set aside specific times each day for these exercises, creating a routine. Just like with physical exercise, consistency is key—the more regularly you engage in these activities, the more you'll benefit.

Social gaming can add another layer of fun and engagement to brain exercises. Playing games with friends and family not only stimulates your mind but also provides a wonderful opportunity for connection and laughter. Games like **Scrabble, card games,** or **trivia challenges** turn mental exercises into lively gatherings where everyone can get involved. These games challenge memory, improve word recall, and foster strategic thinking, all while you enjoy the company of others. Setting up regular game nights can become a cherished tradition that combines cognitive stimulation with social interaction, making retirement even more fulfilling.

Tracking your progress in these cognitive games and puzzles can be an excellent motivator. Keep a journal or a notepad where you jot down your puzzle-solving times, high scores, and any personal milestones. Did you solve that particularly tricky logic puzzle faster than last time? Have you noticed an improvement in your memory recall during trivia games? Recording your progress keeps you motivated and highlights your cognitive improvements over time. As you see your skills sharpening, you'll feel a sense of pride and accomplishment that makes these brain exercises more rewarding.

3.5 Video Games for Intellectual Engagement

Video games aren't just for kids anymore—they offer many benefits for retirees, including cognitive stimulation, social interaction, stress relief, improved memory, and enhanced problem-solving skills. Whether it's solving intricate puzzles or outsmarting opponents in a strategic game, video games provide engaging mental exercises that help keep your brain sharp and active. The satisfaction of overcoming challenges and the excitement of achieving victories make gaming a fun and effective way to stay intellectually engaged during retirement.

Research has increasingly shown the positive impact of video games on seniors' cognitive health. A study conducted by the University of California, San Francisco, found that seniors who played video games designed to improve multitasking skills showed significant improvements in memory and attention span. Another study published in *Frontiers in Aging Neuroscience* indicated that playing video games could enhance cognitive flexibility and even slow down cognitive decline in older adults. Games that challenge memory, problem-solving, and strategic thinking provide a mental workout, helping to keep the brain engaged and sharp.

These findings suggest that incorporating gaming into a senior's routine can be more than just a leisure activity—it's a powerful tool for maintaining mental acuity and promoting overall well-being during retirement. Whether it's using virtual environments to explore new worlds or simply engaging with interactive puzzles, gaming is proving to be an exciting and beneficial way for retirees to stay mentally sharp and socially connected.

Needless to say, you need to choose the right games to enjoy them and to maximize these benefits. If you love puzzles, games like **Lumosity** and **Brain Age** are designed specifically to improve mental agility through a variety of brain-training exercises. These games offer daily challenges that test your memory, attention, and problem-solving skills. For those who love strategic thinking, titles like **Civilization** and **Age of Empires** are perfect. These games require you to plan, manage resources, and out-think your opponents, providing hours of intellectually stimulating entertainment. If you lean toward creative pursuits, games like **Minecraft** and **The Sims** offer limitless opportunities for building and exploration. VR takes this a step further with titles like **Beat Saber** and **Superhot VR**, which combine mental engagement with physical activity, making it a great way to stay both mentally and physically active.

Getting started with video gaming, whether traditional or VR, is easier than you might think. If you choose a console like the **Nintendo Switch** or **PlayStation**, simply connect it to your TV and follow the setup instructions. For computers, platforms like **Steam** offer vast game libraries, and tablets make it even simpler with app store downloads. VR headsets like the **Oculus Quest 2** or **PlayStation VR** require a bit more setup but are worth it for the immersive experience they provide. Create a comfortable gaming environment with a cozy chair, good lighting, a glass of water, and perhaps some healthy snacks nearby. For VR, ensure you have enough space to move safely as many games require physical movement.

Joining online gaming communities can take your gaming experience to the next level. Many games offer forums, chat features, and multiplayer modes that allow you to connect with others who share similar interests. Imagine playing a cooperative game where you and your friends work together to complete a mission or participating in a lively discussion in a game forum about the best strategies for conquering a difficult level. These interactions can lead to new friendships and a sense of belonging in a community of like-minded video game enthusiasts. Websites like **Reddit** or specific game forums are great places to start. Engaging with these communities enhances your gaming experience and keeps you socially active, providing a fun and interactive way to connect with others.

3.6 The Joy of Playing Chess in Local Clubs

Chess is more than just a game; it's a workout for your brain. It's a rich, engaging activity that stimulates the mind and brings people together. Whether you're a seasoned player or just learning the rules, chess offers incredible mental benefits. It sharpens your concentration, enhances your ability to think strategically, and improves your foresight as you plan multiple moves. These skills don't just stay on the chessboard—they translate into everyday life, helping you make decisions more effectively and solve problems with greater clarity.

One of the most rewarding aspects of playing chess is how it brings people together. At a local chess club or over a friendly game with a neighbor, you'll find that chess naturally sparks conversation and camaraderie. As you engage with others, you're exercising your mind and building meaningful relationships.

If you've never played chess before or haven't picked up a chess piece in years, don't worry! Learning the basics of chess is easy, and with the right resources, you'll be ready to start playing in no time. For beginners, there are plenty of resources to help you get started. Websites like **Chess.com** and **Lichess.org** offer interactive tutorials, puzzles, and practice games that walk you through the fundamentals. There are also countless apps available that let you play against the computer or other people, helping you practice whenever you like. For those who prefer a more traditional route, books like **Bobby Fischer Teaches Chess** are excellent for breaking down the strategies and tactics that make chess so engaging. No matter which route you choose, learning chess is accessible and fun.

Once you've grasped the basics, consider joining a local chess club. These clubs aren't just for seasoned players; they welcome people of all skill levels and provide a fantastic environment to learn, compete, and socialize. Many local community centers or libraries offer chess clubs, and you'll find the atmosphere relaxed and welcoming. It's not about winning or losing every game, but about enjoying the process, learning from others, and, of course, having fun.

Beyond improving your game, chess clubs are also a great way to meet people from different walks of life. You'll have the chance to share tips and strategies, talk about past games, or simply enjoy the company of fellow players. And, as you play regularly, you'll notice your game improving naturally, just through the act of playing and discussing tactics with others. The friendships you form at a chess club often extend beyond the board, turning casual opponents into lifelong friends.

If you're feeling confident in your chess skills and want to challenge yourself further, why not try participating in a chess tournament? Local clubs and community centers often host friendly tournaments, which is a fantastic way to test your skills in a more competitive setting. These tournaments don't have to be stressful, as they're typically designed to be fun and engaging, providing a sense of accomplishment whether you win or lose.

For those who prefer a more flexible schedule, online chess tournaments are another exciting option. Websites like **Chess.com** regularly host competitions, allowing you to play against opponents from around the world. Whether you're competing locally or online, participating in tournaments can give you a great sense of achievement and add an extra layer of excitement to the game. You'll find that the competitive spirit keeps you engaged, while the supportive chess community is always there to cheer you on, offering advice and encouragement every step of the way.

3.7 Organizing a Local Bridge Club

Bridge is a card game that blends strategy, communication, and social interaction. It has captivated players for generations. The game is typically played by four players, divided into two teams of two. Each player is dealt 13 cards, and the objective is for teams to bid and win "tricks" based on the cards they hold. The catch? You and your partner must work together without directly communicating, relying instead on shared strategies and subtle signals through your bids and plays.

Bridge is a game that stimulates the mind and strengthens social bonds, making it a perfect activity for retirees who are looking for both intellectual challenges and meaningful connections. Whether you're competing in a friendly match or playing with friends over coffee, bridge has a way of turning every hand into an opportunity for creative thinking, collaboration, and—of course—fun.

Bridge is often described as the ultimate team game because it requires players to not only think ahead but also collaborate with their partners without speaking a word. The teamwork involved in bridge fosters a deep level of cooperation, as partners must learn each other's playing styles and strategize together. This collaboration enhances communication skills and helps sharpen your ability to read social cues.

The intellectual challenge of bridge lies in its complexity. With endless combinations of bidding, play, and defense strategies, each game is a mental workout that sharpens memory, enhances problem-solving skills, and improves critical thinking. The thrill of outmaneuvering your opponents and executing a well-planned strategy adds an extra layer of satisfaction to the game.

If you're passionate about bridge and want to bring others into the game, organizing a local bridge club can be a rewarding way to foster a sense of community. The first step is to gauge interest among your friends, neighbors, or members of your community. You'd be surprised how many people are eager to play or learn bridge. Spread the word by putting up flyers at community centers, posting on **Meetup.com**, and social media groups, or mentioning your idea during local events.

Once you have a few interested players, the next step is to find a venue. Many local libraries, community centers, or even coffee shops have spaces available for group activities. Choose a venue that is comfortable and accessible for all members. Then, establish a regular schedule—whether it's a weekly evening game or a monthly gathering, consistency helps build momentum and keeps people engaged.

Club rules are important for ensuring everyone has an enjoyable experience. Start by setting some basic guidelines, such as how to rotate partners, handle bidding disputes, or resolve ties. You don't have to be too rigid, but a few ground rules will ensure the club runs smoothly. As your club grows, you can add new members or expand into hosting small tournaments. It's all about creating a welcoming space where people can enjoy the game and socialize.

Starting a bridge club doesn't mean you have to figure everything out on your own. There are plenty of resources available to help new clubs thrive. One of the best places to start is with bridge teaching software and apps like **Bridge Baron** or **Funbridge**, which can help beginners learn the rules and improve their skills. These tools are useful for players who want to practice outside of club meetings.

Online forums and communities are also invaluable. Websites like **BridgeBase Online** or **Bridge Winners** offer forums where you can ask questions, discuss strategies, and even play virtual games with people from around the world. These platforms provide support and foster a larger sense of community among bridge enthusiasts.

For more formal support, consider affiliating your club with a national or local bridge organization, such as the **American Contract Bridge League (ACBL)**. These organizations offer resources for managing clubs, organizing tournaments, and providing official rankings for players. They can help you create a bridge club that is organized, inclusive, and part of a larger network of players.

With the right tools, a supportive community, and a little organization, your local bridge club can become a vibrant social hub that brings people together for both fun and intellectual stimulation.

3.8 Attending Workshops and Lectures

Are you a lifelong learner? Or looking for new ways to engage your curiosity? Attending workshops and lectures is another way to enrich your retirement. These events offer the opportunity to dive deeper into subjects you're passionate about or discover new ones you've never explored. The good news is that finding these events, both locally and virtually, has never been easier.

Start by checking out local resources like university websites, libraries, and community centers. Many institutions offer free or low-cost public lectures on everything from history and science to the arts and technology. Your local library might even host its own workshops or be able to direct you to events happening in your community. Organizations like museums, historical societies, and cultural centers frequently offer public talks or workshops that align with their missions.

For virtual events, platforms like **Eventbrite** or **Meetup** list thousands of online workshops and lectures on a broad range of topics. Universities and major cultural institutions, such as the **Smithsonian** or the **TED platform**, regularly offer virtual events you can access from anywhere. And don't forget about **YouTube** and **podcast platforms**, where you can find expert-led talks and lectures on practically any subject under the sun.

With so many events available, how do you choose the ones that are right for you? The key is to align your choices with both your current interests and your desire to explore new areas. Don't limit yourself to familiar territory. There's value in diversifying the subjects you engage with, as learning something entirely new can spark creativity and stimulate different areas of your brain. For example, if you typically enjoy science talks, why not attend a lecture on literature, art, or philosophy?

This variety keeps things interesting and broadens your perspectives, making you a more well-rounded thinker.

Once you've chosen an event, a little preparation can go a long way toward maximizing your experience. For in-person workshops or lectures, it might be helpful to do some preliminary reading on the subject. A quick article or a short video can give you context and help you follow along more easily during the event. If the workshop involves active participation, like a writing class or an art workshop, consider practicing beforehand or gathering the necessary materials. Being well-prepared allows you to fully immerse yourself in the learning experience, whether you're attending in person or online.

For virtual events, especially those involving interactive elements, it's important to get your tech in order. Here's a quick checklist to ensure you're ready:

- **Test your computer's audio and video** ahead of time. Make sure your microphone and camera work if the event involves interaction.

- **Check your internet connection** for stability. A dropped connection can interrupt the flow of a virtual event, so it's best to ensure everything is working smoothly beforehand.

- **Download any required software** early. Some events may require **Zoom, Microsoft Teams**, or another platform. Installing and testing these apps ahead of time can save you from scrambling at the last minute.

- **Set up a quiet, comfortable space** for yourself. Having a calm environment will help you stay focused and enjoy the experience.

One of the most satisfying aspects of attending a workshop or lecture is taking what you've learned and putting it into action. Don't let the knowledge slip away—applying it is key to reinforcing and deepening your understanding. If the event covered a practical skill, such as photography or creative writing, why not start a personal project? Set yourself a challenge, like writing a short story or taking a series of photographs, to practice what you've learned. If you attended a more academic lecture, consider writing a brief summary or reflection on what you found most interesting. This kind of review helps solidify the information and makes it easier to recall later.

You might also consider sharing what you learned with others. Teaching a new concept or skill to a friend, family member, or even a group can be an excellent way to reinforce your understanding while passing knowledge along. You could start a small discussion group with other retirees who share your interests—this can be a fun and social way to dive deeper into topics and keep the learning process alive. No matter how you choose to apply it, the knowledge gained from workshops and lectures is a powerful tool for personal growth and intellectual engagement. By taking the next step and putting that knowledge into practice, you'll find yourself continually growing and expanding your horizons during your retirement years.

As you continue to explore the many fulfilling activities that retirement offers, consider tapping into the creative side of life. While intellectual engagement keeps your mind sharp, creative expression nourishes your soul. Whether you've always dreamed of painting a masterpiece, learning to play an instrument, or finally writing that novel, the next chapter will guide you through the enriching world of art, music, and writing. These pursuits offer joy and personal satisfaction and open up new avenues for self-expression and connection with others, making them a perfect complement to your journey of lifelong learning and growing.

Chapter Four

Creative Expression: Finding Joy Through Imagination

There's nothing quite like being surrounded by paints, clay, or a blank canvas, with your favorite music gently playing in the background. The day is yours, and the possibilities for what you can create are endless. As a professional in design, I've always had a deep appreciation for all forms of art—whether it's visual arts like painting or sculpting, digital creations such as graphic design or photography, or musical and literary expression through writing and composing. Creative expression has always been a source of joy and inspiration for me, and I'm looking forward to spending more time exploring various artistic forms when I retire. These golden years are the perfect opportunity to immerse yourself in creativity through the vibrant world of colors, the rhythms of sound, or the power of storytelling and letting your imagination soar in new and exciting ways. Welcome to the world of creative expression, where your imagination knows no bounds and your golden years are filled with colors, textures, sounds, and endless possibilities.

4.1 Exploring Art Forms: From Painting to Digital Creativity

Art exploration brings an invigorating sense of discovery and creativity that can enhance life at any age, especially in retirement. Delving into various art forms awakens a world of personal expression that helps keep the mind sharp and the spirit engaged. Studies have shown that engaging in artistic pursuits can improve cognitive function, reduce stress, and boost emotional well-being, making it a perfect activity for seniors seeking joy and enrichment.

Exploring different art forms can be as exhilarating as discovering a hidden talent. From the fluidity of watercolor to the bold strokes of acrylic painting, each medium offers a unique way to express your personality and experiences. **Watercolor**, with its transparent layers and soft edges, is perfect for capturing the delicate beauty of nature. Start with high-quality watercolor paper, soft brushes, and a basic palette of paints. Experiment with techniques like wet-on-wet for dreamy blends, or wet-on-dry for sharp edges. **Acrylic painting**, on the other hand, dries quickly and can be used to create vibrant and textured pieces. You'll need a canvas, a variety of brushes (including flat and round), and a palette knife for adding texture. The fast-drying nature of acrylics allows for easy layering, making it ideal for bold, expressive works.

Sculpting and pottery bring a tactile dimension to art, allowing you to shape and mold different materials into tangible forms. For pottery, start with air-dry clay if you don't have a kiln, or invest in a small electric kiln and stoneware clay if you want to fire your pieces. Basic tools like wire cutters, loop tools, and rib tools will help you carve and shape your creations. Sculptors working with other mediums, such as stone or wood, will need specialized carving tools and safety equipment like goggles and gloves. There's immense satisfaction in creating something functional, like a vase, or purely decorative, like a whimsical sculpture, with your own hands.

The digital realm offers endless possibilities. **Digital art** allows for boundless experimentation without the mess. Tools like **Procreate.com** (for iPad) or **Adobe Photoshop** and **Illustrator** (for desktop) give you access to a wide range of brushes, colors, and effects that mimic traditional art forms, but with the added bonus of undo buttons and layers. Start with a drawing tablet or iPad with a stylus for hands-on control. Digital artists can experiment with everything from sketching and painting to graphic design and animation. Programs like **Corel Painter** emulate the experience of using real paints, while apps like **ArtRage** offer a more simplified, intuitive approach to digital creation. Beginners can explore their creativity with platforms like **Krita** (a free, open-source program), offering professional-grade tools at no cost.

Engaging in artistic activities brings a wealth of cognitive and emotional benefits. The act of creating art reduces stress and promotes relaxation, providing a therapeutic escape from daily worries. It's like a mini-vacation for your mind. Artistic expression also improves motor skills, especially fine motor coordination, as you manipulate brushes, pencils, or sculpting tools. The process of planning and executing a piece of art stimulates creativity and problem-solving skills, keeping your brain sharp and agile. Plus, there's a profound sense of accomplishment and joy that comes with seeing your finished work, a testament to your imagination and effort.

Setting up a home studio doesn't have to be difficult or require a lot of space. You can transform a corner of a room with good natural light into your creative haven. **For painting**, you'll need canvases, brushes, paints, and a palette. A sturdy easel is also helpful for larger works, while a flat table is ideal for smaller pieces or watercolors. **For pottery**, purchase a small electric kiln, a wheel if space allows, and a variety of clays and glazes. As mentioned earlier, air-dry clay is an easy option for beginners. **Sculptors** should organize their tools—chisels, gouges, files, and rasps—and ensure they have a sturdy work surface. **For digital artists**, a digital drawing tablet or iPad with a stylus, paired with art software will transform any corner into a high-tech studio. Keep your space organized and inspiring by adding personal touches like artwork, plants, or a pinboard for ideas. Remember, your studio should be a place where you feel free to experiment and express yourself without judgment.

Finding local art classes and communities can greatly enhance your artistic journey. Many community centers, senior centers, and local colleges offer classes in various art forms, providing a structured environment to learn new skills. These classes are taught by experienced instructors who offer guidance and constructive feedback. Online courses are also a great option, with platforms like **Skillshare**, **Udemy**, or **MasterClass** offering tutorials on everything from watercolor techniques to digital illustration. Joining an art group or a club is incredibly rewarding by sharing your work and drawing inspiration from others. Being part of a creative community creates a sense of belonging and motivation. You might find opportunities to exhibit your work in local galleries or participate in art fairs, showcasing your talent to a wider audience.

One of my favorite activities is working with watercolors on **Masa paper**, a unique Japanese paper that offers a different experience compared to traditional watercolor paper. Masa paper is soft, absorbent, and slightly textured, which allows the watercolor to flow and spread in a way that creates beautiful, organic effects. It gives the artwork a sense of depth and movement, making each piece feel alive. The way the paint interacts with the paper's fibers creates unpredictable but stunning results—perfect for capturing the fluidity of nature, which I love to explore.

For me, painting on Masa paper is more than just creating art—it's a meditative, zen-like practice that helps reduce any stress or worries. The delicate brushstrokes, the absorption of color, and the flow of the paint on the textured surface bring a sense of calm and presence. I've been drawing since I was a kid, and as I got older, I took classes to refine my skills, particularly in painting on Masa paper. The peaceful process of working on this paper, combined with the beauty of watercolors, offers a profound sense of satisfaction and relaxation. It's my way of disconnecting from the noise of the world and entering a space of quiet creativity, where the focus is on the simple joy of creating.

Take a moment to reflect on your artistic journey. What mediums intrigue you the most? What subjects inspire your creativity? Jot down your thoughts and perhaps sketch a few ideas. Keep this journal as a testament to your growth and exploration in the world of art.

Engaging in painting, pottery, sculpture, and digital arts opens up a world of creative possibilities, offering personal satisfaction and community connection. These activities invite you to explore, create, and share your unique vision with the world. Grab your brushes, mold that clay, and let your imagination soar!

4.2 Creating Melodies and Memories

Picture yourself standing on a stage, surrounded by friends, harmonizing beautifully as your voices blend into a symphony of sound. The audience is smiling, swaying to the rhythm. This isn't a professional concert, it's your local choir, and it could be one of the most fulfilling experiences of your retirement. Joining a local choir or band can be a beautiful way to fill your days with music and camaraderie. Local community centers, churches, and senior centers often host choirs and musical ensembles that welcome members of all skill levels. Are you a seasoned singer or someone who hums in the shower? Either way, these groups provide a supportive environment where you can share your love of music. And the regular rehearsals and performances give you something to look forward to, adding structure and excitement to your week.

The health benefits of singing and playing musical instruments are nothing short of remarkable. When taking a deep breath, filling your lungs, and letting out a powerful note, you improve your respiratory function and increase lung capacity. Singing and playing instruments also enhance cognitive abilities, as reading music and coordinating movements require mental sharpness. It's like giving your brain a workout while having a blast. Music has a magical way of lifting your spirits and increasing emotional well-being. It releases endorphins, the body's natural feel-good chemicals, which can alleviate stress and anxiety. There's a special joy in creating music, a sense of accomplishment that comes from mastering a piece or nailing a difficult note. And let's not forget the sheer fun of it all—music brings laughter and a sense of playfulness that can make you feel youthful and vibrant.

If singing isn't quite your thing, or if it has already sparked your love for music, why not learn to play an instrument? Choosing an instrument to learn is a deeply personal and exciting journey. Start by thinking about the types of sounds that resonate with you. Reflect on the music you naturally gravitate towards—do you enjoy the smooth tones of jazz, the vibrant beats of rock, or the calming chords of folk? Different genres often highlight specific instruments, which could be a helpful hint in narrowing down your choice. If you're still unsure, try sampling a few instruments before committing. Many music stores allow visitors to try out instruments, so don't hesitate to ask for a demonstration. You can also watch online videos to get a feel for different sounds and the playing style each instrument demands.

Consider your lifestyle and physical preferences, too. Some instruments require regular upkeep, like a violin or saxophone, while others, like a keyboard, need less maintenance. Think about the physical aspects as well: if you're concerned about dexterity, instruments with simpler finger positions, like the ukulele, might be a good starting point. Ask yourself how you envision playing your instrument. Do you want to play solo pieces or join a local group? If you're dreaming of playing along with others, a versatile instrument like the guitar or keyboard can open up more collaborative opportunities. Above all, let your intuition guide you—choosing an instrument that excites you is the best way to stay motivated and enjoy the learning process.

Once you've selected your instrument, it's time to dive into learning. Look for a music teacher experienced with adult learners, someone who tailors lessons to accommodate your pace and style. Many local music schools offer beginner classes, and you can even explore online platforms that cater specifically to new players. Apps like **You-**

sician and **Simply Piano** provide interactive tutorials and exercises, while **YouTube** offers a treasure trove of free lessons for every instrument imaginable. Joining a community ensemble or jam group can add a layer of joy to your practice, where the feedback and encouragement from fellow musicians will keep you motivated. With each song you learn, you'll discover the joy of musical expression and the thrill of mastering a skill that brings beauty to your life, and to those who listen.

Once you've begun to develop your skills and feel more comfortable with your instrument, share the joy of music by organizing informal music nights with friends or community members. Picture a cozy evening where everyone brings an instrument or simply their voice, ready to make music and memories. Nobody needs to be a virtuoso to enjoy these gatherings—just a willingness to participate and have fun. Start by setting a regular date and inviting friends who share your interest in music. Choose a mix of familiar songs and new pieces to keep things interesting. Provide sheet music or lyrics so everyone can join in, regardless of their skill level. Create a supportive atmosphere where everyone feels comfortable sharing their talents, whether they're playing a solo, singing a duet, or joining a group chorus. The focus should be on enjoyment and connection, rather than perfection. These music nights can become a cherished tradition, a time to unwind, express yourself, and bond with others over the universal language of music.

I learned to play both piano and guitar early in life. As life got busier, my focus shifted to other pursuits, especially visual arts. Still, music has always been part of our home. We keep a keyboard in the living room, and my husband—who also learned to play as a child—often sits down to improvise melodies, filling our home with warm, spontaneous sounds. With retirement on the horizon, he's excited to spend more time developing his skills and exploring composition, diving deeper into the joy of creating music. For both of us, these musical moments have become a way to connect, reflect, and share something we love, and it's inspiring to think about what's possible as we step into this new chapter.

4.3 Photography Classes: Capturing Life's Moments

Photography opens a unique window into the world, inviting you to see beauty in the small, often overlooked moments of everyday life. It's an art that allows you to capture the warmth of a grandchild's smile, the serene hues of a setting sun, or the delicate intricacies of a blooming flower—all while inviting you to pause and observe more deeply. Unlike a fleeting glance, a photograph transforms a single moment into a lasting memory, one you can revisit and share with others. As you learn to master a camera, you'll begin to notice how light dances across different surfaces, how shadows add drama to familiar scenes, and how the world changes from morning to night. Photography not only enhances your appreciation for the world around you but also offers a creative outlet that can be deeply fulfilling. Each photograph becomes a way to tell a story, to communicate an emotion, and to connect with others, capturing experiences that, through your lens, become timeless.

Photography is not only a creative pursuit but it also offers remarkable benefits for mental sharpness and physical vitality. The act of composing a shot, focusing on details, and processing images stimulates cognitive functions, helping to keep the mind sharp. It encourages physical movement as well, whether it's walking to find the perfect vantage point or adjusting your posture to capture a unique angle. In this way, photography nurtures both mental agility and gentle physical activity, making it an ideal hobby for anyone looking to stay engaged, active, and inspired.

Choosing the right equipment is the first step on this exciting path. If you're aiming for professional-quality shots, a **DSLR** (Digital Single-Lens Reflex) camera offers versatility with interchangeable lenses and manual controls. Brands like **Canon** and **Nikon** are reliable options. For those who prefer something lighter but equally capable, mirrorless cameras from brands like **Sony** and **Fujifilm** provide high-quality images without the bulk. However, don't underestimate the power of a good smartphone camera. Modern smartphones like the **iPhone** or **Samsung Galaxy** boast impressive photography capabilities and are perfect for spontaneous shots. The key is to match your choice of equipment with your photography goals and budget, ensuring you get the most out of your investment.

Once you have your camera in hand, the next step is to learn some basic photography techniques. Composition is the backbone of any great photo. The rule of thirds is a simple yet powerful guideline: imagine your frame divided into nine equal parts by two horizontal and two vertical lines. Placing your subject along these lines or at their intersections creates a balanced and engaging image. Lighting is another crucial element. Natural light, especially during the golden hour (shortly after sunrise or before sunset), can add a magical quality to your photos. Avoid harsh midday sun that casts unflattering shadows. Instead, seek out soft, diffused light for more even illumination. Angling your shots from different perspectives, such as getting low to the ground or shooting from above, can add depth and interest to your photos. Experiment with these techniques to find what works best for your style.

To build a solid foundation, consider exploring online courses or local workshops. Websites like **Udemy, Skillshare,** and **MasterClass** offer beginner-friendly photography courses that cover everything from camera settings to editing techniques, often led by professional photographers. Local community colleges and art centers frequently offer in-person classes, which can provide hands-on experience and personalized feedback. Some nature or travel organizations also run photography workshops, giving you the chance to practice in beautiful settings with expert guidance. These resources offer a wealth of knowledge to help you elevate your skills and develop your unique photographic eye.

Editing and organizing your photos is where the magic happens. Basic photo editing tools like **Adobe Lightroom** or free alternatives like **GIMP** can enhance your images, allowing you to adjust brightness, contrast, and color balance. Start with simple edits to improve overall quality, such as cropping out distractions or straightening a tilted horizon. Organizing your digital photos is equally important to prevent them from becoming a chaotic mess. Create folders by date or event, and use tags to make searching easier. Cloud storage services like **Google Photos** or **Apple iCloud** offer convenient ways to back up and access your photos from any device. By keeping your photos organized, you can easily find and enjoy your treasured memories without sifting through countless files.

Sharing and displaying your photos is the final touch that brings your creative efforts to life. Online galleries, such as those on **Flickr** or **Instagram**, provide platforms to showcase your work to a broader audience. These platforms also offer the opportunity to connect with other photography enthusiasts, gain feedback, and participate in contests. Social media is a great way to share your photos with friends and family, keeping them updated on your adventures and creative projects. For those who prefer tangible displays, creating physical albums or prints can be incredibly satisfying. Many online services offer customizable photo books, prints on canvas, or calendars featuring your best shots. Imagine flipping through a beautifully printed album filled with photos from your travels or seeing your favorite image proudly displayed on your living room wall. These physical mementos not only preserve your memories but also serve as daily reminders of the beauty you've captured.

Photography opens up a world of creative expression where every click of the shutter can tell a story, evoke emotions, and freeze moments in time. With the right equipment, a grasp of basic techniques, and a knack for editing and organizing, you can create stunning images that reflect your unique perspective. And by sharing and displaying your photos, you invite others to see the world through your eyes.

4.4 Crafting Stories: Creative Writing Workshops

Engaging in creative writing can be one of the most rewarding ways to explore and preserve the richness of life's experiences. For many, the urge to write stems from a desire to capture meaningful memories, share wisdom, or simply express emotions and thoughts that words make more vivid. Creative writing allows you to turn life's journey into stories, reflections, and insights, giving voice to the moments that have shaped you. Through various forms of writing—whether it's memoirs, poetry, fiction, or essays—each genre offers a unique outlet. Memoirs provide a way to revisit past events, honoring both the joys and challenges that have defined you. Poetry distills feelings and moments into words that can be as healing as they are expressive. Fiction invites you to imagine characters and worlds, and non-fiction allows you to share knowledge, ideas, or perspectives you're passionate about.

For seniors, creative writing is especially valuable. It sharpens the mind, enhances emotional resilience, and gives a lasting legacy to family and friends. In a workshop setting, guided exercises help you experiment with styles, refine your voice, and bring depth to your writing. Crafting a poem, weaving a story, or capturing real-life reflections can open new pathways to connection and self-expression, making creative writing a profound way to enrich this chapter of life.

Sitting down in a room filled with people, each carrying their own unique stories, can spark a remarkable journey into the world of creative writing. Writing workshops offer a fantastic way to explore different genres and styles. They are structured to provide a nurturing environment where you can improve your skills and gain confidence. Typically, workshops involve a combination of writing exercises, group discussions, and peer critiques. The feedback you receive from fellow participants and instructors is invaluable—it helps you see your work from different perspectives and identify areas for improvement. Workshops also foster a sense of community and camaraderie among writers, creating a supportive network that encourages you to keep writing. Regular attendance keeps you motivated and disciplined, turning writing from a solitary activity into a social and interactive experience.

For those times when inspiration seems elusive, creative writing prompts and exercises can be useful tools to spark creativity and help you dive into new perspectives. Try envisioning a day in the life of someone completely different from you, or writing a story that begins with a surprise discovery in an unexpected place. Challenge yourself to describe a memory using only sensory details—what did you hear, smell, and feel in that moment? Or imagine crafting a letter to a loved one who's no longer here, sharing something you wish you'd said. A simple prompt like "Write about a day in the life of your favorite childhood toy" can lead to unexpected and delightful stories. These prompts open doors to fresh ideas, emotions, and memories, making every writing session an exploration. These exercises stimulate the imagination and encourage you to think outside the box. The goal is to get your creative juices flowing and push the boundaries of your imagination. These prompts can be used outside of workshops as well, providing a handy tool to keep you writing regularly. They can be found in books, online resources, or even created by you, tailored to your interests and experiences.

Publishing your work is an exciting possibility that brings your writing to a broader audience. Whether you dream of seeing your name in print or simply want to share your stories with friends and family, there are numerous avenues to explore. Community newsletters and local publications often welcome submissions from amateur writers, providing a platform to get your work out there. Blogs offer a flexible and accessible way to share your writing online, allowing you to reach readers all over the world. If you're interested in a more formal approach, self-publishing platforms like **Amazon Kindle Direct Publishing** or **Lulu** enable you to publish your books. These platforms guide you through the process, from formatting your manuscript to designing a cover and setting your book's price. Self-publishing gives you complete control over your work and the satisfaction of holding a printed copy of your book in your hands. Navigating the publishing world can seem daunting, but with a bit of research and perseverance, you can find the right path for your writing.

Creative writing workshops open up a world of possibilities, inviting you to explore different genres, improve your skills, and share your stories. They provide a supportive community and structured environment that turns writing into a joyful and rewarding activity. With the right prompts and exercises, you can overcome any creative blocks and keep your imagination alive. And when you're ready, publishing opportunities await, offering the chance to share your unique voice with a wider audience. Open your notebook or your laptop, let your imagination run wild, and see where your words can take you.

As you explore creative expression, you're not only diving deeper into your passions and talents but also opening doors to share these discoveries with others. Art, music, writing, and crafting all have a unique way of connecting us—sparking conversations, bridging generational gaps, and creating shared experiences that can transform solitary pursuits into communal joys. In the next chapter, we'll look at how building new connections can foster a supportive network and enrich your life.

Chapter Five

Socializing and Building New Connections

Retirement marks the beginning of a social renaissance, a time to rediscover former connections and build new ones in fulfilling and fun ways. This stage of life offers endless possibilities to expand your social circles: hosting parties at home, joining local clubs, attending online meetups, or exploring the world of dating. From community events and book clubs to virtual interest groups and travel companions, there's no shortage of ways to stay connected and engaged. These activities bring joy and laughter and enrich daily life, infusing each day with fresh energy and perspective. The beauty of retirement is having the freedom to embrace the kinds of connections that add meaning and excitement to every season.

5.1 Hosting Parties and Theme Nights

Hosting parties and theme nights brings joyful energy to any gathering, transforming your home or chosen venue into a vibrant space where friends, family, and new acquaintances come together to socialize, laugh, and create lasting memories. Think of yourself as an artist, and your event as a canvas. Start by choosing a theme that sets the atmosphere for the gathering. It can be a cozy autumn dinner with pumpkin soup and warm apple pie, or a tropical luau complete with leis, a Piña Colada bar, and fresh pineapple centerpieces. Each theme creates an opportunity to make your event unique and memorable.

Once you have a theme, bring it to life with thoughtful décor. For a rustic autumn gathering, consider plaid table runners, cinnamon-scented candles, and mini pumpkins to create a warm, inviting space. A luau could feature vibrant sarongs, seashells, and bright hibiscus flowers for a tropical vibe. Music is key to setting the mood, so curate a playlist on **Spotify** or another streaming service to match the theme—mellow jazz for a dinner party or lively island tunes for a luau. If you're planning a dance night, explore genres that suit the energy you want to create, like upbeat swing, classic rock, or rhythmic salsa.

The types of gatherings you can host are as varied as your imagination. Classic dinner parties offer an intimate setting for meaningful conversations and can be tailored to any theme, from a cozy Italian night with pasta and wine to a tapas-style Spanish evening. Themed parties add an extra layer of fun! Try a 70s disco night, an elegant masquerade, or a tropical luau complete with Hawaiian shirts and tiki drinks. Game nights bring laughter and light-hearted competition, perfect for playing classics like charades and trivia, or organizing a mini-casino night with poker and blackjack. For book lovers, hosting an author-themed dinner where guests bring food inspired by their favorite novels can create a unique twist. If you prefer the great outdoors, a garden picnic or a backyard BBQ offers a relaxed way to enjoy good company and beautiful weather. By catering to different interests and social circles, you ensure there's something for everyone to enjoy and remember.

Food and drinks play a central role in any gathering. For themed events, consider potluck-style dining where guests bring dishes that complement the theme, like hearty stews and crusty bread for an autumn dinner or tropical fruit skewers and coconut desserts for a luau. Accommodate diverse dietary needs by offering vegetarian, gluten-free, and allergy-friendly options. Don't forget non-alcoholic drink choices like sparkling water with fresh fruit, mocktails, or a "make-your-own" soda bar with different syrups and garnishes. These thoughtful touches help ensure everyone feels comfortable and included.

Few activities bring people together more than dancing. Moving to the rhythm, sharing laughter, and embracing the joy of dance create bonds that go beyond words. Dancing not only provides a fun social experience but also a fantastic workout, enhancing cardiovascular health, balance, and flexibility, all of which are beneficial as we age. The variety of dance styles—ballroom, line dancing, salsa, or swing—ensures there's something everyone can enjoy. Dance nights can be the centerpiece of your gathering or a spontaneous addition to any evening, infusing energy and joy into the atmosphere.

Dance nights are easy to organize and can be hosted almost anywhere—a spacious living room, community hall, or a backyard. Make sure the floor is smooth and obstacle-free for safe dancing. Arrange seating around the perimeter for those who want to take breaks, and decorate the space to fit your theme. A live band adds a special touch, but a well-chosen playlist can also create the perfect vibe. For extra flair, add a few themed decorations or set up a DIY photo booth for guests to capture memories. Consider offering a brief dance lesson at the start of the evening to encourage everyone to join in, especially those who might be shy or uncertain of their dancing skills. You can often find local dance instructors through community centers or online platforms like **Meetup** and **Facebook groups**. Introducing everyone to a few basic steps helps break the ice and gets the night off to a lively start.

Creating an inclusive environment is essential. Ensure your space is easy to navigate for guests with mobility issues, with ample seating and open pathways. Choose music with a range of tempos so everyone can find something to dance to, and provide cozy blankets or fans if your event is outdoors. Minor considerations like these show your guests that their comfort and enjoyment are important to you.

Leverage technology to make organizing and hosting easier. Digital invitations from platforms like **Evite** or **Paperless Post** add elegance to your event planning. Music streaming services let you tailor the soundtrack to your theme, while video calls can bring distant friends and family into the celebration, no matter where they are. Create a shared online photo album where guests can upload their snapshots, giving everyone a digital keepsake of the night.

Hosting parties and dance nights goes beyond the events themselves; it's about building connections, creating joy, and turning your home into a place of shared happiness. The gatherings you host, whether it's a lively dance night, an intimate dinner, or a themed event, invite friends and family to come together, socialize, and celebrate. These occasions become cherished memories, adding richness and community to your life in retirement.

5.2 Sharing Stories and Opinions in Book and Film Clubs

Gathering with friends who share your love for stories is a special time. Book and film clubs offer a chance to dive deep into conversations that inspire, entertain, and challenge. And starting your own club is not that difficult. Begin by inviting friends, neighbors, or former colleagues who enjoy a good book or a thought-provoking film. Spread the word at local community centers, libraries, or social media groups, and soon you'll have a lively circle of members. Set a meeting schedule that suits everyone, whether monthly or bi-weekly and start building your list of books and films to explore. Keep the lineup diverse—a classic novel one month, a contemporary thriller, or an inspiring documentary the next. This variety keeps discussions fresh and ensures there's something to captivate everyone.

Facilitating discussions in your club can be a breeze with a few thoughtful guidelines. Start with open-ended questions that invite everyone to share their perspectives. For books, you might ask, *"How did the protagonist evolve throughout the story, and what drove that change?"* or *"What underlying themes resonated with you, and why?"* For films, questions like, *"How did the cinematography or score enhance the mood of the film?"* or *"What symbolic moments or motifs caught your attention?"* can spark deeper conversations. You could also explore connections by asking, *"Did any of the characters or situations remind you of real-life experiences or people?"* or *"How might this story be different if set in today's world?"* Ensure everyone has a chance to speak by gently steering the discussion and keeping an eye on clock-watchers who might not speak up on their own. Respect is key. Remind members to listen actively and avoid interrupting. Everyone's opinion is valuable, and it's these diverse perspectives that make discussions so rich.

Integrating technology can enhance and enrich your club experience. Organize virtual meetings via video calls, especially if members are spread out geographically or have mobility issues. Platforms like **Zoom** or **Google Meet** are user-friendly and offer features like screen sharing, which can be great for film clubs wanting to watch trailers or clips together. Social media groups or messaging apps like **WhatsApp** can be used to share additional resources, such as articles, interviews with authors or directors, and discussion questions. These tools also allow for ongoing conversations between meetings, keeping the excitement alive. Imagine watching a film at home, then jumping into an online chat to share your initial thoughts—instant engagement!

Additional club activities can further enrich the experience and deepen social bonds. Plan outings to attend film screenings at local theaters, especially for new releases or special showings of classic films. Arrange meetings with local authors to discuss their books; many writers are thrilled to share their insights and answer reader questions. Host themed nights where everyone dresses up related to the book or film. For instance, don flapper dresses and tuxedos for a "Great Gatsby" evening, channel your inner detective with a Sherlock Holmes mystery night, or step back into the 1950s for a "Grease" movie night, complete with poodle skirts and leather jackets. For a literary touch, try an Agatha Christie murder mystery party, with guests portraying characters from her famous novel "Murder on the Orient Express." And you can celebrate historical periods with "Downton Abbey" themed evenings or a classic Western film night featuring cowboy hats and boots.

Few things compare to the thrill of unpacking a novel's twist or dissecting a film's visuals with a group that's just as invested as you are. Book and film clubs create a space where stories come alive through shared insights, laughter, and the occasional debate. These gatherings are as much about building connections as they are about the stories themselves.

5.3 Dance Lessons: In Rhythm with Your Community

Exploring dance lessons or joining a dance school can open doors to new friendships, healthy movement, and endless fun. Whether you're interested in the formal ballroom, energetic salsa, laid-back swing, or upbeat line dancing, there's a dance style for every taste and ability. Dance schools and clubs provide structured environments where you can learn, grow, and share the joy of movement with others who love to dance.

Before embarking on a new dance journey, it's wise to check in with your doctor, especially if you have joint issues, arthritis, or other health concerns. Dancing is generally a low-impact exercise that promotes flexibility, balance, and cardiovascular health, making it a fantastic choice for retirees. However, certain movements—like quick turns, jumps, or repetitive steps—can put stress on the joints. Consulting a healthcare provider allows you to choose a dance style and intensity level that aligns with your fitness and mobility. Your doctor may recommend gentle styles like ballroom or line dancing, which provide all the benefits of movement with less impact on the joints. Don't hesitate to communicate any physical limitations to your instructor; they can offer modified steps to help you enjoy dancing safely.

Your search for the perfect dance school or club can start in your local area. Many community centers, recreation facilities, and gyms offer beginner-friendly dance classes, so check their schedules for lessons that catch your interest. Dance studios often specialize in particular styles, from tango to hip hop to salsa, and frequently welcome beginners with no prior experience. Ask for a trial class if you're curious about a style but aren't ready to commit. Websites like **Meetup,**

Facebook Events, or **Eventbrite** also make it easy to find local dance clubs or themed events. For more structured programs, look into adult education programs, as some offer affordable dance courses open to the public.

Starting dance lessons might feel daunting, but most dance schools cater to various skill levels, from absolute beginners to seasoned dancers. Begin by choosing a class labeled as "beginner" or "introductory." These classes usually start with the fundamentals, such as learning basic steps, understanding rhythm, and coordinating movements with a partner if the style involves it. Expect a supportive, social atmosphere as dance instructors encourage camaraderie and create a relaxed environment where everyone feels comfortable learning. Classes are typically structured to build skills progressively, so you'll feel yourself improving and becoming more confident with each session.

When deciding on a style, think about the vibe and physical level that appeals to you. **Ballroom dance** offers an elegant and structured experience, where you can learn classics like the waltz, foxtrot, or tango. If you're drawn to something with a livelier beat, **Latin dances** like salsa or bachata deliver fast-paced footwork and vibrant music, making it a great choice for those who enjoy an energetic atmosphere. **Swing dance** brings a fun, jazzy feel perfect for upbeat personalities, while **line dancing** provides a more casual, social style where everyone dances in unison. The key is to choose a style that resonates with your personality and energy level. Many people find that exploring a few different styles helps them discover what they truly enjoy.

Once you've chosen a school or club, commit to regular classes or events to get the most from your experience. Regular participation allows you to build your skills, but it's also a way to become part of the dance community. Dance clubs often host social gatherings, practice nights, or themed events, providing plenty of chances to meet new friends and try out your skills in a supportive setting. Attending these events can help reinforce what you're learning in lessons and add an extra layer of fun to your dance journey.

Consider investing in comfortable dance shoes designed for your chosen style as they provide the support and movement you'll need on the dance floor. Many studios can recommend where to find affordable options that suit both beginners and regular dancers. Dressing comfortably and confidently is also key; while some dance styles have specific attire, most studios recommend clothing that allows you to move freely without restriction.

One of the best aspects of joining a dance school or club is the social connection it brings. Dance lessons create a shared experience, helping people bond over common interests and challenges. Whether it's the satisfaction of mastering a new step or the laughter following a misstep, dancing with others cultivates a unique sense of camaraderie. Don't be afraid to chat with classmates or attend studio events—most dancers are friendly and supportive, eager to welcome new faces. These social connections often extend beyond the dance floor, as many clubs and schools organize group outings, dinners, or performances that build lasting friendships.

As you progress, you may feel ready to try intermediate or advanced classes, explore new dance styles, or participate in performances or showcases offered by the studio. Some schools hold semi-annual or annual events where students can showcase what they've learned, adding excitement and a sense of accomplishment to the dance experience. Many dancers find joy in the continuous journey of learning, improving, and sharing their love of dance with others. Dancing is about having fun and expressing yourself, so embrace each step as part of the adventure! By joining a dance school or taking lessons, you're not just learning new steps—you're joining a community, building confidence, and opening yourself up to a world of rhythm, connection, and joy.

5.4 Connecting Online in Virtual Meetups

With today's technology, connecting with friends and joining lively discussions has never been easier, no matter where you are. Virtual meetups bring people together from across the globe, allowing you to build vibrant online communities right from home. While online socializing might seem unfamiliar to those who didn't grow up with smartphones or laptops, there are plenty of simple, user-friendly platforms that make it a breeze. Tools like **Zoom** and **Skype** are designed with straightforward setups and include interactive features like screen sharing and breakout rooms to keep your virtual gatherings dynamic and engaging. **Facebook Messenger** offers video calling, so staying in touch with loved ones is just a few clicks away.

One platform that stands out for organizing both in-person and virtual activities is **Meetup.com**. This social media site is a treasure trove of groups centered around various interests, hobbies, and professions. Whether you're passionate about knitting, hiking, or discussing the latest bestseller, you'll likely find a group that suits your interests. Joining is simple—create a profile, browse through the available groups, and hit the "Join" button. Before you know it, you'll be receiving invitations to virtual book discussions, game nights, and fitness classes. Meetup.com's user-friendly interface makes it easy to RSVP, receive notifications, and keep track of upcoming events. It's like having a personal social calendar at your fingertips.

Speaking of virtual activities, the possibilities are endless. Imagine hosting a virtual book discussion where everyone logs on from their cozy reading nooks, ready to dive into a spirited conversation about the latest novel. Or picture a game night where you and your friends engage in a friendly competition of online trivia or digital board games. For those with niche hobbies, consider starting a hobby group where you can share tips, showcase your projects, and learn from others. Virtual meetups can also include cooking classes, language exchange sessions, and virtual travel tours. The key is to choose activities that engage everyone and foster a sense of community, even through a screen.

Building and maintaining online communities is an art. To ensure that everyone feels welcomed and respected, start by setting clear guidelines. Encourage open communication and active participation by creating discussion threads, sharing resources, and organizing regular virtual meetups. Use social media groups or messaging apps to keep the conversation going between meetings. Platforms like **Facebook Groups** or **WhatsApp** can be excellent for this purpose. Regularly check in with members to see how they're doing and what they'd like to see more of. Creating a welcoming and inclusive atmosphere is crucial for the success of any online community.

Virtual engagement offers many benefits, especially for those with mobility issues or living in remote areas. It provides a way to maintain social connections and reduce feelings of isolation without the need for travel. If you live in a rural area where social opportunities are limited, virtual meetups can be a lifeline to the outside world. They offer a sense of belonging and community, allowing you to participate in activities and discussions that might not be available locally. Plus, the convenience of logging in from home means you can join in your pajamas if you like!

5.5 Rediscovering Romance in Retirement

Rediscovering romance in retirement can feel like a fresh, exciting chapter, where every moment offers a sense of renewal. Retirement presents unique challenges and opportunities for deepening connections, rekindling affection, and building new shared experiences with your partner. On one hand, you have the freedom to explore relationships without the constraints of a demanding work-life balance. On the other, differing life experiences and past relationships can add layers of complexity. But this phase of life also offers a chance to connect deeply, free from the pressures that once weighed on you. With more time on your hands, you can focus on building a relationship based on mutual interests, shared adventures, and genuine companionship. Whether rekindling an existing flame or forging new connections, the possibilities of romancing in retirement are many.

Navigating online dating might seem like venturing into uncharted waters. What makes it less intimidating is that many sites and apps cater specifically to seniors, such as **OurTime**, **SilverSingles**, and **eHarmony**. Start by creating a profile that reflects your true self. Be honest about your interests, hobbies, and what you're looking for in a partner. Privacy is paramount, so choose a username that doesn't reveal too much about you and take advantage of the site's privacy settings. When it comes to first meetings, choose a public place and let a friend or family member know where you'll be. Keep the initial meetings short and sweet—think coffee or a light lunch, allowing you to gauge compatibility without feeling overwhelmed.

Shared activities are the heartbeat of any thriving relationship. Imagine spending a Saturday morning in a cooking class, learning to whip up a gourmet meal together. Or perhaps you both enjoy staying active—consider signing up for dance classes or taking long, leisurely walks in the park. Travel is another fantastic way to bond. Exploring new destinations, experiencing different cultures, and creating memories together can strengthen your connection. Even simple activities like gardening or attending community events can provide opportunities for quality time and shared experiences. The key is to find activities you both enjoy, fostering a sense of teamwork and mutual enjoyment.

Maintaining independence in a relationship is crucial for its health and longevity. It's important to remember that while you share many aspects of your life, you're still individuals with your own interests and social circles. Encourage each other to pursue personal hobbies and spend time with friends. This enriches your life and brings fresh perspectives and stories to share. Balancing togetherness with independence creates a healthy dynamic where both partners feel valued and fulfilled. It ensures that the relationship enhances your life, rather than becoming the sole focus of it.

Rediscovering romance in retirement is about embracing the freedom to explore love without constraints. It's about finding joy in shared activities while maintaining your independence. Whether you're navigating online dating or deepening an existing relationship, the possibilities for connection and companionship are boundless. So, take the plunge, open your heart, and let romance add a new sparkle to your golden years.

In these golden years, cultivating social connections and embracing romance bring a unique richness to your life. Gathering friends around a lively dinner table, rekindling old friendships, or exploring the excitement of newfound romance, all these relationships add warmth, laughter, and a sense of belonging to every day. These moments of connection remind us of the joy in shared experiences and the comfort of companionship.

As we delve further into this stage of life, there's another thrilling path to explore—one that reaches beyond personal connections and taps into the spirit of community. Retirement is a chance to channel your time and talents into causes that matter, to strengthen bonds within your community, and to contribute in ways that bring purpose and impact. So, let's turn the page and discover how meaningful engagement can shape this journey, transforming retirement into a time of growth, generosity, and connection with the world around you.

Chapter Six

Community Engagement and Leadership

Retirement offers a unique chance to engage with your community in meaningful ways, by sharing your expertise, exploring new roles, or building connections that enrich both your life and the lives of those around you. Perhaps you'll lead a neighborhood initiative, volunteer at local charities, or mentor others, bringing your skills and passions to light in impactful ways. Stepping into community involvement and leadership is about reigniting a sense of purpose, making connections, and transforming retirement into a time of fulfillment and growth. In this chapter, we'll explore how community engagement can be both rewarding and empowering, helping you build lasting connections and make a meaningful impact.

6.1 Volunteering: A Powerful Way to Give Back and Connect with Your Community

We've all seen people out there cleaning up beaches or planting flowers along a walking path in a park. Maybe you've noticed volunteers helping at local events or lending their skills to support community projects. Volunteering in retirement is about giving back, staying active, meeting new people, and adding more excitement to your day. Whether it's lending a hand at a community event, sharing your career skills with a nonprofit, or simply spending a morning making a park more beautiful, each small act brings people together and gives your day a boost of purpose.

There's something out there for everyone when it comes to volunteering. Love animals? Local shelters are always looking for help. Have a knack for teaching? Libraries and schools could use you to tutor or mentor students. If you're coming from a healthcare career, hospitals have volunteer roles where you can offer companionship to patients or help with admin tasks. Whatever you're into, there's a place that needs it. And if you have a specialized skill, like finance, law, or business, your knowledge can be a lifeline for local organizations that could use expert guidance. The best part? You're keeping your mind sharp while doing something truly amazing.

Volunteering has you covered no matter if you're a routine-lover or a spur-of-the-moment type. If you like consistency, there are roles where you can volunteer weekly or monthly—like helping at a food bank or reading to kids at a library. If you like variety, you can try different one-off opportunities, such as working on a local environmental project or lending a hand at community events here and there. Either way, you're contributing, and you get to choose a setup that works for your lifestyle.

Finding volunteer gigs that match your interests is easy. Community centers, libraries, animal shelters, and schools are great places to start. Or, check out online resources like **VolunteerMatch**, which lets you search for opportunities that align with your interests. A quick phone call or visit to a community board can connect you to projects you'd enjoy. Sometimes, all you need to do is reach out and let folks know you're interested. They'll be thrilled to have you on board!

One of the best things about volunteering is that you're never doing it alone. You become part of a community of people who share your interests and are just as eager to lend a hand. Volunteering is one of those rare activities where everyone benefits: you're helping others, connecting with people, and bringing a fresh sense of purpose to your days. It's not about how much time you can give, but the impact you can make. Even a few hours a month can mean so much. Retirement opens the door to new experiences, and volunteering is a meaningful, rewarding way to spend that time. And one of the best ways to dive in? Start with seasonal events and local festivals. These community gatherings bring people together in celebration, and they're always in need of enthusiastic volunteers.

6.2 Participating in Seasonal Local Events and Festivals

Seasonal festivals have always held a special place in my heart. There's something magical about the way each season brings its unique celebrations. In the fall, I enjoy visiting local harvest fairs, where the abundance of crops is on full display. Rows of vibrant pumpkins, freshly picked apples, and tables filled with homemade jams and pies create a rich tapestry of the season's bounty. Winter brings cozy holiday markets, filled with the warmth of spiced cider and festive lights twinkling in the evening sky. Spring is a time of renewal, with garden shows and flower festivals that celebrate nature's rebirth, while summer offers open-air concerts, food fairs, and lively parades that make the most of long, sunny days. Attending these events fills each season with excitement and connection, turning the passage of time into a series of shared experiences. By creating your seasonal calendar, you can immerse yourself in the beauty of local festivals and discover new ways to enjoy your community throughout the year.

But why just attend when you can actively participate? Volunteering at local events and festivals not only immerses you in the community spirit but also gives you a deeper sense of purpose and connection. Imagine being part of a local festival—perhaps you're helping to set up stalls, greeting attendees, or managing a schedule of live performances. These roles may seem small, but they're the heartbeat of any successful event, and they offer a front-row seat to the community's energy and creativity.

If you're crafty or enjoy cooking, consider setting up a booth at a farmer's market, artisan fair, or a fundraising event. Selling homemade jams, baked goods, or hand-crafted items lets you share your passions while helping a charity and striking up conversations with visitors and other vendors. It's a perfect way to meet like-minded people, share skills, and become woven into the local fabric. For those with a love of performing, local festivals often need talent for everything from musical acts to storytelling sessions. Volunteering as a singer in a community choir, acting in a small theater production, or joining a band adds excitement and camaraderie. The thrill of performing and the joy of being part of a team create unforgettable memories and build strong friendships. Helping with event logistics is another rewarding way to volunteer. From organizing schedules and coordinating vendors to decorating spaces and managing clean-up, you'll gain behind-the-scenes insights into how festivals come to life. Imagine the pride of seeing an event unfold successfully, knowing you played a part in making it happen. The friendships and connections you build through these roles often last long beyond the event itself.

Each year, my husband and I volunteer at local jazz and blues festivals. It's the perfect fit for our schedule, lifestyle, and love of music. It's very special to be behind the scenes, setting up for performances, and seeing the excitement build as crowds gather. Working side by side with others who appreciate the same music creates an easy camaraderie, and by the end of each event, we find ourselves with new friends and great stories to share. It's not just volunteering; it's an experience we look forward to every year.

Engaging in seasonal activities offers a host of benefits beyond mere entertainment. Staying connected with the community rhythm helps you feel more anchored and involved. These events provide a rich tapestry of experiences, from diverse cultural festivals that broaden your horizons to educational workshops that keep your mind sharp. Each season brings its unique offerings, ensuring your social calendar remains vibrant and varied. These activities bring together people of all ages and backgrounds, fostering a sense of unity and shared values.

Safety and accessibility are crucial considerations to ensure you enjoy these events comfortably. Start with practical attire—comfortable shoes for walking, layers for changing weather, and a hat for sun protection. If you have mobility issues, look for events that offer accessible facilities, such as ramps, seating areas, and accessible restrooms. Many events provide maps and guides highlighting accessible routes and services. It's also wise to plan your transportation, whether it's ensuring there's parking close by or using public transport that accommodates your needs. Staying hydrated and taking regular breaks can make a world of difference, especially during longer events. And always have a small first-aid kit handy, just in case.

Holiday markets, summer fairs, and seasonal festivals bring communities together in a unique way—and behind every one of these events is a team of volunteers making it all happen. Volunteering at local events offers you be part of the energy and excitement that these events bring to the community. You're giving back in a way that's fun, rewarding, and meaningful.

6.3 Starting a Small Non-profit Organization

Have you ever thought of transforming your passion into a force for good in your community? The first step in starting a non-profit is identifying a cause that sparks your enthusiasm and addresses a real need. Think about what issues matter to you. Is it homelessness, animal welfare, or perhaps environmental conservation? Once you've pinpointed your passion, it's time to dig into some research. Look at existing organizations to see what's already being done and where there might be gaps. Maybe there's a ton of support for stray animals but not enough for endangered local wildlife. The goal is to ensure your non-profit fills a unique niche and has a clear, compelling mission.

Setting up the legal and financial foundations for your non-profit might sound like a Herculean task, but it's manageable if you break it down. Start by registering your non-profit according to the legal requirements in your country. Each country has its own process, so it's important to check with local government offices or online resources for guidance. For example, in the UK, you would register with the Charity Commission, while in Canada, you'd apply for charitable status through the Canada Revenue Agency.

Registering a non-profit organization in the USA involves filing Articles of Incorporation in your state and securing an Employer Identification Number (EIN) from the IRS. Applying for 501(c)(3) status with IRS Form 1023 (or Form 1023-EZ for smaller organizations) will grant federal tax-exempt status, allowing for tax-deductible donations. Be sure to check for any additional state or local registration requirements. For guidance, resources like the IRS website and state-specific online resources can provide detailed assistance.

Financial management is another crucial aspect. Open a dedicated bank account for your non-profit and keep meticulous records of income and expenses. You might want to hire an accountant or use financial software designed for non-profits to ensure everything stays in order. These steps ensure your non-profit is built on a solid legal foundation, ready to make a lasting impact no matter where you are.

Building a team and network is where the magic happens. You'll need passionate volunteers and dedicated board members who believe in your cause. Start by reaching out to friends, family, and community members who share your vision. Clearly define roles and responsibilities to ensure everyone knows what's expected of them. Networking with other non-profits and community leaders can also be incredibly beneficial. Attend local non-profit meetings, join online forums, and participate in community events to build relationships and gain support. Collaboration is key. By working together, you can share resources, ideas, and volunteers, making your mission more achievable and impactful.

Fundraising and grant writing are the lifeblood of any non-profit. Start with the basics—community fundraisers like bake sales, car washes, or silent auctions are great ways to raise initial funds and spread awareness. For larger sums, grant writing is essential. Identify potential grants by researching foundations, corporations, and government programs that align with your mission. Many foundations list available grants on their websites, and resources like **Grants.gov**, **Foundation Center**, and **GrantWatch** provide searchable databases of public and private grants. Look for grants that fit your mission and align with the specific projects you want to fund.

Writing a compelling grant proposal involves clearly stating your mission, outlining your goals, and showing exactly how the funds will be used. Start by identifying the problem your non-profit addresses, showing why it's relevant, and then explaining how your project provides a unique solution. Include budgets, timelines, and measurable outcomes to strengthen your proposal's credibility. Success stories and testimonials can also help, as they paint a picture of the impact your organization has already made. Including these elements helps potential funders see your organization's effectiveness and illustrates how their investment will directly benefit the community.

Here's an example of a local non-profit that successfully raised funds through a community art auction. They invited local artists to donate pieces, which were then auctioned off at a gala event. The combination of beautiful art, a fun evening, and a worthy cause led to a highly successful fundraiser. Additionally, the organization applied for a grant from a local arts foundation, highlighting its mission to support underprivileged youth through art programs. By crafting a detailed proposal complete with a budget, timelines, and testimonials from past participants, they successfully secured the funding they needed to expand their impact.

Strong grant proposals reflect careful research, clear writing, and alignment with the funder's values. The more thoroughly you understand the funding landscape and each specific grant's requirements, the more effectively you can position your organization for success. With a little dedication, your efforts in fundraising and grant writing will provide the solid financial foundation your non-profit needs to thrive.

As you can see, starting a non-profit in retirement is not just about filling your days; it's about filling them with purpose and passion. By identifying a cause, laying a solid legal and financial foundation, building a strong team, and mastering fundraising, you can create a lasting impact on your community. It's a journey that offers rewards far beyond personal fulfillment, enriching the lives of those your organization touches.

6.4 Creating a Garden for a Thriving Community

Transforming a vacant lot into a lush, vibrant garden where neighbors can gather and connect is a rewarding endeavor. In my community, we saw an empty lot that had been neglected for years, filled with overgrown weeds and trash. With some dedicated volunteers and careful planning, that same space was turned into a thriving garden, bursting with flowers, vegetables, and benches where people now relax and socialize. What was once an eyesore has become a beautiful gathering place that brings neighbors together.

Planning and organizing a community garden starts by identifying the perfect plot of land. This could be an under-used park space, a neglected corner of your neighborhood, or even a section of a local schoolyard. Before rallying support, it's essential to determine the land's availability and ownership. Begin by researching property records, which you can find at your city's or county's land registry office or online through government databases. If the land belongs to the city or another organization, contact the relevant department or property owner to discuss your idea and explore any necessary permits or leasing agreements.

Once you've clarified these legal considerations, you'll be ready to rally support from your community. To get your garden off the ground, start by hosting a meeting to gauge support and gather potential volunteers. People love to get behind a cause that beautifies their neighborhood and provides fresh produce. Advertise the meeting through local channels like neighborhood social media groups, community centers, and bulletin boards at libraries or coffee shops. You might also reach out to local schools, garden clubs, or environmental organizations—they often have members who are passionate about community projects.

During the meeting, share your vision for the garden, highlighting the benefits it will bring, such as beautifying the neighborhood, providing fresh produce, and creating a space for community gatherings. Ask attendees to think about their unique skills and how they might contribute. Some may be seasoned gardeners, while others may have experience with fundraising, event planning, or building structures like garden beds and benches. By inviting people to play an active role, you're fostering a sense of ownership and excitement for the project, making it more likely they'll stay involved over the long term. Consider organizing volunteer roles based on interests and availability, like coordinating planting schedules, managing social media updates, or organizing fundraising events. Make it easy for new volunteers to join by setting up an email list or online group for regular updates, ensuring that even those who can't attend every meeting feel informed and engaged.

Once you have the land and the people, it's time to plan the layout. Think about sections for vegetables, flowers, and herbs. Raised beds are a great option for those with mobility issues, and they help to keep the garden organized. Choose plants that are well-suited to your climate and soil conditions. Native plants are often the best choice—they're hardy, low-maintenance, and great for local wildlife.

Organizing educational workshops and events within the garden can turn it into a hub of learning and interaction. Invite local gardening experts to give talks on topics like composting, pest control, and organic farming. These sessions can be informal, like a chat over a garden bed, or more structured, with demonstrations and Q&A segments. You could host seasonal events, like a spring planting day or a fall harvest festival. These events teach valuable skills and bring the community together. Imagine children learning to plant seeds, adults exchanging gardening tips, and everyone enjoying the fruits of their labor at a communal picnic. These gatherings foster a sense of community, making the garden a cherished local resource.

The benefits of community gardens are wide-ranging and profound. For starters, they improve local food security by providing fresh, healthy produce to those who might not have easy access to it. Gardens also beautify neighborhoods, transforming eyesores into green sanctuaries. This uplifts the area aesthetically, can increase property values, and reduce crime rates. Beyond these tangible benefits, community gardens create a sense of ownership and pride. When people come together to create and maintain something beautiful, they form bonds that strengthen the fabric of their community. You'll find that the garden becomes a place where friendships bloom alongside the flowers.

Engaging all ages in the community garden is crucial for its success and sustainability. Consider creating areas specifically designed for children's gardening. These can be small plots where kids can plant and care for their veggies or flowers. Activities like scavenger hunts, storytelling sessions, and craft projects can make the garden a magical place for the younger generation. Intergenerational interaction is a beautiful byproduct of these efforts. Imagine a grandparent showing a grandchild how to plant tomatoes, or a teenager teaching an older adult how to use a gardening app. These interactions build mutual respect and understanding, enriching the lives of everyone involved. The garden becomes not just a place for plants to grow, but for relationships to flourish.

In retirement, you have the opportunity to create something lasting and impactful. Engaging with your community through a shared project or a leadership role adds purpose to these years. Community initiatives like gardens bring people together to connect and learn, but for those ready to take on a greater challenge, leadership positions offer a unique chance to shape and improve the community on a broader scale. Let's dive into how running for local office can allow you to lead with purpose and make an even bigger difference.

6.5 Running for a Local Office: Leading with Purpose

Retirement offers a unique opportunity to step into roles that make a lasting impact, and for those passionate about their communities, running for local office can be one of the most fulfilling paths. Positions in local government—whether on the city council, school board, or a community planning commission—play a crucial role in shaping the daily lives of neighbors, families, and friends. These roles allow you to directly influence the policies and projects that make your town or city a vibrant, supportive place to live.

If you've ever looked around and thought, *"I could really help make this better,"* running for office is a way to turn that thought into action. From improving local parks and schools to championing affordable housing or green initiatives, local offices are where meaningful changes start. Bringing a lifetime of experience, leadership, and a true love for your community, you have the opportunity to tackle important issues and work toward solutions that make a difference.

Embarking on a path in local politics might seem daunting, but the journey can be incredibly rewarding and empowering. In this guide, I'll walk you through the essentials of launching your campaign, connecting with your community, and making a positive impact through service in the local government. Now's the time to take that next step and lead with purpose, vision, and a deep commitment to the community you call home.

Understanding the Requirements

Before launching your campaign, it's essential to understand the basic requirements for running for local office. While these may vary depending on your location, most positions have some general guidelines:

- **Age**: Most local offices require candidates to be at least 18 years old, though some positions may have higher age thresholds. So, you'll fit easily here.

- **Residency**: Candidates typically must have lived in the district or city for a certain period, often at least one year, to be eligible to run.

- **Citizen status**: In most cases, candidates must be U.S. citizens (or citizens of their country) to run for office.

- **Additional qualifications**: Depending on the position, some offices may require specific educational backgrounds or professional qualifications, though this is less common for local roles.

Here's a quick checklist to ensure you meet the prerequisites:
- Verify your age and residency status with your local government office.

- Check the requirements for the position you're interested in, whether it's city council, school board, or another role.

- Confirm you're registered to vote in the district or city where you plan to run.

- Gather necessary documentation, such as proof of residency and voter registration, which you'll need to submit when filing your candidacy.

Campaign Strategies

Running for office requires more than just meeting the qualifications—you need a solid campaign strategy to gain support and win over voters. Start by building a team, even if it's a small one. Trusted friends, family, or community members who share your passion can assist with organizing events, managing social media, and fundraising efforts.

Here are a few key components of a successful campaign:
- **Craft a clear message**: What do you stand for? What changes do you want to bring to the community? Make sure your campaign message is concise, impactful, and resonates with the concerns of your neighbors.

- **Fundraising**: Even local campaigns need funding for things like signs, flyers, and advertisements. Host fundraising events, or consider online platforms like **GoFundMe** to collect donations.

- **Social media presence**: Platforms like Facebook, X, and Instagram allow you to reach voters and keep them updated on your campaign. Regular posts, live chats, and short videos can make you more accessible to the community.

- **Volunteer outreach**: Your supporters can help spread the word. Organize door-to-door canvassing efforts, distribute campaign materials, and attend local events to increase visibility.

Building a local presence is essential. You don't need a massive advertising budget; focusing on personal connections and community engagement is often more effective for local campaigns.

Engaging with the Community

Successful local campaigns are all about connection. People want to vote for someone they feel understands their needs and shares their values. Start by making yourself a visible and active member of your community—if you aren't already. Here are a few ways to engage with your constituents:

- **Attend community events**: Whether it's a local fair, charity event, or town hall, show up, introduce yourself, and listen to people's concerns. This face-to-face interaction is invaluable in building trust.

- **Host town hall meetings**: Organize your own events to

discuss issues that matter to the community. These meetings allow potential voters to ask questions, voice concerns, and get to know you in a more personal setting.

- **Door-to-door canvassing**: As old-fashioned as it may seem, nothing beats the personal touch of knocking on doors and introducing yourself. It shows dedication and creates a personal connection that voters will remember.

The more involved you are in the community, the more likely people are to see you as someone who represents their interests and values.

Handling Election Outcomes

Elections can be exhilarating, but they can also be unpredictable. Whether you win or lose, it's important to approach the outcome with grace and positivity. Here's how to handle each scenario:

- **If you win**: Congratulations! Your hard work has paid off, and now it's time to deliver on your campaign promises. Stay engaged with your constituents, continue attending community events, and remain transparent in your communication with the public.

- **If you lose**: Running for office is a significant achievement, win or lose. Take pride in your efforts and the connections you made along the way. Reflect on the experience, and if you're still passionate about making a difference, consider running again in the future. In the meantime, continue volunteering and being active in the community. You don't need a title to contribute meaningfully.

- **If you're undecided about running again**: Consider the impact you've made during your campaign, the relationships you've built, and whether your passion for the community still drives you. Again, even without a formal position, you can influence positive change by staying involved.

Running for local office is a meaningful way to lead and shape the future of your community. By understanding the requirements, developing a strong campaign strategy, engaging with the people, and approaching the election results with grace, you can ensure your efforts make a difference, no matter the outcome.

6.6 Mentoring the Younger Generation: Shaping the Future Through Guidance

Becoming a mentor allows you to share the insights and hard-earned lessons from your life journey, offering guidance that can genuinely shape someone else's path. Retirement opens up the time and space to connect with the younger generation in meaningful ways. From sharing career insights to supporting someone through life's twists and turns, mentorship creates a bridge between your experiences and their aspirations. Being there as a steady, encouraging presence can make all the difference, both for them and for you.

Mentoring is a two-way street. While you're helping guide the next generation, you'll find that you also gain personal satisfaction, a sense of purpose, and often, a fresh perspective. There's a special kind of fulfillment that comes from seeing someone grow and succeed with your support. For retirees, mentoring offers an opportunity to stay connected, engaged, and intellectually stimulated.

Beyond personal rewards, mentoring has a profound impact on the community. Young people benefit from having a trusted, experienced individual to turn to—someone who believes in their potential and offers guidance without judgment. As a mentor, you're contributing to the development of future leaders, creators, and innovators. You're helping to build a stronger, more connected community, one relationship at a time.

The first step is to find mentoring opportunities. Many schools, community centers, and organizations are always looking for mentors who can provide guidance and support to young people. Here's where you can start:

- **Schools and educational programs**: Many schools offer formal mentoring programs where you can work with students one-on-one or in small groups, helping with academic subjects, career guidance, or personal development.

- **Youth clubs and community centers**: Local organizations like **Boys & Girls Clubs**, **YMCAs**, and youth centers often have mentorship programs designed to connect young people with positive role models.

- **Nonprofit organizations**: Groups like **Big Brothers Big Sisters**, **Mentor.org**, and other local nonprofits match mentors with mentees based on shared interests and goals. These organizations often provide training to help you become an effective mentor.

- **Career-focused programs**: If you're coming from a specific industry, consider mentoring through professional associations or job placement programs that help young people navigate career choices.

Each of these opportunities will have specific criteria, such as a background check, a time commitment, or participation in training sessions. However, the reward of watching a young person thrive under your guidance makes the process well worth it.

Being an effective mentor goes beyond simply giving advice; it's about building an environment where your mentee feels genuinely heard and supported. This relationship thrives on active listening—taking the time to ask thoughtful questions, giving them room to express their ideas, and acknowledging their feelings. The goal is to ensure they feel validated and understood.

Together, you'll set meaningful, achievable goals, whether they involve academic progress, career planning, or personal growth. Having clear objectives not only keeps you both focused but also motivates and empowers your mentee to see their potential path forward. And as they make strides toward these goals, you're there to offer constructive feedback. This isn't about criticism but about encouragement, highlighting their strengths, and gently guiding them on areas where they can grow, helping them develop confidence.

Mentorship is also about leading by example. You're modeling resilience, compassion, and a strong work ethic—qualities you hope to inspire in your mentee. By watching you embody these traits, they get a firsthand look at what it means to be driven and thoughtful. Encourage their independence, allow them to make decisions, reflect on outcomes, and build essential problem-solving skills.

The bond you create in mentorship often extends beyond the official timeline, becoming a lasting source of support. Even after the formal mentorship period ends, keeping in touch through a quick message or an occasional coffee meet-up can make all the difference. It's about showing you're there for them, no matter what life brings.

When the time comes to conclude the formal mentorship, it's natural to feel mixed emotions. Have an open conversation about how your relationship might continue more casually if that's what feels right. Let them know you're still there, respecting their independence as they start new life chapters. With this approach, mentoring becomes a truly enriching experience, offering support, growth, and a bond that lasts a lifetime.

Mentorship is a journey for both the mentor and the mentee, and it can have profound, lasting impacts. By providing wisdom, support, and encouragement, you're not only shaping a young person's future but also enriching your own post-retirement life with purpose and connection. Whether you're guiding a student through the challenges of school, helping a young professional navigate their career, or simply being a sounding board for life's ups and downs, mentoring is a powerful way to give back. It's about more than just sharing your knowledge—it's about making a difference, one conversation at a time.

Engaging with your community through volunteering, mentoring, or running for local office brings purpose and fulfillment that can make retirement truly rewarding. These outward pursuits build connections, create lasting impacts, and allow you to leave a legacy in your community. But just as important are the hobbies and activities we nurture at home—personal projects that balance and complement our community efforts. Home-based hobbies bring a different kind of joy and relaxation, offering creativity and comfort right in your own space. Now, let's explore how these fulfilling at-home pursuits can be a source of inspiration and well-being, enriching both your days and your community involvement.

Chapter Seven

Home-Based Hobbies: Inspirations in the Heart of Your Home

You finish your morning coffee as sunlight spills through the curtains, bringing warmth to the room and sparking that familiar excitement for the day's project. Welcome to the world of home-based hobbies and activities—where every corner of your home becomes a place to create, explore, and unwind. Home-based hobbies offer retirees a wonderful blend of comfort, creativity, and freedom, making each day feel rewarding at a relaxed, flexible pace. Learning new skills like quilting, winemaking, or home decorating brings cognitive benefits, helping to keep the mind sharp and engaged. These activities offer a sense of purpose, whether you're piecing together a vibrant quilt, transforming your living space, or perfecting a batch of homemade wine. The results go beyond your own enjoyment—they can be shared as thoughtful gifts, savored with friends, or donated to fundraisers, adding a layer of meaning and community impact. For those who love to travel or stay active in the community, home-based hobbies fit seamlessly into your lifestyle, ready to pick up as soon as you return. They're a way to keep the mind engaged, bring joy to others, and enhance retirement with layers of creativity, connection, and generosity.

7.1 Home Gardening: Creating Your Peaceful Oasis

Step into your backyard, seeing potential in every corner, or glance at your balcony, ready to bring a touch of greenery to your view. Whether you're working with a wide-open space or a cozy window box, designing your garden is all about maximizing what you have. Start by looking at your space and considering the local climate, sunlight, and what each area can support. For a backyard, you could create zones—a vegetable patch, a flower bed, and perhaps a cozy corner with a chair for morning coffee. If space is limited, as with a balcony, go for compact plants that thrive in containers. Herbs like basil and mint are wonderful choices, adding greenery and fresh flavors to your kitchen. Ultimately, the goal is to shape a small sanctuary, a peaceful escape where nature welcomes you whenever you need it.

Now, let's talk about making your garden not just beautiful but also kind to Mother Earth with sustainable gardening practices. Start with composting, which is like giving your garden a multivitamin. Collect kitchen scraps, yard waste, and other biodegradable materials, and let them break down into nutrient-rich compost. Your plants will thank you! Rainwater harvesting is another fantastic practice. Set up a rain barrel to collect runoff from your roof and use it to water your garden. It's a win-win: you save on your water bill, and your plants get a drink of chemical-free water. Eco-friendly pesticides are a must—ditch the harsh chemicals and opt for natural alternatives like neem oil or insecticidal soap. These practices benefit the environment and create a healthier garden for you and your family.

Beyond the blooms and the harvest, gardening offers profound therapeutic benefits. Imagine sinking your hands into the soil, feeling the cool earth between your fingers—it's like a natural stress reliever. Studies have shown that gardening can reduce stress, improve mood, and help combat depression. Daily interaction with your garden can become a form of mindfulness, where you focus on the present moment and let go of worries. The rhythmic act of planting, watering, and weeding becomes a meditative practice, offering a sense of calm and satisfaction. Plus, it's incredibly rewarding to watch a seed you planted grow into a thriving plant. It's a reminder of the beauty of life's cycles and the joy of nurturing something from start to finish.

Gardening with grandchildren is a delightful way to bond and teach them about nature. Picture you and your grandkids, hands dirty with soil, planting a butterfly garden—so fun! Choose plants like milkweed, zinnias, and lavender that attract butterflies, and watch as these beautiful creatures flutter around, delighting young and old alike. Or perhaps you'd prefer to create a fairy garden. Gather miniature plants, tiny furniture, and whimsical decorations, and let your imaginations run wild as you design a magical world together. These projects are not only fun but also educational, teaching children about plant life cycles, pollinators, and the importance of caring for the environment. The memories you create will be cherished for years to come, long after the flowers have bloomed and the fairies have moved on to new adventures.

Garden Planning Checklist

To help you get started, here's a simple checklist for planning your garden space:

- **Assess Your Space**: Look at what you have to work with, whether it's a spacious backyard, a cozy balcony, or just a simple window box. Think about the size, layout, and any specific limitations or advantages your space offers.

- **Determine Sunlight Availability**: Observe your garden area throughout the day to see how much sunlight it receives. Different plants thrive in different conditions, so note if your space has full sun, partial shade, or mostly shade.

- **Choose Plants Suited to Your Climate and Space:** Research plants that thrive in your local climate, considering your space's sunlight exposure. Check gardening websites like **Garden.org** or apps like **PlantSnap** to find plant options for your specific conditions.

- **Plan Your Garden Zones:** If you have room, consider creating distinct areas—a vegetable patch in the sunniest spot, a flower bed to add color, or a cozy seating nook for relaxation. Sketch out a rough layout or use free garden planning tools like **SmartGardener** to help you visualize.

- **Gather Necessary Tools and Supplies**: Collect essential gardening tools, such as a trowel, gloves, compost, plant containers, and soil. Look up tutorials on **YouTube** or garden blogs for tips on using these tools effectively.

- **Set Up Sustainable Systems:** Consider eco-friendly practices like adding a compost bin for organic waste or installing a rain barrel to collect water. These systems are not only sustainable but also save costs and reduce waste in your garden.

- **Find Project-Specific Instructions:** If you're new to gardening or tackling a specific project (like raised beds or container gardening), check out instructional guides on platforms like **YouTube**, gardening blogs, or **Pinterest** for step-by-step tips.

Gardening is as much about the journey as it is about the results. Revel in the calm and therapeutic satisfaction it brings, and invite loved ones to share in the beauty of your growing garden.

7.2 Creating Personal Touches: Adventures in DIY Home Decor

Many designers, myself included, began their journeys simply by falling in love with the process of decorating their own homes. What started as a few DIY projects to personalize my space turned into a career in interior design and home staging, where every project became a new adventure in creativity and style. You don't have to plan for a design career, though—unless inspiration strikes, then why not? Home decor projects can be a joyful and fulfilling way to transform your home into a reflection of you.

The best part? Inspiration and guidance are just a click away. Websites like **Pinterest** and **Instagram** are treasure troves for DIY decor ideas, with countless accounts dedicated to everything from farmhouse style to modern minimalist makeovers. **YouTube** is another resource, offering step-by-step tutorials on almost any project you can think of, whether it's refinishing furniture, creating wall art, or making custom shelving. If you prefer a more structured approach, platforms like **Skillshare** and **MasterClass** offer in-depth courses on everything from basic home decor techniques to advanced design skills.

Imagine filling your space with unique, handcrafted pieces that aren't just beautiful but tell a story, each one a personal touch added with your own hands. DIY decor lets you shape a cozy sanctuary that speaks to your style while exploring new skills. Whether you're adding a fresh coat of paint, reimagining a piece of furniture you got at a garage sale, or creating custom art for your walls, these projects allow you to express yourself and make each room uniquely yours. Ready to dive in? Let's explore the world of DIY decor and see how a few creative touches can elevate your home.

Let's start with simple upcycling projects. You know those old jars that have been collecting dust in your pantry? It's time to give them a new life. Turn them into beautiful vases by wrapping them in twine or painting them in your favorite colors. Or how about customizing some cushion covers? Grab some plain cushions, stencils, and fabric paint, and let your creativity flow. You'll end up with one-of-a-kind pieces that add a fresh touch to your space.

Next, let's dive into furniture restoration ideas. Let's say you found an old, worn-out chair at a flea market and decided to transform it into a stunning statement piece. The first step is sanding to remove the old finish and smooth out any imperfections. You'll need sandpaper, a sanding block, and a bit of elbow grease. Once you've got a smooth surface, it's time to paint. Choose a color that complements your decor and apply it evenly with a brush or roller. For a more rustic look, consider distressing the edges by lightly sanding them after painting. If the chair has a padded seat, reupholstering it gives it new life. Choose a fabric that speaks to your style, remove the old fabric, and staple the new one in place. You'll need a staple gun, fabric scissors, and a bit of patience, but the result is well worth it.

Now, how about creating art for home decor? Whether it's a painting, sculpture, or handmade craft, it adds a unique touch to your home. If you're into painting, start with a blank canvas and some acrylic paints. Don't worry if you're not a seasoned artist—abstract art is all about free expression. For those who prefer three-dimensional art, try your hand at sculpting with clay. You can create beautiful pieces like vases, figurines, or decorative bowls. Handmade crafts are also a creative way to personalize your space. Think about creating a mosaic with broken tiles or sea glass, or making a macramé wall hanging. The key is to choose materials and techniques that allow you to learn new skills and enjoy the process.

Seasonal decor projects offer a creative way to bring the changing beauty of each season into your home, making your surroundings feel fresh and inspiring year-round. For the holiday season, try crafting a Scandinavian-inspired wreath by weaving dried orange slices, cinnamon sticks, and sprigs of eucalyptus into a minimalist ring. This blend of earthy elements not only looks stunning but fills your entryway with a subtle, cozy scent. In summer, create a statement piece by arranging a tabletop "mini desert garden" with succulents, pebbles, and driftwood. This vibrant touch brings a splash of greenery indoors and requires little maintenance, perfect for the hotter months. For autumn, elevate your space with a dried floral wall hanging made of bundles of pampas grass, wheat, and soft autumnal flowers tied to a wooden branch and hung above your dining table. And in spring, consider creating a botanical display by pressing fresh, colorful blooms and framing them as a series of floral artwork for your walls. These projects go beyond the usual decor ideas, celebrating each season's unique beauty in creative, unexpected ways. Don't be afraid to think outside the box—try experimenting with unconventional materials or combining seasonal elements in new ways to give your home a personal, one-of-a-kind touch.

Updating your walls with creative paint and wallpaper choices is one of the simplest ways to breathe new life into your space, and it's another chance to think beyond the basics. Try color-blocking with bold shapes or soft gradients for an artistic flair that feels custom-designed. For a playful touch, paint an accent ceiling in a contrasting color, or go for an ombré effect on the walls for a dreamy, eye-catching gradient. Experiment with textures, too—chalkboard paint in a kitchen or workspace adds function and fun, while metallic or pearlescent finishes add a hint of luxury without overwhelming the room.

Wallpaper offers even more options for exploring personality and style. Try peel-and-stick murals for an easy-to-change look or create a cozy reading nook with a vintage-inspired botanical wallpaper. If you're feeling adventurous, layer patterns with wallpaper in frames as wall art, or mix wallpaper panels with wainscoting for a blend of modern and traditional aesthetics. For inspiration, check out design blogs like **Apartment Therapy, Houzz, Emily Henderson's Blog,** and **The Spruce,** or wallpaper-focused sites like **Spoonflower** and **Wallshoppe.** Don't be afraid to go bold—your walls can be a canvas for creativity that turns any room into a space that feels uniquely yours.

Quilting and sewing offer endless opportunities to infuse your home with warmth and personality. Think of a custom quilt as a canvas for storytelling—each fabric square can represent a cherished memory, favorite color palette, or theme, making it both beautiful and meaningful. For a unique twist, try creating a "memory quilt" using fabric from old clothes, scarves, or even ties, weaving personal history into a cozy keepsake. Or go modern with bold, geometric designs in bright colors for a fresh, contemporary look. Cushions and curtains can also be personalized with unique fabrics, such as vintage finds, hand-dyed textiles, or embroidered patterns that add texture and depth to your decor.

For inspiration, explore **Pinterest, Instagram,** or online quilting communities like **QuiltCon** and **Modern Quilt Guild,** where you can find an array of designs and techniques to suit any style. If you're new to quilting, online platforms like **Bluprint, Craftsy**, or even **YouTube** offer tutorials that guide you through both basics and more intricate techniques. Many local fabric stores also host sewing and quilting classes, making it easy to learn in a supportive environment. These projects not only transform your home but also provide a deeply satisfying creative outlet that you'll enjoy each time you see or use your handcrafted pieces.

DIY Project Checklist

Here's a handy checklist to help you get started with your DIY home decor projects:

- **Choose a Project:** Think about what excites you most, whether it's upcycling jars, customizing cushions, restoring furniture, creating unique wall art, adding seasonal decor, painting, wallpapering, quilting, or sewing.

- **Find Instructions:** Check out websites like **YouTube, Pinterest**, or **Instructables** for step-by-step guides, or refer to DIY blogs and tutorials specific to your project type. Clear instructions can make all the difference, especially for new techniques.

- **Gather Materials:** Collect your supplies based on the project—this might include jars, fabric paint, old furniture, sandpaper, paint, fabric, canvas, clay, tiles, mason jars, string lights, quilting fabric, or anything else that sparks creativity.

- **Set Up Your Workspace:** Find a well-lit area to work in, equipped with all your tools and supplies for a smooth process.

Embrace the creativity and take pride in crafting something uniquely yours. Whether it's your first project or your fiftieth, remember that each piece adds a personal touch to your home.

7.3 World Cuisines: Virtual Cooking Classes

The enticing aroma of fresh herbs and spices fills your kitchen as you prepare a vibrant Mediterranean feast, or the satisfying sizzle of a Japanese Teppanyaki grill brings an element of excitement to your cooking. Exploring global flavors through virtual cooking classes can turn everyday meals into culinary adventures. You might find yourself mastering an Italian risotto that's creamy and rich, a fragrant Thai curry layered with spices, or a delicate French soufflé that rises just right.

These classes go beyond teaching new recipes, they immerse you in the cultural roots and health benefits of each dish. The Mediterranean diet, known for its heart-healthy fats and fresh produce, supports cardiovascular health, while Japanese cuisine, with emphasis on fresh fish and vegetables, is celebrated for promoting longevity. From vegetarian dishes packed with flavor to keto-friendly recipes that keep carbs in check, virtual cooking classes open up a world of vibrant, healthy, and diverse culinary traditions waiting to be explored.

How do you get started with virtual cooking classes? The first step is selecting a platform that suits your style. Websites like **MasterClass** offer courses taught by renowned chefs like **Gordon Ramsay** and **Alice Waters**, while platforms like **Skillshare** provide a variety of classes ranging from beginner to advanced levels. For live, interactive experiences, check out platforms like **Airbnb Experiences** and **Cozymeal**, where chefs host real-time cooking classes, allowing you to ask questions and get immediate feedback as you cook along. If you prefer to learn at your own pace, pre-recorded classes on sites like **Udemy** and **Rouxbe** allow you to pause, rewind, and repeat as needed. Many of these platforms offer free trials, so you can explore different classes before committing. When enrolling, pay attention to course descriptions to find classes that focus on the cuisines and techniques you're most excited to learn.

One of the joys of learning to cook is sharing the experience with others. Cook-along sessions are a fantastic way to socialize and bond over a shared love of food, even if you're miles apart. You can set up a virtual cook-along with friends or family members, each person in their kitchen, following the same recipe together. It's like having a dinner party without leaving your home. You can chat, laugh, and compare notes as you chop, sauté, and season your way to a delicious meal. To set this up, choose a recipe in advance and share the ingredient list with everyone. Use video conferencing tools like **Zoom** or **Google Meet** to connect, and designate someone to lead the session. It's a fun, interactive way to stay connected and create new memories, all while honing your culinary skills.

As you dive deeper into the world of cooking, you might want to document and share your culinary adventures. Starting a cooking blog or a vlog is a wonderful way to do this as you will create a digital diary of your favorite recipes, cooking tips, and cultural insights. This provides a creative outlet and allows you to connect with a wider community of food enthusiasts. To get started, choose a blogging platform like **WordPress** or **Blogger** for written content or **YouTube** for video content. Begin by sharing simple recipes and gradually include more complex dishes as you gain confidence. Don't worry about being perfect as authenticity is what resonates with readers and viewers. Share your personal experiences, the challenges you faced, and the triumphs you celebrated. Include photos or videos of your dishes, and don't forget to engage with your audience by responding to comments and questions. This can become a rewarding hobby that keeps you engaged and inspired.

Recipe Sharing Circle

Why not start a recipe-sharing circle with your friends and family? It's a fun and delicious way to stay connected and inspire each other in the kitchen! Here's how to get started:

- **Choose a Theme**: Pick a theme for each round of sharing to add excitement and variety. It could be something classic, like "Italian Night" or "Vegetarian Delights," or something more adventurous, like "Global Street Foods" or "Family Favorites." Themes make it easy for everyone to get inspired and stay on track.

- **Select Recipes:** Each participant selects a recipe within the theme to share. Encourage everyone to choose something they love or are excited to try, whether it's a traditional family recipe or a new dish they've discovered.

- **Share Recipes Digitally:** Use email, a shared **Google Doc**, or a **WhatsApp** group to share each person's recipe. This way, everyone can access, save, and print each recipe easily. Include photos, ingredient substitutions, and any unique tips to help everyone recreate the dish as closely as possible.

- **Organize a Virtual Meet-Up**: Schedule a time to meet virtually (**Zoom, Skype, or Google Meet** are all great options). During the meet-up, discuss the recipes, swap cooking tips, share successes or hilarious mishaps, and chat about any modifications or variations people tried. These conversations add a personal touch and make everyone feel more connected.

- **Cook, Taste, and Explore:** After the meet-up, dive into the recipes you received, trying a new dish each week or whenever you feel like a culinary adventure. It's a great way to expand your culinary repertoire, learn new techniques, and add to your collection of tried-and-true recipes.

Cooking world cuisines from the comfort of your home is about embarking on a delicious adventure that enriches your life and connects you with others. Whether you're exploring new flavors, learning new techniques, or sharing your culinary creations, your kitchen becomes a gateway to the world of cuisines.

7.4 Home Brewing and Wine Making: Crafting Your Beverages

My husband and I first got into home winemaking as a weekend project, and what a rewarding journey it's been! Crafting a drink that suits our tastes brings a unique sense of satisfaction. Each batch feels like an accomplishment, from selecting the flavors to savoring that first sip. Home brewing and winemaking have become more than hobbies for many people. They're a creative way to experiment and enjoy the results together with friends and family. And who knows? Like us, you might find this hands-on craft adds an extra layer of enjoyment to your weekends.

If you're curious about trying it yourself, getting started is easy. For beer brewing, you'll need essentials: a fermenter, airlock, brewing kettle, siphoning tubes, and bottles. Winemaking requires a few basics, too: a primary fermenter, glass carboys, airlocks, and bottles. Once you've gathered your equipment, it's time to dive into some beginner-friendly recipes and techniques.

For beer, a simple pale ale is a great starting point. Begin by brewing a wort, which involves boiling malt extract with water and hops. After cooling, transfer it to your fermenter and add yeast. Let it ferment for about a week, then siphon it into bottles, add a bit of sugar, and cap them. After another week or two, you'll have your own homemade beer ready to enjoy.

For wine, start with a basic grape wine recipe. Crush fresh grapes or use grape juice concentrate, then add sugar, water, and yeast to your fermenter. Let it ferment for about a week, then transfer it to a carboy to continue fermenting for several weeks. Once fermentation is complete, siphon the wine into bottles and cork them. Patience is key here, as aging the wine for a few months will enhance its flavor and smoothness.

Getting started is easier when you have the right resources and connections. Many local brewing supply stores offer everything from equipment and ingredients to expert advice for beginners and enthusiasts alike. They often host workshops and tasting events, where you can learn the basics and get tips on crafting flavors. Online resources are also plentiful; websites like **Homebrewers Association**, **Wine-Maker Magazine**, and **YouTube** channels dedicated to brewing and fermenting provide tutorials and guidance for all skill levels. For those who enjoy a social aspect, consider joining a local brewing club or online community, such as **Reddit** or **Facebook groups**. Here, you can swap recipes, troubleshoot challenges, and share your successes. Building connections with fellow brewers and local businesses can add depth and fun to your brewing journey, enriching the experience with shared knowledge and camaraderie.

While brewing and winemaking are fun and rewarding, it's important to keep safety and legal considerations in mind. Always sanitize your equipment thoroughly to prevent contamination, which can spoil your brew. Use food-grade sanitizers and follow the instructions carefully. Ensure you're storing your ingredients and finished products in a cool, dark place to maintain their quality. When it comes to legalities, check your local regulations. In many places, you're allowed to brew a certain amount for personal use without a license, but it's wise to confirm the details.

Home brewing and winemaking is also the opportunity to share your creations with friends and family. Consider hosting tasting parties where you can showcase different batches and get feedback. It's a great way to socialize and share your passion. Beyond your immediate circle, look into joining local homebrew clubs or online communities. These groups are goldmines of tips, recipes, and camaraderie. They often host events, competitions, and meetups where you can learn from more experienced brewers and share your successes and challenges.

Starter Recipe for Pale Ale

Here's a simple recipe to get you started with brewing your first batch of pale ale:

Ingredients:

- 6 lbs of light malt extract
- 1 oz of cascade hops
- 1 packet of ale yeast
- 5 gallons of water
- Priming sugar (for bottling)

Instructions:

- In a large brewing kettle, bring 3 gallons of water to a boil.
- Stir in the malt extract and return to a boil.
- Add cascade hops and boil for 60 minutes.
- Cool the wort quickly by placing the kettle in an ice bath.
- Transfer to a sanitized fermenter and add enough water to make 5 gallons.
- Pitch the yeast and seal the fermenter with an airlock.
- Let it ferment at room temperature for about a week.
- Siphon into bottles, add priming sugar, and cap.
- Store the bottles at room temperature for two weeks, then enjoy!

Home brewing and wine-making offer more than just a beverage; they bring together creativity, patience, and a touch of science. There's a true satisfaction in each step, from mixing ingredients to watching fermentation unfold, all culminating in a drink that's distinctly your own. With a few essential tools and a bit of dedication, you'll soon be raising a glass to celebrate both your efforts and the unique flavors you've crafted. Cheers to your new adventure!

7.5 Beginner's Guide to Baking Artisan Breads

Baking artisan bread at home is a simple way to create delicious, homemade loaves with minimal tools and ingredients. To get started, you'll need a few basic tools: a mixing bowl, a wooden spoon, a bench scraper, a kitchen scale (optional but helpful for precise measurements), and a Dutch oven or a baking stone for the actual baking process. For ingredients, the essentials include flour, water, salt, and yeast. With just these simple components, you can create a flavorful artisan loaf that's crunchy on the outside and soft on the inside. It's important to note that quality ingredients can make a big difference, so opting for unbleached organic flour and high-quality sea salt can elevate your loaf.

Step-by-Step Baking Process

Baking an artisan loaf may seem intimidating but it is surprisingly simple. Here's a simple guide to get you started:

1. **Mix the dough**: In a large bowl, combine 3 1/2 cups of flour, 1 1/4 teaspoons of salt, and 1/4 teaspoon of instant yeast. Slowly pour in 1 1/2 cups of lukewarm water and stir until the dough comes together. It should be sticky but manageable.

2. **First rise (bulk fermentation)**: Cover the bowl with plastic wrap or a damp towel and let the dough rise at room temperature for 12 to 18 hours. The long rise time develops the flavor and gives the loaf its signature crusty texture.

3. **Shaping the dough**: After the first rise, turn the dough onto a lightly floured surface. Gently shape it into a ball by folding the edges toward the center. Let it rest for 15 minutes.

4. **Final proof**: Place the shaped dough seam-side down in a well-floured proofing basket or a bowl lined with a kitchen towel. Cover and let it rise for another 1-2 hours, or until it has doubled in size.

5. **Preheat the oven**: While the dough is in its final proof, preheat your oven to 450°F (230°C). Place a Dutch oven or baking stone inside the oven to heat for at least 30 minutes before baking.

6. **Baking**: Carefully transfer the dough into the preheated Dutch oven or onto the baking stone. If using a Dutch oven, cover it with a lid to trap steam, which helps create a crispy crust. Bake for 30 minutes with the lid on, then remove the lid and bake for an additional 15-20 minutes until the crust is golden brown and the internal temperature reaches 200°F (93°C).

7. **Cooling**: Let the bread cool on a wire rack for at least an hour before slicing to allow the interior to set and avoid a gummy texture.

Once you've mastered the basic artisan loaf, it's time to get creative with variations. You can experiment with different flours like whole wheat, rye, or spelt to introduce new flavors and textures. For those seeking gluten-free options, try incorporating flours like almond, buckwheat, chickpea, rice, or oat, which can add unique flavors and make your loaf accessible to everyone. Adding seeds (sunflower, flax, sesame), nuts (walnuts, pecans), or dried fruits (raisins, cranberries) can further personalize your loaf. For a savory twist, try incorporating herbs (rosemary, thyme) or cheese (cheddar, Parmesan) into the dough. These additions are easy to fold in during the shaping stage and can transform a simple loaf into a gourmet experience. Don't be afraid to mix and match ingredients to find your signature combination.

Enjoy artisan bread fresh for the best experience, but you can store it for several days if you wrap it properly. For short-term storage, keep your loaf in a paper bag or a bread box to maintain the crispy crust. If you want to extend its freshness, consider slicing the bread and freezing individual slices in a freezer bag. When you're ready to enjoy it, just pop a slice in the toaster or oven for a few minutes, and it will taste as good as fresh.

Sharing homemade bread is one of the most fulfilling aspects of baking. Whether you gift a loaf to a neighbor, bring it to a family gathering, or donate it to a community event, your bread can become a symbol of care and connection. Consider wrapping it in a linen towel or tying it with twine and a small tag to make your gift feel extra special. It's a simple gesture that can bring warmth and joy to those around you.

If you're ready to dive deeper into artisan bread baking, there are many resources to help you perfect your technique. Websites like **King Arthur Baking** and **Breadtopia** offer detailed recipes, tutorials, and expert tips. For video tutorials, check out **YouTube** channels such as **Bake with Jack** and **The Bread Code**, which provide easy-to-follow instructions for beginners. For those looking for structured courses, **Udemy** and **Craftsy** offer online classes, while **Skillshare** has a variety of bread-making workshops. And if you prefer a book, classics like **Flour Water Salt Yeast** by **Ken Forkish** or **Tartine Bread** by **Chad Robertson** offer in-depth guidance for passionate beginners and experienced bakers alike.

Baking artisan bread at home is a simple and satisfying process that opens up endless possibilities for creativity and sharing. With the right tools, a bit of patience, and some experimentation, you can create delicious loaves that bring comfort to your home and to those around you. Sharing your homemade bread can be as fulfilling as the baking itself—consider selling your loaves at local farmers markets, where you can connect with other food enthusiasts, or donating batches to community fundraisers, adding a personal touch to a cause. You might even start a "bread swap" with friends and neighbors, trading flavors and techniques to keep the creativity flowing and build connections in the process.

Home-based hobbies bring joy, creativity, and purpose into your daily life, making retirement a time for exploration and fulfillment right from the comfort of your home. Whether you're experimenting in the kitchen, tending to a garden, or crafting a handmade masterpiece, these hobbies offer a deeply personal way to express yourself, relax, and stay engaged. But sometimes, a favorite hobby or a lifetime of professional skills can spark something more—a desire to share your talents with others or to turn them into a thriving business venture. It might be selling handmade crafts, teaching a cooking class, offering consulting services, or starting a freelance career—the world of entrepreneurship offers exciting paths for growth. In the next chapter, we will explore how you can turn your unique skills, experiences, and passions into meaningful entrepreneurial endeavors.

Chapter Eight

Entrepreneurial Endeavors and Part-Time Work

Now, as you've traded in office hours for a more relaxed lifestyle, it might be the perfect moment to explore a new adventure—one where you create something entirely your own. Retirement offers a chance to dive into a project that's fueled by your skills, interests, and lifelong passions. It may be the time to build something meaningful at your own pace, whether it's a small business, a creative venture, or a personal project. It's about bringing together what you love and what you've learned over the years and shaping it into something that feels rewarding and truly yours.

In this chapter, we're diving into the world of part-time businesses and side gigs that bring purpose, creativity, and financial reward to your retirement years. From turning a favorite hobby into a source of income to sharing your professional expertise as a consultant or freelancer, you'll find endless ways to keep that entrepreneurial spark alive. Retirement is a chance to reinvent yourself, create, grow, and enjoy a playground of new possibilities. Let's explore how to turn your passions into profitable ventures and make these years your most exciting yet.

8.1 Starting a Small Business in Retirement: Turning Your Passion into Profit

Identifying viable business opportunities in retirement can feel like striking gold, especially when you align them with your passions. Think back to what you loved doing during your career or hobbies that have always brought you joy. Were you the go-to person for organizing events at work? Perhaps event planning is in your future. Or maybe you've always had a knack for woodworking—why not open an online shop to sell your handmade creations? Platforms like **Etsy** allow you to showcase unique, handcrafted products to a global audience. For those offering services like consulting or event planning, **Fiverr** is a great marketplace for freelancers to connect with clients seeking specific skills. If you're new to entrepreneurship or want to learn more about running a business, platforms like **Coursera** offer courses on small business management and entrepreneurship, helping you turn your passion into a thriving business.

But passion is just one part of the equation. Planning is where the rubber meets the road. A solid business plan acts as a roadmap from idea to execution, guiding your decisions along the way. Start by clearly defining your goals: are you looking to supplement your income, stay mentally engaged, or both? Next, identify your target audience—understanding who will benefit from your product or service is key to creating a successful business. Then, consider funding sources, whether you're dipping into savings, seeking small business loans, or bootstrapping. Tools like **LivePlan** help you create a professional business plan with financial projections to ensure your venture is viable. For additional support, **SCORE**, a nonprofit organization, offers free mentoring and templates to help you develop your plan. You can also find detailed advice and templates through the **U.S. Small Business Administration (SBA)**, which provides resources on funding options and business development. For readers outside the U.S., similar resources are available globally: **Canada's Business Development Bank (BDC)** offers guides on financing and planning; **Australia's Business.gov.au** offers step-by-step business planning tools; the **United Kingdom's GOV.UK** platform provides resources through **the Department for Business and Trade**, and **the European Union's Your Europe** portal includes information on starting and growing a business across EU member countries.

Navigating the legal and financial landscape may seem too complicated at first, but it's a necessary step to ensure you set up your business for success. Registering your business legally—whether it's filing for a business license, registering a business name, or securing the right permits—not only protects you but also establishes credibility. Services like **LegalZoom** can help streamline the process, making it easier to file for LLC formation, trademarks, and other legal necessities. Understanding your tax obligations is critical. Will you need to pay quarterly taxes? What deductions can you claim as a business owner? The **IRS Small Business** and **Self-Employed Tax Center** provides guidance on navigating the complexities of business taxes, offering resources specifically for small business owners and freelancers. If you're outside the U.S., look to similar authorities: **Canada's CRA Business Tax Hub**, the **UK's HMRC for Self-Assessment and VAT guidance**, **Australia's ATO Small Business Newsroom**, and the **EU's Taxation and Customs Union portal** for guidance within **the European Union**.

Managing finances efficiently is just as essential. Tools like **QuickBooks** simplify tracking expenses, managing invoices, and handling tax filings all in one place, but there are other options too. **Xero** is popular for its user-friendly interface and multi-currency support, while **Wave** offers a free suite of accounting tools ideal for small businesses. **FreshBooks** provides invoicing and expense tracking with a focus on freelancers and service-based businesses. Each of these platforms helps streamline your financial management, ensuring your focus can remain on growing your venture.

Balancing risk and reward is a vital part of any business venture. Every business has risks, but thorough planning can mitigate them. Conducting market research is a good starting point. Knowing your competitors' strengths and weaknesses can help you position your product or service effectively. Tools like **Google Trends** allow you to track consumer interest and market demand, ensuring that your business idea is in line with current trends. If you're unsure about demand, start small by testing your product or service with minimal investment. For example, if you're thinking about selling handmade crafts, you can begin by producing a small batch and selling it at local markets or online to gauge interest. Platforms like **Oberlo** offer insights into trending products, while **SurveyMonkey** allows you to gather customer feedback before making larger commitments.

When venturing into a new business, it's important to be mindful of your personal commitments and health. Running a business can be demanding, and it's essential to strike a balance that fits into your lifestyle. Structuring your time efficiently will help you maintain that balance while growing your business.

Business Idea Brainstorming Exercise

To help you get started, try this exercise, which will guide you through identifying the best opportunities aligned with your passions, skills, and market needs:

- **Passion and Skills Assessment**: Start by listing three things you are passionate about. Whether it's baking, teaching, crafting, or technology, your passions will fuel your motivation. Then, identify three skills you've honed over the years, such as project management, communication, or creative design. These are the foundations of your future business. Use tools like **MindMeister** to create a visual mind map of your passions and skills to see how they intersect.

- **Market Needs**: Think about the problems or needs you've noticed in your community or among friends and family. Is there a gap that you could fill? Perhaps there's a need for a local handyman service, or maybe you've noticed a demand for personalized gifts.

- **Business Ideas**: Combine your passions, skills, and the market needs you identified to brainstorm three potential business ideas. For example, if you love gardening and have strong organizational skills, perhaps starting a local gardening consultation business could be a good fit. Use **Trello** to organize your ideas, track goals, and set deadlines.

- **Feasibility Check**: For each business idea, consider the resources you'll need, the potential market size, and the initial costs. Use tools like **SurveyMonkey** to gather feedback from potential customers and validate your ideas.

- **Action Plan**: Choose the most viable idea and outline the first five steps to bring it to life. These steps might include creating a website, registering your business, and purchasing initial inventory. Platforms like **Google Trends** can help you research trends related to your idea, while **SCORE** mentors can provide personalized advice on your next moves.

By aligning your business with your passions and skills, creating a detailed plan, and understanding the legal and financial landscapes, you're setting yourself up for success. Retirement is the perfect time to pursue something that brings you both joy and fulfillment. Let's turn those retirement dreams into reality!

8.2 Starting a Blog, Vlog, or Podcast: Share Your Journey and Earn Along the Way

If you're excited about the idea of sharing your thoughts and experiences with the world, starting a blog, vlog, or podcast might be the perfect way to connect with others and generate some extra income. The first step is to decide on your content focus. What makes your life unique and engaging? Maybe you have a knack for turning everyday moments into captivating stories, or perhaps your travel experiences could inspire others to explore new destinations. Family stories, health tips, and hobbies are also rich sources for content. Platforms like **Udemy** or **Skillshare** offer courses to help you brainstorm and structure your content, ensuring that it keeps your audience engaged. The key is to create content that reflects your personality and passions. For example, you could share that unforgettable moment when you got lost in a foreign city but stumbled upon an amazing local restaurant, or offer practical tips on staying fit in your golden years while avoiding the gym. Your content should be relatable, entertaining, and informative, making your readers, viewers, or listeners feel like they're part of your journey.

Next, you'll need to choose the right platform for your content. If blogging is your style, platforms like **WordPress** and **Blogger** provide user-friendly, customizable options for beginners. For a cleaner, more writing-focused experience, **Medium** offers a streamlined interface perfect for those who want to dive straight into writing without worrying too much about design. If you're more interested in creating video content, **YouTube** is the leading platform for vloggers, offering an enormous audience and tools that make uploading and editing videos simple. For aspiring podcasters, platforms like **Anchor** and **Podbean** allow you to record, edit, and distribute episodes with ease. The **YouTube Creator Academy** offers free, invaluable insights into growing a successful channel, while **Buzzsprout** and **The Podcast Host** provide essential tips for starting and growing a podcast. When choosing your platform, consider your technical skills, time commitment, and the audience you want to reach.

Once you've selected your platform, it's time to dive into the technical setup. If you're starting a blog, you'll need a domain name and a hosting provider. **Bluehost** makes setting up your domain and hosting simple, allowing you to get your site live quickly. For those opting for a vlog or podcast, having the right equipment is crucial. A quality camera or microphone can make a huge difference in the clarity and professionalism of your content. But don't worry—you don't need to break the bank. Many smartphones today have excellent cameras and affordable microphones like the **Blue Yeti** are available for podcasting. When editing audio for podcasts, **Audacity** is a free and beginner-friendly tool to get you started. For video and image enhancements, **Canva** is perfect for creating polished thumbnails and visual assets that will grab your audience's attention.

Content creation doesn't stop at posting—you'll need to engage with your audience to build a community around your blog, vlog, or podcast. Responding to comments and messages shows your viewers or readers that you value their input, creating a stronger connection. Social media platforms like **Facebook**, **Instagram**, and **X** are powerful tools for promoting your content and reaching a wider audience. For visually focused content, **Pinterest** can be another great avenue to drive traffic. Collaborations with other content creators can also expand your reach. You can team up with a fellow retiree who shares your love for travel or partner with a health expert to provide your audience with valuable insights. **BuzzSumo** is a useful resource for finding influencers in your niche, helping you establish partnerships that can elevate your content.

While sharing your thoughts and experiences is rewarding on its own, monetizing your content can turn your blog, vlog, or podcast into a source of income. Instead of treating monetization as an afterthought, think of it as an integral part of your strategy. Advertising is one of the most straightforward ways to generate revenue. Platforms like **Google AdSense** allow you to display ads on your blog or vlog, with earnings generated from clicks or views. Sponsorships are another lucrative avenue. If you build a niche audience, brands may approach you to promote their products or services. Affiliate marketing is also a powerful way to earn money. By partnering with platforms like **Amazon Associates** or **ShareASale**, you can promote products relevant to your audience and earn commissions on any sales made through your referral links. You could also offer premium content, such as exclusive blog posts, behind-the-scenes videos, or personalized coaching. **Patreon** allows your audience to support you financially in exchange for access to special perks, while **Teachable** gives you the tools to create and sell courses or workshops based on your expertise.

By leveraging these resources and taking a strategic approach to both content creation and monetization, you'll be well on your way to building a blog, vlog, or podcast that not only reflects your passions but also generates income. Retirement offers the perfect opportunity to explore new ventures, and with the right tools, your platform can grow into something both creatively and financially rewarding.

8.3 Transforming Your Hobbies into Income Streams

Exploring marketable hobbies is a fantastic way to blend passion with potential income. Start by thinking about the activities that genuinely captivate you—those that make hours fly by without you even noticing. For some, it's creative arts like **painting, woodworking, or pottery**; for others, it's **culinary skills** like baking artisan bread, brewing craft beer, or making homemade jams. These skills can easily become sources of income with the right approach and audience.

Take a moment to assess what's in demand. With people embracing eco-friendly lifestyles, **organic gardening** can become more than a backyard activity. Selling fresh, organic produce or specialty herbs can attract local buyers or small restaurants looking for local suppliers. Similarly, **handcrafted items** like quilts, knitted garments, or hand-painted decor can appeal to customers searching for unique, high-quality, handmade goods.

Consider also hobbies with high customization potential, such as **personalized calligraphy, stationery design, or custom jewelry**. People love one-of-a-kind items that reflect their tastes and interests, making custom products a great way to add personal value to what you create. If you love photography, think beyond traditional prints—consider creating **photo books, calendars, or postcards** that showcase local scenes or thematic collections.

Your unique style and mastery over specific techniques are invaluable assets. Perhaps you've honed a technique in **weaving, soap-making, candle-making,** or **upcycling old furniture**. Customers love supporting skilled artisans who bring a creative, personal touch to their products.

Finally, let your enthusiasm shine. When your love for a hobby is visible in the final product, it becomes naturally more appealing. This passion-driven quality can be your unique selling point, distinguishing your offerings from mass-produced alternatives. Whether it's through storytelling on social media, sharing progress updates, or giving customers a behind-the-scenes look into your creative process, showing your genuine joy for your craft can help foster a loyal following and make your products even more desirable.

Planning your business around a hobby doesn't have to be overwhelming. Start with setting realistic goals. Do you want to make a full-time income or just a little extra pocket money? Understanding your target market is crucial. Who are the people most likely to buy your products or services? Outline a simple business plan that includes your goals, target market, and a basic financial overview. Consider starting small to test the waters. You don't need a massive inventory or a full-fledged online store right away. Begin with a few items and see how they sell. This way, you can adjust your offerings based on what's popular and refine your approach without significant financial risk.

Tools and platforms for selling your creations are plentiful and varied, making it easier than ever to turn your hobbies into income. If you're into crafts or handmade goods, **Etsy** is a fantastic marketplace that caters specifically to artisans and creatives, with a user-friendly interface and an audience eager for unique, handcrafted items. For collectibles or vintage finds, **eBay** is a go-to platform, offering a global reach and the option to auction rare items. If your hobby involves creating home-grown produce or homemade foods, local farmers' markets are ideal for building a loyal, local customer base, allowing you to meet customers face-to-face and establish personal connections.

For those interested in setting up a full online store, **Shopify** provides a robust platform to create a branded e-commerce site, with options to manage inventory, process payments, and track orders—all customizable to fit your style and needs. And don't underestimate the power of social media: platforms like **Instagram, Facebook**, and **TikTok** can be highly effective for showcasing your products, interacting with followers, and conducting direct sales. Each of these tools offers unique ways to share your creations, reach new audiences, and grow a business around the things you love making.

As mentioned earlier, legal and financial considerations are essential when turning a hobby into a business. First, consider if you need to register your business. This step varies by location but registering can provide legal protection and lend credibility. Understanding tax implications is also crucial. Even small-scale operations need to keep track of income and expenses for tax purposes. You might need to pay self-employment taxes or collect sales tax, depending on your products and location. Managing income and expenses effectively is vital. Keep detailed records of sales, costs, and any business-related expenses. This practice not only helps with taxes but also gives you a clear picture of your business's financial health.

Hobby to Business Checklist

1. **Identify Marketable Hobbies:**

- List your hobbies and assess their market potential.

- Consider market demand, uniqueness, and your passion.

2. Plan Your Business:
- Set realistic goals (full-time income vs. extra money)

- Understand your target market

- Outline a simple business plan

3. Tools and Platforms:
- Crafts: Etsy, Shopify, Collaborative Markets

- Collectibles: eBay

- Home-grown produce: Local farmers' markets, restaurants

- Social media: Instagram, Facebook, Pinterest

4. Legal and Financial Aspects:
- Register your business if necessary

- Understand tax implications

- Keep detailed financial records

Transforming a hobby into a business isn't just a way to earn extra income—it's a chance to bring new energy and purpose into your days. With thoughtful planning, the right tools, and a true love for what you do, your favorite pastime can become a fulfilling and profitable venture. Whether it's knitting, pottery, gardening, or any passion you hold dear, retirement can be the start of a whole new adventure. Get ready to take what you love and make it something even more impactful.

8.4 Part-Time Jobs That Don't Feel Like Work: Enjoying Your Second Act

Part-time work in retirement brings a wealth of benefits that can make this phase of life more fulfilling. One of the biggest perks is the social aspect; a part-time job often comes with a built-in social network. Whether you're chatting with customers or collaborating with coworkers, these interactions keep you mentally sharp and socially active, which is a huge plus. Then there's the physical side. Many part-time roles keep you on your feet and moving and offer opportunities to stay active without a formal workout. It's an easy way to avoid that sedentary lifestyle, keeping you fit and energized. There's also the benefit of maintaining a routine. While retirement offers lots of freedom, it can sometimes feel like a blank slate. Having a part-time job, even for just a few hours a week, gives structure to your days and a purpose to your time. It's something to look forward to, a way to stay engaged and organized.

And, of course, there's the financial boost. Part-time work lets you supplement your retirement income, giving you more flexibility with your spending. Whether you're saving for a special vacation, supporting a hobby, or just enjoying some extra 'fun money,' a part-time job provides that extra financial freedom—without the commitment of full-time hours.

In short, part-time work in retirement is about staying connected, active, and purposeful, with the added perk of extra income to enjoy along the way.

The secret to enjoying part-time work in retirement is finding something that aligns with your passions and interests. Are you a nature lover, a bookworm, or a social butterfly? There's likely a part-time job that fits your lifestyle. Here are some ideas to get you started:

- **Pet Sitting or Dog Walking**: If you're an animal lover, pet sitting or dog walking can feel more like spending time with a furry friend than work. You get to enjoy the company of pets, stay active, and earn a little extra income.

- **Event Planning**: For those who thrive on organizing and socializing, part-time event planning is a perfect match. Whether it's weddings, local community events, or birthday parties, this job allows you to tap into your creativity and meet new people.

- **Working at a Bookstore or a Library**: If you're an avid reader, working part-time in a bookstore or library can be a dream job. Surrounded by books and fellow book lovers, you'll have the chance to discuss literature, discover new reads, and enjoy a relaxed environment.

- **Coffee Shop Barista**: Working at a local coffee shop offers a chance to meet new people, engage in friendly conversation, and be part of a bustling social environment. It's a great way to stay connected with your community while enjoying a flexible schedule.

- **Tour Guide**: If you love history, culture, or local landmarks, becoming a part-time tour guide can be an exciting way to share your knowledge with others. This job is especially enjoyable if you live in or near a popular tourist destination.

When selecting a part-time job, think about what excites you. Ask yourself: What do I enjoy doing in my free time? How can I turn my passions into a paid opportunity? By choosing a job that fits your interests, it won't feel like work—it'll feel like an extension of your hobbies.

Now that you know what kind of part-time work you're interested in, where do you look? Fortunately, there are plenty of resources to help you find the perfect gig:

- **Senior-Friendly Job Websites**: Websites like **RetirementJobs.com, FlexJobs,** and **Workforce50.com** specialize in part-time and flexible job listings for retirees. These platforms often list opportunities that are tailored to older adults, offering positions in various industries.

- **Local Business Listings**: Don't forget to check out job boards at your local coffee shops, community centers, and grocery stores. Many local businesses look for part-time workers and often prefer hiring retirees because of their reliability and experience.

- **Volunteer to Job Opportunities**: Sometimes volunteering can lead to part-time employment. Nonprofits, community organizations, and cultural institutions like museums often offer volunteer positions that could turn into paid opportunities once you've shown your skills and enthusiasm.

- **Community Center Boards**: Your local senior or community center may have job postings specifically for retirees. These boards can be a valuable resource for part-time work within the center itself or connections to nearby businesses.

One of the best things about part-time work in retirement is the flexibility to balance work with leisure. But to truly enjoy the benefits without feeling stretched thin, it's all about setting boundaries and managing your time well. First, it's important to set clear boundaries around how many hours you want to work each week and stick to that limit. Think of it as enhancing your lifestyle, not overburdening it. Let your employer know your availability upfront so everyone's on the same page—after all, you've earned the right to set your own terms!

Managing your time effectively is key, too. Create a schedule that lets you fit in both work and relaxation, prioritizing personal time for hobbies, social engagements, and activities you enjoy. Blocking off hours for yourself makes it easier to keep work in its place, ensuring it's just one part of your routine, not the whole picture.

And for the right fit, consider roles that offer flexibility. Jobs like pet sitting or working in retail can often work around your personal schedule. Flexibility is a game-changer, allowing you to maintain that sense of freedom while still earning a little extra.

Balancing part-time work with your retirement lifestyle is all about making sure the job enhances your life, rather than detracting from it. By choosing jobs that align with your passions and maintaining control over your schedule, you can create a fulfilling, flexible retirement that includes both enjoyable work and plenty of personal time.

8.5 Freelancing: Flexibility and Freedom

Freelancing is a flexible way to continue earning an income while pursuing projects you're passionate about. Whether you're looking to leverage the skills you've honed over your career or explore a new field, freelancing offers the perfect balance of work and leisure. The best part? You get to set your own hours, choose the clients and projects that interest you, and, in many cases, work from the comfort of your home. The beauty of freelancing lies in the sheer variety of opportunities available, particularly for retirees. Here are some common freelancing roles to consider:

- **Consulting**: If you've spent decades building expertise in a particular industry, consulting allows you to offer advice and solutions to businesses in need. Whether you're a retired business executive, teacher, or engineer, consulting can be a lucrative and fulfilling way to stay engaged in your field.

- **Writing and Editing**: If you have a flair for words, freelance writing or editing could be a perfect fit. You can write blog posts, articles, or even ghostwrite books. Editors are always in demand for proofreading, content editing, and fact-checking.

- **Graphic Design**: For those with a creative streak, graphic design is a popular freelancing option. You can create logos, brochures, websites, and marketing materials for businesses looking to boost their visual appeal.

- **Tutoring**: Retired teachers or professionals with expertise in specific subjects can find freelancing opportunities in tutoring. Whether it's helping students with math, language, or exam preparation, tutoring allows you to use your knowledge to make a difference.

- **Virtual Assistant**: Many businesses and entrepreneurs need help with administrative tasks, and becoming a freelance virtual assistant can be an excellent way to stay organized while working on a part-time basis.

Freelancing offers retirees the opportunity to stay active and engaged, working on projects they enjoy without the constraints of a 9-to-5 job. The flexibility means you can work on your terms, whether that's a few hours a day or only when a project excites you.

Ready to dive into freelancing? The first step is setting yourself up professionally. Here's a quick guide to help you get started:

- **Create a Professional Profile**: Whether you're setting up a profile on LinkedIn, a freelancing platform, or building a personal website, it's important to showcase your skills and experience. Highlight your strengths, include a professional photo, and write a compelling bio that explains what you offer. Be sure to include testimonials or references if you have them.

- **Choose Freelancing Platforms**: Websites like **Upwork**, **Freelancer**, and **Fiverr** are great places to find freelance gigs. These platforms connect freelancers with clients across various industries, offering jobs that range from small one-off projects to long-term engagements. You can set your rates, bid on jobs that interest you, and build a portfolio.

- **Set Up a Workspace**: Even if you're freelancing part-time, it's essential to have a dedicated workspace where you can focus on your projects. Whether it's a home office or a corner of your living room, having a quiet, organized space will help you stay productive.

- **Invest in the Right Tools**: Depending on your freelance niche, you'll need the right tools. Writers may need good grammar-checking software like **Grammarly**, while graphic designers might require programs like **Adobe Creative**

Cloud. For virtual assistants, tools like **Trello** or **Asana** can help keep you organized.

By setting up a professional workspace and utilizing the right platforms and tools, you'll be ready to dive into the freelancing world with confidence. Once you're set up, the next challenge is attracting clients. Here are a few strategies to help you build and maintain a strong client base:

- **Networking**: Leverage your existing network of former colleagues, friends, and acquaintances. Let them know you're freelancing and available for projects. Attend industry events, your local Chamber of Commerce networking events, local meetups, or online webinars to connect with potential clients.

- **Ask for Referrals**: Satisfied clients are your best advocates. As soon as you get your first clients, ask for referrals or recommendations. Word-of-mouth marketing can be incredibly powerful in helping you build a reputation and attract new clients.

- **Maintain an Online Presence**: Having an online presence is essential in today's digital world. Build a personal website that showcases your work, skills, and testimonials. Keep your LinkedIn profile updated and consider starting a blog and social media accounts where you can share your expertise.

- **Deliver High-Quality Work**: The key to maintaining a steady stream of clients is delivering reliable, high-quality work on time. Building trust with your clients will not only lead to repeat business but also help you grow through positive reviews and recommendations.

Freelancing comes with the freedom to set your hours, but it's important to manage your time effectively to avoid feeling overwhelmed. Here are some tips for managing your freelance workload:

- **Set and Negotiate Rates**: One of the first things you'll need to do is determine your rates. Research what others in your industry are charging and set a rate that reflects your experience and skills. Be confident in negotiating your fees—don't undersell yourself.

- **Manage Multiple Clients or Projects**: Juggling multiple clients can be challenging. Use project management tools like **Trello**, **Asana**, or **Monday.com** to keep track of deadlines and client expectations. Setting clear boundaries with clients regarding response times and deliverables can help prevent burnout.

- **Balance Work and Leisure**: One of the perks of freelancing is the ability to balance work with leisure. However, it's important to set boundaries so work doesn't consume your personal time. Establish a routine where you dedicate specific hours to work and leave ample time for relaxation and hobbies.

Freelancing offers the perfect balance between maintaining a flexible schedule and staying engaged with meaningful work. By managing your workload effectively and delivering high-quality results, you'll be able to enjoy both the freedom of retirement and the rewards of freelancing.

Retirement opens doors to endless possibilities, and whether through entrepreneurial pursuits or flexible part-time work, there's a unique opportunity to shape this stage of life in a way that's both fulfilling and purposeful. Starting a small business or taking on part-time work offers more than just financial benefits—it brings a renewed sense of purpose, connection, and growth. You're not just keeping busy; you're engaging your skills, meeting new people, and continuing to make a meaningful impact while earning income. These endeavors are as flexible as you need them to be, with options to fit every lifestyle, interest, and schedule. So whether you're inspired to launch a side business, take on a few weekly work hours, or consult in your field, the possibilities are only limited by your imagination. Retirement is your time—let it be as dynamic and rewarding as you've always dreamed.

Chapter Nine

Building Your Legacy for Future Generations

You know that feeling when you find an old photo album and suddenly you're swept into a whirlwind of memories and emotions? It's like uncovering a treasure chest of your life's greatest hits. Now, imagine creating something that brings that same sense of warmth and nostalgia to future generations. These endeavors are your chance to leave something meaningful behind, reflecting your values and passions, and ensuring that a part of you continues to inspire and impact others. Welcome to the world of legacy projects.

9.1 Legacy Projects: Making a Lasting Impact

Legacy projects are more than just tasks or hobbies; they are purposeful endeavors designed to encapsulate your essence and share it with the world. Think of them as your personal time capsules, filled with what you hold dear. You could be writing a memoir to share your life's journey, planting a memorial garden that blooms with every season, or establishing a scholarship to support future scholars. Whatever it may be, these projects are as unique as you are. They reflect your passions, values, and the indelible mark you wish to leave on the world. It's like your own personal brand of immortality, minus the need for any magic potions or eternal youth elixirs.

Starting a legacy project might sound exciting but also intimidating. Approach it as any other extensive project: it's all about breaking it down into small and manageable steps. First, identify what truly matters to you. Are you passionate about education? Consider a scholarship fund. Love gardening? A community garden could be your green legacy. Next, gather your troops—family, friends, and community members who share your vision. Their support can turn your dream into reality. Outline your project, set realistic goals, and create a timeline. Remember, Rome wasn't built in a day, and neither will your legacy project. Allocate resources wisely, whether it's time, money, or manpower. And most importantly, stay flexible. Sometimes the path to legacy-building has a few unexpected detours, but that's where the adventure lies.

It's important to remember that you're not alone on this journey. Many resources and support systems are available to help bring your legacy project to life. Community grants can provide the financial backing needed for larger initiatives. Nonprofit partnerships can offer expertise, networking opportunities, and additional resources. Online platforms like **GoFundMe** or **Kickstarter** allow you to crowdsource funding and gather community support. Local libraries and community centers often have workshops and seminars on project management, grant writing, and nonprofit management. Don't hesitate to reach out to organizations that align with your project's goals—they're usually more than willing to lend a helping hand. After all, every great legacy starts with a little help from your friends.

Documenting your legacy project is not just about keeping records; it's about telling a story that can inspire others. Keep a journal or blog about the progress, challenges, and milestones. Share photos and videos on social media to engage your community and keep them updated. This transparency not only fosters support but also creates a living record of your journey. Consider creating a dedicated website or a digital scrapbook that future generations can access. By sharing your story, you extend the reach and influence of your legacy, turning it into a beacon of inspiration for others to follow. Remember, your legacy isn't just what you leave behind; it's the light that guides others long after you're gone.

Your Legacy Blueprint

1. **Identify Your Passion:** What cause or project truly excites you?

2. **Gather Your Team:** Who in your circle shares your vision?

3. **Outline the Project:** What are the key steps and necessary resources?

4. **Set Realistic Goals:** What milestones will mark your progress?

5. **Document the Journey:** How will you share your story and inspire others?

Creating a legacy project is your chance to leave a lasting impact, one that resonates with your values and passions. It's about building something meaningful, involving your community, and sharing the journey. So, let's turn those dreams into reality, one step at a time.

9.2 Teaching Workshops and Classes

So, you've got a treasure trove of knowledge and skills just waiting to be shared with the world. Teaching workshops and classes in your area is a fantastic way to make a difference while staying engaged and active. First things first, let's identify your teaching niche. What are you exceptionally good at? Maybe you have a knack for crafting, whipping up gourmet meals, or navigating the digital world like a tech-savvy whiz. Think about the compliments you've received over the years and the activities that make you lose track of time. These are your bread and butter, the skills you can impart to others.

Once you've pinpointed your area of expertise, it's time to set up your workshops or classes. Start by finding a suitable venue. Community centers, local libraries, and even your living room can serve as excellent spaces. Consider the materials you'll need—think supplies for crafting, ingredients for cooking, or tech devices for a technology class. Pricing your class can be a delicate balance. You want to cover your costs and value your time but also make it accessible. Research similar classes in your area to gauge a fair price. Marketing your classes is where the fun begins. Create eye-catching flyers, post on social media, and tap into community bulletin boards. Word of mouth is powerful, so don't be shy about asking friends and family to spread the word.

Teaching effectively means catering to diverse learning styles and creating an engaging environment. Some people are visual learners who thrive on diagrams and videos, while others are kinesthetic learners who need hands-on activities. Mix it up with interactive demonstrations, group exercises, and lively discussions. Keep the atmosphere relaxed and fun—nobody wants to feel like they're back in a stuffy classroom. Encourage questions and be patient. Remember, your goal is to inspire and educate, not to overwhelm. And hey, don't forget the power of humor. A well-timed joke can break the ice and make everyone feel more comfortable.

Measuring the success and impact of your teaching efforts is crucial. Gather feedback from participants through surveys or casual conversations. Ask them what they enjoyed, what they found challenging, and what they'd like to learn next. This feedback is gold—it helps you refine your classes and meet the needs of your audience. Assess the broader benefits to the community. Are participants using their new skills to start businesses, improve their lives, or contribute to community projects? Track these outcomes to see the ripple effect of your efforts. Your legacy as a teacher is not just in the knowledge you impart, but in the lasting impact you make on those you teach.

9.3 Crafting Your Ethical Will

Writing an ethical will is a chance to capture your deepest beliefs, values, and life philosophies—a meaningful message to future generations. An ethical will differs from a legal will, which handles the distribution of assets; instead, it shares the core of who you are. This document allows you to convey your wisdom, hopes, and the guiding principles that have defined your life. There's no legal jargon here, just heartfelt stories, lessons, and dreams meant for those you love. Think of it as a personal manifesto, a way to ensure that your values and perspectives will continue to inspire, even after you're gone.

Before you start writing, take a moment to reflect on what truly matters to you. This is where the soul-searching happens. Ask yourself questions like, *"What are the core values that have guided my decisions?"* and *"What lessons have I learned that I want to share?"* Maybe it's the importance of kindness, the value of hard work, or the joy of lifelong learning. Jot down memories that highlight these values—times when you felt most proud, moments of struggle that taught you resilience, or even simple joys that brought meaning to your life. This reflective process helps clarify what you want to convey, ensuring that your ethical will is a genuine representation of your inner self.

Now comes the fun part—putting pen to paper. Start by addressing your audience, whether it's your family, friends, or your community. Use language that feels natural and true to your voice, as if you were having a heartfelt conversation. Express your emotions openly—this is your chance to be vulnerable and authentic. Share stories that illustrate your values, and don't shy away from discussing both triumphs and failures. They all contribute to the tapestry of your life. Be clear and concise, but also allow your personality to shine through. Remember, this document is a piece of you, a way to connect with your loved ones on a deeply personal level.

Once you've crafted your ethical will, the next step is to ensure it's preserved and shared with the right people. Store it alongside your important documents, like your legal will, so it's easily accessible. Share copies with trusted individuals—family members, close friends, and your attorney. Another meaningful option is to incorporate it into family traditions. Perhaps you read it aloud during family gatherings or create a digital version that can be passed down through generations. The goal is to make sure your ethical will is not a static document but a living testament to your values, continually inspiring those who come after you.

9.4 Building a Family Tree

Have you ever wondered where your ancestors came from? Genealogy, or the study of family history, turns you into a detective, piecing together your lineage and discovering the tales that make your family unique. With a wealth of online resources available today, building your family tree can be a significant, but easy-to-complete, project. Platforms like **Ancestry.com** and **FamilySearch** provide access to public records, census data, and DNA testing services, helping you trace your ancestors whether they lived locally or halfway around the world. Begin by gathering as much information as you can from living relatives—names, birthdates, and places of residence are invaluable starting points. From there, delve into these databases and local archives to complete the picture.

Genealogy is more than just tracing names and dates; it's about bringing those names to life with the stories that make each generation memorable. Conversations with older relatives who are still alive can yield rich narratives, preserving memories that might otherwise fade. If you have elderly relatives, now is the perfect time to connect with them and capture their stories. Prepare a few open-ended questions to encourage detailed responses, like "What was your childhood like?" or "Are there any unique family traditions?" Recording these interviews, either with audio or video, adds an irreplaceable layer of personality, capturing not only the stories but also the voices and expressions that make them feel real. These accounts will provide future generations with a personal connection to their roots, enriching your family tree with color and depth. Don't wait—these precious memories won't last forever, and you can create a lasting legacy for those who come after you.

Technology can be a powerful ally in organizing and preserving your findings. Software like **Family Tree Maker** or **MyHeritage** lets you create visually appealing family trees, attach photos and documents, and add recordings to each ancestor's profile. Cloud storage platforms like **Google Drive** or **Dropbox** are excellent for backing up and sharing your progress, enabling other family members to contribute additional details and stories. Collaborative genealogy strengthens family ties, as relatives come together to share memories, research, and insights.

Once you've gathered information and collected personal stories, consider compiling it all into a family legacy document or book. This doesn't have to be complicated; it can be as simple as a digital document or as elaborate as a professionally printed book. Organize your work chronologically, beginning with your oldest known ancestors and working down to the present day, weaving photos, documents, and interview transcripts into a narrative that future generations can appreciate. This legacy document becomes more than a record—it's a gift that preserves your family's unique story.

For an extra touch, celebrate the completion of your family history project with a gathering, whether in person or virtual. Sharing the final product honors your ancestors and strengthens connections with the family members of today. Your family tree will be a cherished legacy, ensuring that the memories, traditions, and stories of past generations live on.

9.5 Engaging in Philanthropy: Small Acts, Big Impacts

Identifying causes that align with your values is like finding that perfect pair of shoes—they fit just right and make you feel fantastic.

To start, think about what truly resonates with you. Maybe you've always had a soft spot for animals or a passion for education. Reflect on your life experiences and the causes that have touched you personally. Researching charities is crucial to ensure your contributions are effective. Websites like **Charity Navigator** or **GuideStar** provide ratings and reviews of charities, helping you find organizations that align with your values and have a proven track record of making a difference. Evaluating a charity involves looking at its transparency, financial health, and the impact of its programs. This ensures your efforts are not just well-intentioned, but also effective and transformative.

Philanthropy isn't solely about writing big checks; sometimes, the smallest acts of kindness can create ripples of change. Volunteering your time at a local shelter, mentoring a young individual, or even organizing a community clean-up event can make a world of difference. These small, impactful acts of kindness bring immediate benefits and foster a sense of community and purpose. Imagine spending a few hours a week helping students improve their reading skills or delivering meals to homebound seniors. These actions, though small, create meaningful connections and significantly impact those you help. The beauty of small acts is that they are accessible to everyone, regardless of financial capability, and they remind us that even the tiniest gestures can have a grand impact.

Creating a philanthropic plan is about being intentional in your efforts. Start by setting clear, achievable goals. Do you want to volunteer a certain number of hours each month, make regular financial contributions, or perhaps start a charitable fund? Outline your objectives and create timelines to keep yourself on track. Consider integrating your philanthropic activities into your daily or weekly routine—this makes giving back a natural part of your life rather than an occasional effort. If you're financially contributing, decide on a budget that aligns with your financial situation. Regularly review and adjust your plan to ensure it remains aligned with your values and circumstances. A strategic plan keeps your philanthropic efforts focused and consistent, maximizing their impact.

Leaving a philanthropic legacy ensures your efforts continue to make a difference long after you're gone. Setting up endowed funds or including charitable giving in your estate plans can provide lasting support to causes you care about. Encourage your family and friends to continue the work you've started, inspiring the next generation to uphold the values and commitments you hold dear. Sharing your philanthropic vision with your loved ones and involving them in your charitable activities can instill a sense of responsibility and passion in them. This way, your legacy of kindness and generosity lives on, fostering a culture of giving and community service.

Engaging in philanthropy is about finding causes that speak to your heart, making small yet impactful differences, and planning your efforts to create lasting change. Your golden years are the perfect time to give back and ensure that your values and passions continue to make the world a better place.

Chapter Ten

Conclusion

As we reach the end of this book, I want to remind you that this is the beginning of the rest of your life; a new, exciting chapter of your life after work. I'll never forget the moment I realized retirement wasn't some far-off dream—it was approaching faster than I'd expected. I watched friends step into their new lives, and it got me thinking, "What's next for me?" That question launched me on a journey of discovery, where I realized retirement could be much more than a break from work—it could be an opportunity for reinvention. This book was born from that journey, and I hope it inspires you to explore, create, and connect in new ways that make this next chapter your best yet.

Together, we've explored ways to keep life intellectually engaging, socially rich, and purpose-driven. We looked at everything from diving into creative projects that stir the soul to sharing wisdom through community involvement and legacy building. Maybe you're feeling drawn to explore new ideas, start that small business you've dreamed of, or simply connect with others who are on the same journey. Each chapter offers ways to make this time a period of discovery and fulfillment.

As you step into retirement, remember it's not just about filling the hours but about doing things that make you feel alive. I encourage you to start with one small, meaningful step—perhaps it's trying that first community class, beginning a family history project, or joining a club you've always been curious about. Whatever it is, let it add joy, purpose, and a sense of adventure to your days.

Personally, one of the most rewarding parts of my own journey has been sharing experiences with people who inspire me. This sense of connection is priceless, and I encourage you to find those moments with family, friends, and newfound acquaintances who lift you up and keep you engaged. As I've learned, the best discoveries often come through the people we meet and the stories we share.

So here's my final thought: let's make these years extraordinary. Retirement is your chance to explore, create, and leave a meaningful impact, no matter how big or small. I'd love to hear about the new directions you take, the lessons you uncover, and the connections you form. Reach out, share your story, or even drop me a line about your next adventure—you'll find my contact info at the end of this book.

Thank you for joining me on this journey. Approach this chapter of your life with curiosity and openness, knowing that the best chapters are often the ones we write ourselves. Here's to the joy, discovery, and boundless potential that retirement brings—may it be everything you've imagined and much, much more!

References

1. Re-Defining Yourself in Retirement https://www.forbes.com/sites/robpascale/2019/04/25/re-defining-yourself-in-retirement/

2. How to Arrange Your Daily Schedule after Retirement https://ifa.ngo/wise-words/how-to-arrange-your-daily-schedule-after-retirement/

3. Online Learning for Seniors: The 6 Best Free Online Courses https://www.storypoint.com/resources/health-wellness/online-learning-for-seniors/

4. Master Your Chess with Our Exclusive Guides https://knight-master.com/

5. Video game training enhances cognitive control in older adults https://pmc.ncbi.nlm.nih.gov/articles/PMC3983066/

6. Intrinsic Resting-State Activity in Older Adults With Video Game Experience https://www.frontiersin.org/journals/aging-neuroscience/articles/10.3389/fnagi.2019.00119/full

7. 15 Best Video Games that are Perfect for Older Adults https://www.g2a.com/news/features/video-games-for-older-people/

8. The Benefits of Art and Painting for Older Adults https://allseniorscare.com/the-benefits-of-art-and-painting-for-older-adults/

9. Five Benefits of Volunteering in Retirement https://seniorcommunity.org/five-benefits-volunteering-retirement/

10. The #1 Reason to Pick Up an Instrument After 50 https://www.aarp.org/health/brain-health/info-2023/brain-health-benefits-of-learning-an-instrument.html

11. 5 Surprising Benefits of Singing https://achgroup.org.au/blog/health-benefits-of-singing/

12. 8 Tips for Getting Started With Creative Writing https://www.masterclass.com/articles/tips-for-getting-started-with-creative-writing

13. Where to Find Virtual Activities for Older Adults [2024] https://www.televeda.com/posts/where-to-find-virtual-activities-for-older-adults

14. How to start a seniors' social club - Niagara Frontier Publications https://www.wnypapers.com/news/article/2023/03/06/154455/how-to-start-a-seniors-social-club

15. How Do I Start Dating When I'm Over 60? https://www.springrose.co/blogs/blog/how-do-i-start-dating-when-im-over-60

16. 15 Community Event Ideas That Bring People Together https://www.socialtables.com/blog/event-planning/community-event-ideas/

17. How to Start a Nonprofit: Complete 9-Step Guide for Success https://kindful.com/blog/how-to-start-a-nonprofit/

18. How to apply for 501(c)(3) status https://www.irs.gov/charities-non-profits/how-to-apply-for-501c3-status

19. The Benefits of Intergenerational Mentoring https://www.seniorhelpers.com/il/des-plaines/resources/blogs/2024-07-16/

20. Positive aging benefits of home and community gardening https://www.ncbi.nlm.nih.gov/pmc/articles/PMC6977207/

21. How Seniors Benefit from Lifelong Learning https://delaneyatthegreen.com/blog/2024/02/20/the-benefits-of-lifelong-learning-in-retirement/

22. The Best Apps and Tools for Seniors to Learn a New Language https://blog.thebristal.com/the-best-apps-and-tools-for-seniors-to-learn-a-new-language

23. Photography Is a Great Hobby for Retirement. Here's How to Start. https://www.goodhousekeeping.com/life/a46913079/photography-is-a-great-hobby-for-retirement-heres-how-to-start

24. Senior Computer Classes to Try Online for FREE - Medicare.org https://www.medicare.org/articles/senior-comput

er-classes-to-try-online-for-free/

25. Participating in Activities You Enjoy As You Age https://www.nia.nih.gov/health/healthy-aging/participating-activities-you-enjoy-you-age

26. How to Plan a Themed Dinner Party: Tips and Ideas - LinkedIn https://www.linkedin.com/pulse/how-plan-themed-dinner-party-tips-ideas-qrtzc

27. How to Start a Book Club: Advice for Seniors https://atriumatnavesink.org/news/how-to-start-a-book-club-advice-for-seniors/

28. 5 Senior Dance Routines to Try Out https://umcommunities.org/bristolglen/blog/5-senior-dance-routines-to-try-out/

29. Vegetable Gardening for Beginners: The Complete Guide https://www.almanac.com/vegetable-gardening-for-beginners

30. How To Upcycle: Successful Tips for Changing Old Items Into Creative Home Decor https://jennaburger.com/2013/02/01/how-to-upcycle-successful-tips-for-changing-old-items-into-creative-home-decor/

31. Online cooking classes with international chefs https://www.thetablelesstraveled.com/cooking-classes

32. The beginner's REAL guide to hanging wallpaper https://www.ahousefullofsunshine.com/2016/10/the

-beginners-real-guide-to-hanging-wallpaper/

33. The Beginner's Guide to Making Bread https://www.ahyggehomestead.com/beginners-guide-making-bread/

34. Best Online Learning Platforms for Older Adults https://www.ormsbyliving.org/about/news-blog/best-online-learning-platforms-for-older-adults/

35. Creativebug - Craft Classes & Workshops - What will you ...* https://www.creativebug.com/

36. Senior Citizen Course Audit - Niner Central - UNC Charlotte* https://ninercentral.charlotte.edu/courses-registration/registration-information/senior-citizen-course-audit/

37. 7 Profitable Retirement Business Ideas for Your Second Act https://www.shopify.com/ca/blog/retirement-business

38. YouTube Channel as a Retirement Plan https://www.youtube.com/playlist?list=PLe3in6WwMCsvrewpYC2FDw6BeBkofhTNv

39. How To Write An Ethical Will https://www.everplans.com/articles/how-to-write-an-ethical-will

40. How to Build a Family Tree: Tracing Your Ancestors https://www.ngsgenealogy.org/free-resources/build-family-tree/

41. Cyber-Seniors: FREE technology support and training for older adults https://cyberseniors.org/

About the Author

Lara West is a health and wellness advocate dedicated to empowering readers through her insightful writings. With a particular emphasis on women's and midlife health, Lara shares relatable and practical tips drawn from her personal experiences that deeply resonate with her readers.

Her journey began in her mid-forties as she faced perimenopausal symptoms, leaky gut syndrome, an autoimmune disease, and the challenges of caregiving for a family member with dementia. This transformative period ignited her passion for understanding gut health and its significant impact on overall well-being, as well as the importance of self-care for caregivers.

Lara's commitment to holistic wellness inspires her to share practical strategies for navigating the challenges of middle age, caregiving, and maintaining an active lifestyle. She emphasizes the importance of self-care and balanced living, passionately advocating for an active and fulfilling life in retirement, ensuring the best years are ahead. Lara encourages readers to reclaim their vitality and joy at every stage of life.

Through her clear and structured writing style, infused with compassion and relatability, Lara makes complex health topics accessible and engaging, inspiring others to take charge of their health and well-being.

You can reach Lara via her website https://larawestbooks.com or Amazon Author Page https://www.amazon.com/stores/Lara-West/author/B0BV3F1YK7

LaraWestBooks.com

Amazon Author Page

Also by Lara West

1. "The Great Retirement Escape: Your Guide to Journeys Across the Globe, Adventures Close to Home, Inspiring Outdoor Activities, and Fun Active Lifestyle for Your Best Years Yet"

2. "Retirement Reinvented: Your Inspiring Guide to Creative Expression, Intellectual Growth, Entrepreneurial Ventures, and Leaving a Legacy for a Fulfilling and Meaningful Life After Work"

3. **"The Ultimate Collection of Fun Things to Do in Retirement: Your Roadmap to Explore the World, Spark Creativity, Expand Your Mind, Uncover Hidden Talents, Make New Friends, and Savor Your Golden Years"**

4. "7 Healthy Gut Habits For Women Over 40: Get Your Life Back Using Intermittent Fasting, Nutrition, and Self-Care to Restore Gut Microbiome for Weight Loss and Increased Energy"

5. "5 Pathways to Vagus Nerve Mastery for Women Over 40: Holistic Methods to Reduce Anxiety, Clear Brain Fog,

Improve Gut Health, and Balance Weight During Peri-menopause and" Menopause

6. "Gut Health Made Easy for Women over 40: Recipes to Revitalize Your Body and Mind, Manage Menopause Symptoms, Balance Hormones, and Lose Weight with Delicious Smoothies, Salads, and Soups"

7. "Joyful Transition For Women Over 40: Finding Gratitude and Thriving in Menopause with Empowering Affirmations, Journaling, and Positive Mindset Practices"

8. "The Ultimate Gut Health Collection for Women Over 40: Reclaim Your Vitality, Lose Weight, and Manage Menopause Symptoms with Intermittent Fasting, Self-Care, Balanced Nutrition, and Delicious Recipes"

9. "The Ultimate Mind-Body Harmony Collection for Women over 40: Reduce Anxiety, Clear Brain Fog, Improve Gut Health, and Thrive in Menopause with Vagus Nerve Mastery and Positive Mindset Practices"

10. "The Self-Care Guide for Dementia Caregivers: Proven Practices to Reduce Stress, Overcome Burnout, and Find Balance and Joy in the Caregiving Journey"

www.ingramcontent.com/pod-product-compliance
Lightning Source LLC
Chambersburg PA
CBHW071149070526
44584CB00019B/2718